FREE Study Skills DVD Offer

Dear Customer,

Thank you for your purchase from Mometrix! We consider it an honor and a privilege that you have purchased our product and we want to ensure your satisfaction.

As a way of showing our appreciation and to help us better serve you, we have developed a Study Skills DVD that we would like to give you for FREE. This DVD covers our *best practices* for getting ready for your exam, from how to use our study materials to how to best prepare for the day of the test.

All that we ask is that you email us with feedback that would describe your experience so far with our product. Good, bad, or indifferent, we want to know what you think!

To get your FREE Study Skills DVD, email freedvd@mometrix.com with *FREE STUDY SKILLS DVD* in the subject line and the following information in the body of the email:

- The name of the product you purchased.
- Your product rating on a scale of 1-5, with 5 being the highest rating.
- Your feedback. It can be long, short, or anything in between. We just want to know your impressions and experience so far with our product. (Good feedback might include how our study material met your needs and ways we might be able to make it even better. You could highlight features that you found helpful or features that you think we should add.)
- Your full name and shipping address where you would like us to send your free DVD.

If you have any questions or concerns, please don't hesitate to contact me directly.

Thanks again!

Sincerely,

Jay Willis
Vice President
jay.willis@mometrix.com
1-800-673-8175

SIFT

Study Guide 2019 & 2020 SECRETS

Study Guide

Your Key to Exam Success

- SIFT Test Prep Secrets
- Full-Length Practice Test
- Detailed Answer Explanations

Published by

Mometrix Test Preparation

Mometrix Armed Forces Test Team

Written and edited by the Mometrix Armed Forces Test Team

Printed in the United States of America

This paper meets the requirements of ANSI/NISO Z39.48-1992 (Permanence of Paper).

Paperback
ISBN 13: 978-1-5167-1077-5
ISBN 10: 1-5167-1077-0

Dear Future Exam Success Story:

First of all, **THANK YOU** for purchasing Mometrix study materials!

Second, congratulations! You are one of the few determined test-takers who are committed to doing whatever it takes to excel on your exam. **You have come to the right place.** We developed these study materials with one goal in mind: to deliver you the information you need in a format that's concise and easy to use.

In addition to optimizing your guide for the content of the test, we've outlined our recommended steps for breaking down the preparation process into small, attainable goals so you can make sure you stay on track.

We've also analyzed the entire test-taking process, identifying the most common pitfalls and showing how you can overcome them and be ready for any curveball the test throws you.

Standardized testing is one of the biggest obstacles on your road to success, which only increases the importance of doing well in the high-pressure, high-stakes environment of test day. Your results on this test could have a significant impact on your future, and this guide provides the information and practical advice to help you achieve your full potential on test day.

Your success is our success

We would love to hear from you! If you would like to share the story of your exam success or if you have any questions or comments in regard to our products, please contact us at **800-673-8175** or **support@mometrix.com**.

Thanks again for your business and we wish you continued success!

Sincerely,
The Mometrix Test Preparation Team

TABLE OF CONTENTS

Introduction

Thank you for purchasing this resource! You have made the choice to prepare yourself for a test that could have a huge impact on your future, and this guide is designed to help you be fully ready for test day. Obviously, it's important to have a solid understanding of the test material, but you also need to be prepared for the unique environment and stressors of the test, so that you can perform to the best of your abilities.

For this purpose, the first section that appears in this guide is the **Secret Keys**. We've devoted countless hours to meticulously researching what works and what doesn't, and we've boiled down our findings to the five most impactful steps you can take to improve your performance on the test. We start at the beginning with study planning and move through the preparation process, all the way to the testing strategies that will help you get the most out of what you know when you're finally sitting in front of the test.

We recommend that you start preparing for your test as far in advance as possible. However, if you've bought this guide as a last-minute study resource and only have a few days before your test, we recommend that you skip over the first two Secret Keys since they address a long-term study plan.

If you struggle with **test anxiety**, we strongly encourage you to check out our recommendations for how you can overcome it. Test anxiety is a formidable foe, but it can be beaten, and we want to make sure you have the tools you need to defeat it.

Secret Key #1 – Plan Big, Study Small

There's a lot riding on your performance. If you want to ace this test, you're going to need to keep your skills sharp and the material fresh in your mind. You need a plan that lets you review everything you need to know while still fitting in your schedule. We'll break this strategy down into three categories.

Information Organization

Start with the information you already have: the official test outline. From this, you can make a complete list of all the concepts you need to cover before the test. Organize these concepts into groups that can be studied together, and create a list of any related vocabulary you need to learn so you can brush up on any difficult terms. You'll want to keep this vocabulary list handy once you actually start studying since you may need to add to it along the way.

Time Management

Once you have your set of study concepts, decide how to spread them out over the time you have left before the test. Break your study plan into small, clear goals so you have a manageable task for each day and know exactly what you're doing. Then just focus on one small step at a time. When you manage your time this way, you don't need to spend hours at a time studying. Studying a small block of content for a short period each day helps you retain information better and avoid stressing over how much you have left to do. You can relax knowing that you have a plan to cover everything in time. In order for this strategy to be effective though, you have to start studying early and stick to your schedule. Avoid the exhaustion and futility that comes from last-minute cramming!

Study Environment

The environment you study in has a big impact on your learning. Studying in a coffee shop, while probably more enjoyable, is not likely to be as fruitful as studying in a quiet room. It's important to keep distractions to a minimum. You're only planning to study for a short block of time, so make the most of it. Don't pause to check your phone or get up to find a snack. It's also important to **avoid multitasking**. Research has consistently shown that multitasking will make your studying dramatically less effective. Your study area should also be comfortable and well-lit so you don't have the distraction of straining your eyes or sitting on an uncomfortable chair.

The time of day you study is also important. You want to be rested and alert. Don't wait until just before bedtime. Study when you'll be most likely to comprehend and remember. Even better, if you know what time of day your test will be, set that time aside for study. That way your brain will be used to working on that subject at that specific time and you'll have a better chance of recalling information.

Finally, it can be helpful to team up with others who are studying for the same test. Your actual studying should be done in as isolated an environment as possible, but the work of organizing the information and setting up the study plan can be divided up. In between study sessions, you can discuss with your teammates the concepts that you're all studying and quiz each other on the details. Just be sure that your teammates are as serious about the test as you are. If you find that your study time is being replaced with social time, you might need to find a new team.

Secret Key #2 – Make Your Studying Count

You're devoting a lot of time and effort to preparing for this test, so you want to be absolutely certain it will pay off. This means doing more than just reading the content and hoping you can remember it on test day. It's important to make every minute of study count. There are two main areas you can focus on to make your studying count:

Retention

It doesn't matter how much time you study if you can't remember the material. You need to make sure you are retaining the concepts. To check your retention of the information you're learning, try recalling it at later times with minimal prompting. Try carrying around flashcards and glance at one or two from time to time or ask a friend who's also studying for the test to quiz you.

To enhance your retention, look for ways to put the information into practice so that you can apply it rather than simply recalling it. If you're using the information in practical ways, it will be much easier to remember. Similarly, it helps to solidify a concept in your mind if you're not only reading it to yourself but also explaining it to someone else. Ask a friend to let you teach them about a concept you're a little shaky on (or speak aloud to an imaginary audience if necessary). As you try to summarize, define, give examples, and answer your friend's questions, you'll understand the concepts better and they will stay with you longer. Finally, step back for a big picture view and ask yourself how each piece of information fits with the whole subject. When you link the different concepts together and see them working together as a whole, it's easier to remember the individual components.

Finally, practice showing your work on any multi-step problems, even if you're just studying. Writing out each step you take to solve a problem will help solidify the process in your mind, and you'll be more likely to remember it during the test.

Modality

Modality simply refers to the means or method by which you study. Choosing a study modality that fits your own individual learning style is crucial. No two people learn best in exactly the same way, so it's important to know your strengths and use them to your advantage.

For example, if you learn best by visualization, focus on visualizing a concept in your mind and draw an image or a diagram. Try color-coding your notes, illustrating them, or creating symbols that will trigger your mind to recall a learned concept. If you learn best by hearing or discussing information, find a study partner who learns the same way or read aloud to yourself. Think about how to put the information in your own words. Imagine that you are giving a lecture on the topic and record yourself so you can listen to it later.

For any learning style, flashcards can be helpful. Organize the information so you can take advantage of spare moments to review. Underline key words or phrases. Use different colors for different categories. Mnemonic devices (such as creating a short list in which every item starts with the same letter) can also help with retention. Find what works best for you and use it to store the information in your mind most effectively and easily.

Secret Key #3 – Practice the Right Way

Your success on test day depends not only on how many hours you put into preparing, but also on whether you prepared the right way. It's good to check along the way to see if your studying is paying off. One of the most effective ways to do this is by taking practice tests to evaluate your progress. Practice tests are useful because they show exactly where you need to improve. Every time you take a practice test, pay special attention to these three groups of questions:

- The questions you got wrong
- The questions you had to guess on, even if you guessed right
- The questions you found difficult or slow to work through

This will show you exactly what your weak areas are, and where you need to devote more study time. Ask yourself why each of these questions gave you trouble. Was it because you didn't understand the material? Was it because you didn't remember the vocabulary? Do you need more repetitions on this type of question to build speed and confidence? Dig into those questions and figure out how you can strengthen your weak areas as you go back to review the material.

Additionally, many practice tests have a section explaining the answer choices. It can be tempting to read the explanation and think that you now have a good understanding of the concept. However, an explanation likely only covers part of the question's broader context. Even if the explanation makes sense, **go back and investigate** every concept related to the question until you're positive you have a thorough understanding.

As you go along, keep in mind that the practice test is just that: practice. Memorizing these questions and answers will not be very helpful on the actual test because it is unlikely to have any of the same exact questions. If you only know the right answers to the sample questions, you won't be prepared for the real thing. **Study the concepts** until you understand them fully, and then you'll be able to answer any question that shows up on the test.

It's important to wait on the practice tests until you're ready. If you take a test on your first day of study, you may be overwhelmed by the amount of material covered and how much you need to learn. Work up to it gradually.

On test day, you'll need to be prepared for answering questions, managing your time, and using the test-taking strategies you've learned. It's a lot to balance, like a mental marathon that will have a big impact on your future. Like training for a marathon, you'll need to start slowly and work your way up. When test day arrives, you'll be ready.

Start with the strategies you've read in the first two Secret Keys—plan your course and study in the way that works best for you. If you have time, consider using multiple study resources to get different approaches to the same concepts. It can be helpful to see difficult concepts from more than one angle. Then find a good source for practice tests. Many times, the test website will suggest potential study resources or provide sample tests.

Practice Test Strategy

When you're ready to start taking practice tests, follow this strategy:

Untimed and Open-Book Practice

Take the first test with no time constraints and with your notes and study guide handy. Take your time and focus on applying the strategies you've learned.

Timed and Open-Book Practice

Take the second practice test open-book as well, but set a timer and practice pacing yourself to finish in time.

Timed and Closed-Book Practice

Take any other practice tests as if it were test day. Set a timer and put away your study materials. Sit at a table or desk in a quiet room, imagine yourself at the testing center, and answer questions as quickly and accurately as possible.

Keep repeating timed and closed-book tests on a regular basis until you run out of practice tests or it's time for the actual test. Your mind will be ready for the schedule and stress of test day, and you'll be able to focus on recalling the material you've learned.

Secret Key #4 – Pace Yourself

Once you're fully prepared for the material on the test, your biggest challenge on test day will be managing your time. Just knowing that the clock is ticking can make you panic even if you have plenty of time left. Work on pacing yourself so you can build confidence against the time constraints of the exam. Pacing is a difficult skill to master, especially in a high-pressure environment, so **practice is vital**.

Set time expectations for your pace based on how much time is available. For example, if a section has 60 questions and the time limit is 30 minutes, you know you have to average 30 seconds or less per question in order to answer them all. Although 30 seconds is the hard limit, set 25 seconds per question as your goal, so you reserve extra time to spend on harder questions. When you budget extra time for the harder questions, you no longer have any reason to stress when those questions take longer to answer.

Don't let this time expectation distract you from working through the test at a calm, steady pace, but keep it in mind so you don't spend too much time on any one question. Recognize that taking extra time on one question you don't understand may keep you from answering two that you do understand later in the test. If your time limit for a question is up and you're still not sure of the answer, mark it and move on, and come back to it later if the time and the test format allow. If the testing format doesn't allow you to return to earlier questions, just make an educated guess; then put it out of your mind and move on.

On the easier questions, be careful not to rush. It may seem wise to hurry through them so you have more time for the challenging ones, but it's not worth missing one if you know the concept and just didn't take the time to read the question fully. Work efficiently but make sure you understand the question and have looked at all of the answer choices, since more than one may seem right at first.

Even if you're paying attention to the time, you may find yourself a little behind at some point. You should speed up to get back on track, but do so wisely. Don't panic; just take a few seconds less on each question until you're caught up. Don't guess without thinking, but do look through the answer choices and eliminate any you know are wrong. If you can get down to two choices, it is often worthwhile to guess from those. Once you've chosen an answer, move on and don't dwell on any that you skipped or had to hurry through. If a question was taking too long, chances are it was one of the harder ones, so you weren't as likely to get it right anyway.

On the other hand, if you find yourself getting ahead of schedule, it may be beneficial to slow down a little. The more quickly you work, the more likely you are to make a careless mistake that will affect your score. You've budgeted time for each question, so don't be afraid to spend that time. Practice an efficient but careful pace to get the most out of the time you have.

Secret Key #5 – Have a Plan for Guessing

When you're taking the test, you may find yourself stuck on a question. Some of the answer choices seem better than others, but you don't see the one answer choice that is obviously correct. What do you do?

The scenario described above is very common, yet most test takers have not effectively prepared for it. Developing and practicing a plan for guessing may be one of the single most effective uses of your time as you get ready for the exam.

In developing your plan for guessing, there are three questions to address:

- When should you start the guessing process?
- How should you narrow down the choices?
- Which answer should you choose?

When to Start the Guessing Process

Unless your plan for guessing is to select C every time (which, despite its merits, is not what we recommend), you need to leave yourself enough time to apply your answer elimination strategies. Since you have a limited amount of time for each question, that means that if you're going to give yourself the best shot at guessing correctly, you have to decide quickly whether or not you will guess.

Of course, the best-case scenario is that you don't have to guess at all, so first, see if you can answer the question based on your knowledge of the subject and basic reasoning skills. Focus on the key words in the question and try to jog your memory of related topics. Give yourself a chance to bring the knowledge to mind, but once you realize that you don't have (or you can't access) the knowledge you need to answer the question, it's time to start the guessing process.

It's almost always better to start the guessing process too early than too late. It only takes a few seconds to remember something and answer the question from knowledge. Carefully eliminating wrong answer choices takes longer. Plus, going through the process of eliminating answer choices can actually help jog your memory.

Summary: Start the guessing process as soon as you decide that you can't answer the question based on your knowledge.

How to Narrow Down the Choices

The next chapter in this book (**Test-Taking Strategies**) includes a wide range of strategies for how to approach questions and how to look for answer choices to eliminate. You will definitely want to read those carefully, practice them, and figure out which ones work best for you. Here though, we're going to address a mindset rather than a particular strategy.

Your chances of guessing an answer correctly depend on how many options you are choosing from.

How many choices you have	How likely you are to guess correctly
5	20%
4	25%
3	33%
2	50%
1	100%

You can see from this chart just how valuable it is to be able to eliminate incorrect answers and make an educated guess, but there are two things that many test takers do that cause them to miss out on the benefits of guessing:

- Accidentally eliminating the correct answer
- Selecting an answer based on an impression

We'll look at the first one here, and the second one in the next section.

To avoid accidentally eliminating the correct answer, we recommend a thought exercise called **the $5 challenge**. In this challenge, you only eliminate an answer choice from contention if you are willing to bet $5 on it being wrong. Why $5? Five dollars is a small but not insignificant amount of money. It's an amount you could afford to lose but wouldn't want to throw away. And while losing $5 once might not hurt too much, doing it twenty times will set you back $100. In the same way, each small decision you make—eliminating a choice here, guessing on a question there—won't by itself impact your score very much, but when you put them all together, they can make a big difference. By holding each answer choice elimination decision to a higher standard, you can reduce the risk of accidentally eliminating the correct answer.

The $5 challenge can also be applied in a positive sense: If you are willing to bet $5 that an answer choice *is* correct, go ahead and mark it as correct.

Summary: Only eliminate an answer choice if you are willing to bet $5 that it is wrong.

Which Answer to Choose

You're taking the test. You've run into a hard question and decided you'll have to guess. You've eliminated all the answer choices you're willing to bet $5 on. Now you have to pick an answer. Why do we even need to talk about this? Why can't you just pick whichever one you feel like when the time comes?

The answer to these questions is that if you don't come into the test with a plan, you'll rely on your impression to select an answer choice, and if you do that, you risk falling into a trap. The test writers know that everyone who takes their test will be guessing on some of the questions, so they intentionally write wrong answer choices to seem plausible. You still have to pick an answer though, and if the wrong answer choices are designed to look right, how can you ever be sure that you're not falling for their trap? The best solution we've found to this dilemma is to take the decision out of your hands entirely. Here is the process we recommend:

Once you've eliminated any choices that you are confident (willing to bet $5) are wrong, select the first remaining choice as your answer.

Whether you choose to select the first remaining choice, the second, or the last, the important thing is that you use some preselected standard. Using this approach guarantees that you will not be enticed into selecting an answer choice that looks right, because you are not basing your decision on how the answer choices look.

This is not meant to make you question your knowledge. Instead, it is to help you recognize the difference between your knowledge and your impressions. There's a huge difference between thinking an answer is right because of what you know, and thinking an answer is right because it looks or sounds like it should be right.

Summary: To ensure that your selection is appropriately random, make a predetermined selection from among all answer choices you have not eliminated.

Test-Taking Strategies

This section contains a list of test-taking strategies that you may find helpful as you work through the test. By taking what you know and applying logical thought, you can maximize your chances of answering any question correctly!

It is very important to realize that every question is different and every person is different: no single strategy will work on every question, and no single strategy will work for every person. That's why we've included all of them here, so you can try them out and determine which ones work best for different types of questions and which ones work best for you.

Question Strategies

Read Carefully

Read the question and answer choices carefully. Don't miss the question because you misread the terms. You have plenty of time to read each question thoroughly and make sure you understand what is being asked. Yet a happy medium must be attained, so don't waste too much time. You must read carefully, but efficiently.

Contextual Clues

Look for contextual clues. If the question includes a word you are not familiar with, look at the immediate context for some indication of what the word might mean. Contextual clues can often give you all the information you need to decipher the meaning of an unfamiliar word. Even if you can't determine the meaning, you may be able to narrow down the possibilities enough to make a solid guess at the answer to the question.

Prefixes

If you're having trouble with a word in the question or answer choices, try dissecting it. Take advantage of every clue that the word might include. Prefixes and suffixes can be a huge help. Usually they allow you to determine a basic meaning. Pre- means before, post- means after, pro - is positive, de- is negative. From prefixes and suffixes, you can get an idea of the general meaning of the word and try to put it into context.

Hedge Words

Watch out for critical hedge words, such as *likely, may, can, sometimes, often, almost, mostly, usually, generally, rarely,* and *sometimes.* Question writers insert these hedge phrases to cover every possibility. Often an answer choice will be wrong simply because it leaves no room for exception. Be on guard for answer choices that have definitive words such as *exactly* and *always.*

Switchback Words

Stay alert for *switchbacks.* These are the words and phrases frequently used to alert you to shifts in thought. The most common switchback words are *but, although,* and *however.* Others include *nevertheless, on the other hand, even though, while, in spite of, despite, regardless of.* Switchback words are important to catch because they can change the direction of the question or an answer choice.

Face Value

When in doubt, use common sense. Accept the situation in the problem at face value. Don't read too much into it. These problems will not require you to make wild assumptions. If you have to go beyond creativity and warp time or space in order to have an answer choice fit the question, then you should move on and consider the other answer choices. These are normal problems rooted in reality. The applicable relationship or explanation may not be readily apparent, but it is there for you to figure out. Use your common sense to interpret anything that isn't clear.

Answer Choice Strategies

Answer Selection

The most thorough way to pick an answer choice is to identify and eliminate wrong answers until only one is left, then confirm it is the correct answer. Sometimes an answer choice may immediately seem right, but be careful. The test writers will usually put more than one reasonable answer choice on each question, so take a second to read all of them and make sure that the other choices are not equally obvious. As long as you have time left, it is better to read every answer choice than to pick the first one that looks right without checking the others.

Answer Choice Families

An answer choice family consists of two (in rare cases, three) answer choices that are very similar in construction and cannot all be true at the same time. If you see two answer choices that are direct opposites or parallels, one of them is usually the correct answer. For instance, if one answer choice says that quantity x increases and another either says that quantity x decreases (opposite) or says that quantity y increases (parallel), then those answer choices would fall into the same family. An answer choice that doesn't match the construction of the answer choice family is more likely to be incorrect. Most questions will not have answer choice families, but when they do appear, you should be prepared to recognize them.

Eliminate Answers

Eliminate answer choices as soon as you realize they are wrong, but make sure you consider all possibilities. If you are eliminating answer choices and realize that the last one you are left with is also wrong, don't panic. Start over and consider each choice again. There may be something you missed the first time that you will realize on the second pass.

Avoid Fact Traps

Don't be distracted by an answer choice that is factually true but doesn't answer the question. You are looking for the choice that answers the question. Stay focused on what the question is asking for so you don't accidentally pick an answer that is true but incorrect. Always go back to the question and make sure the answer choice you've selected actually answers the question and is not merely a true statement.

Extreme Statements

In general, you should avoid answers that put forth extreme actions as standard practice or proclaim controversial ideas as established fact. An answer choice that states the "process should be used in certain situations, if..." is much more likely to be correct than one that states the "process should be discontinued completely." The first is a calm rational statement and doesn't even make a definitive, uncompromising stance, using a hedge word *if* to provide wiggle room, whereas the second choice is a radical idea and far more extreme.

Benchmark

As you read through the answer choices and you come across one that seems to answer the question well, mentally select that answer choice. This is not your final answer, but it's the one that will help you evaluate the other answer choices. The one that you selected is your benchmark or standard for judging each of the other answer choices. Every other answer choice must be compared to your benchmark. That choice is correct until proven otherwise by another answer choice beating it. If you find a better answer, then that one becomes your new benchmark. Once you've decided that no other choice answers the question as well as your benchmark, you have your final answer.

Predict the Answer

Before you even start looking at the answer choices, it is often best to try to predict the answer. When you come up with the answer on your own, it is easier to avoid distractions and traps because you will know exactly what to look for. The right answer choice is unlikely to be word-for-word what you came up with, but it should be a close match. Even if you are confident that you have the right answer, you should still take the time to read each option before moving on.

General Strategies

Tough Questions

If you are stumped on a problem or it appears too hard or too difficult, don't waste time. Move on! Remember though, if you can quickly check for obviously incorrect answer choices, your chances of guessing correctly are greatly improved. Before you completely give up, at least try to knock out a couple of possible answers. Eliminate what you can and then guess at the remaining answer choices before moving on.

Check Your Work

Since you will probably not know every term listed and the answer to every question, it is important that you get credit for the ones that you do know. Don't miss any questions through careless mistakes. If at all possible, try to take a second to look back over your answer selection and make sure you've selected the correct answer choice and haven't made a costly careless mistake (such as marking an answer choice that you didn't mean to mark). This quick double check should more than pay for itself in caught mistakes for the time it costs.

Pace Yourself

It's easy to be overwhelmed when you're looking at a page full of questions; your mind is confused and full of random thoughts, and the clock is ticking down faster than you would like. Calm down and maintain the pace that you have set for yourself. Especially as you get down to the last few minutes of the test, don't let the small numbers on the clock make you panic. As long as you are on track by monitoring your pace, you are guaranteed to have time for each question.

Don't Rush

It is very easy to make errors when you are in a hurry. Maintaining a fast pace in answering questions is pointless if it makes you miss questions that you would have gotten right otherwise. Test writers like to include distracting information and wrong answers that seem right. Taking a little extra time to avoid careless mistakes can make all the difference in your test score. Find a pace that allows you to be confident in the answers that you select.

Keep Moving

Panicking will not help you pass the test, so do your best to stay calm and keep moving. Taking deep breaths and going through the answer elimination steps you practiced can help to break through a stress barrier and keep your pace.

Final Notes

The combination of a solid foundation of content knowledge and the confidence that comes from practicing your plan for applying that knowledge is the key to maximizing your performance on test day. As your foundation of content knowledge is built up and strengthened, you'll find that the strategies included in this chapter become more and more effective in helping you quickly sift through the distractions and traps of the test to isolate the correct answer.

Now it's time to move on to the test content chapters of this book, but be sure to keep your goal in mind. As you read, think about how you will be able to apply this information on the test. If you've already seen sample questions for the test and you have an idea of the question format and style, try to come up with questions of your own that you can answer based on what you're reading. This will give you valuable practice applying your knowledge in the same ways you can expect to on test day.

Good luck and good studying!

SIFT Overview

The goal of becoming a military aviator is a noble one, and those who achieve it will have earned membership in a very elite class. Many people would like to become aviators, but few are up to the myriad demands and challenges that must be successfully met in order to reach their dream. It is a long and arduous journey, and it begins with performing well on a difficult aptitude test, above and beyond any other requirements for college degrees or percentile rank on broader military aptitude exams. These exams are known as aptitude tests, because they focus less on the knowledge a person already has and more on that person's ability to innately handle certain types of tasks.

There are two primary reasons the military requires aspiring aviators to pass these challenging exams. The first reason hinges on supply and demand. Simply put, the number of men and women interested in becoming aviators in the military is far higher than the number of pilots the various branches of the military actually need. The second primary factor is the enormous cost of training a military pilot. It has long been common knowledge that it costs well over a $1 million to train a pilot, but that now appears to be an outdated figure. It was recently reported that the Air Force spends approximately $6 million to train one fighter pilot. No matter what the exact figure is, training military pilots is extremely expensive. Before they commit to training a pilot, the military branches want to be pretty certain that he or she is up to the challenge, and won't wash out before completing training. These tests have been designed to select the candidates who are most likely to be excellent candidates for pilot training, and they have a long track record of being very accurate.

In the Army, the aptitude test is known as the SIFT, which stands for Selection Instrument for Flight Training. Although SIFT is considered to be an aptitude test, it is also a test of acquired knowledge and skills in some areas, such as aviation knowledge and math. The SIFT has only been around since 2013, when it replaced the Army's previous exam for future pilots, the Army Flight Aptitude Selection Test. There is no paper and pencil version of the SIFT; it is only given via computer. The SIFT is actually a battery of seven different exams, or subtests, and it takes about two and a half hours to complete the entire battery.

The seven sections of the SIFT are: Simple Drawings (SD), which lasts two minutes and has 100 questions, Hidden Figures (HF), which last five minutes and has 50 questions, Army Aviation Information Test (AAIT), which lasts 30 minutes and has 40 questions, Spatial Apperception Test (SAT), which lasts 10 minutes and has 25 questions, Reading Comprehension Test (RCT), which lasts 30 minutes and has 20 questions, and two sections which have a variable number of questions – Math Skills Test (MST) which lasts 40 minutes, and Mechanical Comprehension Test (MCT), which lasts 15 minutes. The reason the number of questions varies on the last two sections is that they are in a format known as computer adaptive. This means that the section will begin with a question of medium difficulty. If the test taker answers it correctly, the computer will give them a harder question. If they answer that question incorrectly, they will be given an easier question. People who answer the first question incorrectly are then given an easier one, and if they get it right, the next question will be harder. The computer will adapt to the test taker in this manner after every question, so a person who answers several of the early questions correctly may not be given as many questions in total as other test takers receive.

Keep in mind that no one will be allowed to take the SIFT more than two times. If a person takes the SIFT, and does poorly, they have one more chance to pass it, but they must first wait six months before attempting it again. If they fail the SIFT the second time, that's it – they can never take it again. So it's critical to be thoroughly prepared to do well on your first attempt at the SIFT.

The next few sections will go over the seven subtests in detail to help prepare you for what you will see on each test.

Simple Drawings Test

The Simple Drawings section of the SIFT couldn't be simpler, on the one hand, yet at the same time, it's also extremely challenging. Every problem asks you to perform one very easy task – look at the five items shown, and choose the one that doesn't match the other four. In other words, four of the five items will be exactly the same, and one will be different, and you must spot the exception and mark the corresponding answer choice.

The task itself sounds easy enough, and, in fact, it really is quite easy. As the name of the section implies, the drawings aren't at all complicated. The differences between the mismatched item and the other four items will be obvious; you won't be searching for minute differences. The problems won't involve looking at five circles and trying to determine which one of them has a circumference that is 31/32 of the circumference of the other four, or any other drawings with only tiny or subtle differences. The correct answer will be apparent. It's just a matter of how quickly you can process what's in front of you and respond correctly.

Answering any single question in this section correctly is easy enough, but answering all of them will be very challenging. That's because there's a time limit of only two minutes, and there are 100 questions. That's what turns this section, which appears disarmingly easy at first glance, into an extremely difficult task. The strictly enforced time limit means a person has a mere 1.2 seconds to spend on each problem if they're going to answer all 100 questions. That's 1.2 seconds to scan the problem, spot the item that doesn't match the others, and mark the correct answer choice, a hundred times in a row.

For the vast majority of people, this is an impossible task. So, you should be aware going in that you probably won't finish all the questions in this section. You should definitely try to go as fast as you can, for as long as you can, because speed is critically important. Of course, accuracy is also critically important, and if going too fast in order to answer all 100 questions causes a drop in your accuracy, you won't have helped yourself at all. Also, if you're running out of time, do not start marking answer choices randomly, hoping to get some right by accident. Wrong answers penalize your score, so you will lower your score if you try randomly guessing.

Giving a person only two minutes to answer 100 questions may seem a bit harsh, but the Army's testing experts deliberately designed this section in such a way that hardly anyone would be able to complete all 100 questions in the allotted time. This section is mainly measuring two abilities or aptitudes – accurate observation under pressure, and reaction time under pressure. These are two of the most important skills a person must possess in order to succeed as a pilot, and the Army's test designers believe that the high-pressure Simple Drawings section is an efficient way of determining which applicants have high levels of skill in these areas, and which ones don't.

It is a good idea to take advantage of the opportunity to practice this subtest before you take your official SIFT. Practicing with a two-minute timer set is your best bet for increasing your chances of earning a great score in this section. You'll gain some experience in racing against the clock while trying to maintain your accuracy.

Bear in mind that the process of answering these questions on paper will not be the same as the process of answering them on a computer, as you will have to for your official SIFT. On paper, you can see the whole page's worth of questions at a time, while on the computer, you will only see one question at a time, and you will have to answer it before you are shown the next one. This may not seem like a big deal, but if each question takes even a tenth of a second longer to process, then that means your timer is effectively starting out at 110 seconds instead of 120 seconds. To try to counteract this effect, it might be a good idea to have an extra blank sheet of paper when you practice that you can use to cover up all the questions on the page except the question you're currently working on. That way, you can better simulate the actual testing experience.

Also, because of the nature of the test questions, there's no reason why you shouldn't be able to retake the same test over a few times. You couldn't do this with a test based on reading passages, of course, because you would tend to remember many of the right answers. However, because the problems in this section involve comparing groups of random symbols, and because you'll be going very fast as you work through the tests, you won't retain very much of what you see. For that reason, we recommend marking your answers on a separate sheet of paper so there will be no clues on the actual questions if you decide to practice again with the same test.

Here are a few examples of what the Simple Drawings questions might look like:

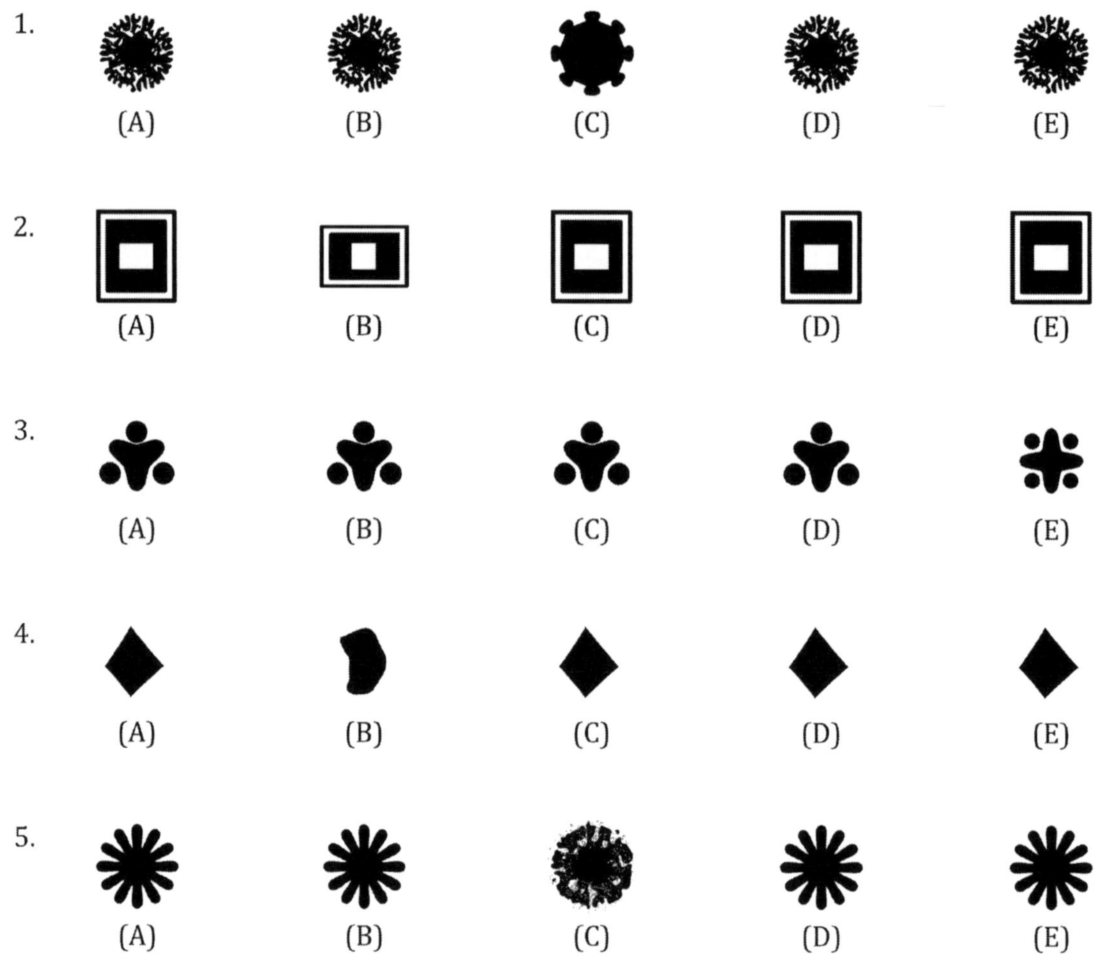

Hidden Figures Test

This section of the SIFT is similar to the Simple Drawings section in that it measures your ability to quickly and accurately apprehend visual information. In Simple Drawings the information you're looking for is obvious, and the difficulty is in trying to complete all of the questions before time expires. That is not the case in the Hidden Figures section; as the name implies, your task in this part of the SIFT is to locate a figure or shape that is hidden in a larger, much more complicated drawing.

These questions are measuring where you fall on the Field Independence – Field Dependence Scale. Field independence refers to a person's ability to ignore non-important visual information, and zero in on the important information within the field. People who are high on the Field Independence end of the scale are able to do this very well, while people on the other end of the scale, the Field Dependence end, have a lot of difficulty in separating important visual information from irrelevant information. Of course, pilots need to be extremely skilled at accurately interpreting visual information instantly, ignoring everything that doesn't matter and honing in on the important data, so you'll need to do well on this section to achieve a high score on the SIFT.

Each group of questions on the test will show five complex arrangements of lines and geometric shapes, where each arrangement looks much like a puzzle that has been put together. Above these, the test will show five different figures. Each arrangement of lines and shapes is hiding one (and only one) of the figures shown above them and you must determine which figure is in each shape arrangement. Not all figures have to be used; some may be used more than once within a set of five questions, so the answer to the fifth question is not necessarily the choice that hasn't been used yet.

This section contains 50 questions, and has a time limit of five minutes. This may sound less intimidating than the Simple Drawings section, which features 100 questions with a two-minute time limit, but for most people, answering all the Hidden Figures questions in the space of five minute will be even more difficult than answering all the Simple Drawings questions in two minutes. That's because in Simple Drawings, it takes a mere glance to find the right answer for each question. In this section, the figure you're looking for is well hidden, and unless you're extraordinarily gifted in field independence, you're going to have to spend some amount of time on each complex drawing to find the hidden figure.

There are a few different strategies that can be used on these questions. Some strategies will work better than others, depending on the different figures and shape arrangements you encounter, and your particular characteristics.

Strategy 1: Examine each shape arrangement in turn. For each arrangement, try to fit each of the figures into the lines in the arrangement. Once you find one that fits (size, shape, and orientation) into the arrangement, go ahead and mark it. There's no need to check the remaining figures since only one will fit into each arrangement. Remember though not to cross a figure off the list after you've used it; figures can be used multiple times in the set.

Strategy 2: Instead of starting with the shape arrangements, start with the figures. Look through the figures and check for any prominent distinguishing characteristics (e.g., a long side at a particular diagonal angle, a pair of sides that run parallel at a particular distance, a side that zigzags). For each figure with a prominent feature, scan the shape arrangements and eliminate that figure for any arrangements that cannot accommodate the prominent feature. Once you've ruled out as many figures as possible for the five arrangements, follow the steps for strategy 1, but check out only the remaining figures (the ones that you haven't eliminated for each arrangement).

You'll want to try out both strategies and see which one gives you better results within the time constraints of the section. One of the most important rules governing these questions is that the hidden figure has to be the exact same size and orientation as where it is shown above with the answer choices, so regardless of what strategy you choose to employ, keep this in mind.

On the next page is an example of a hidden figures question set.

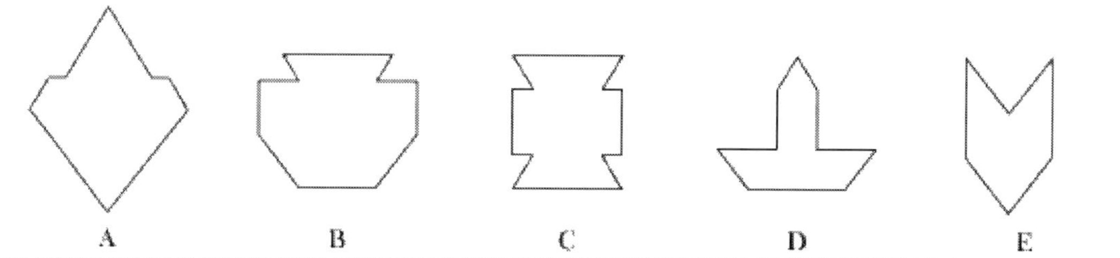

1. 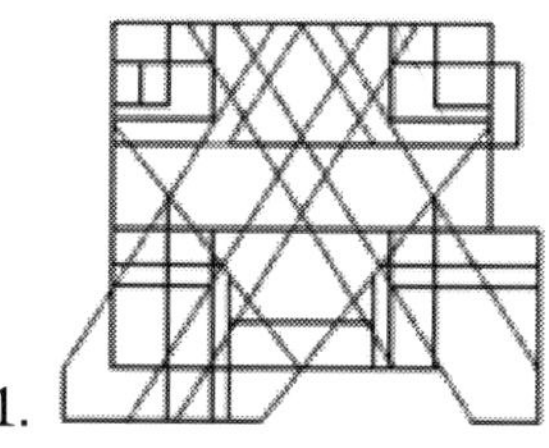

2. 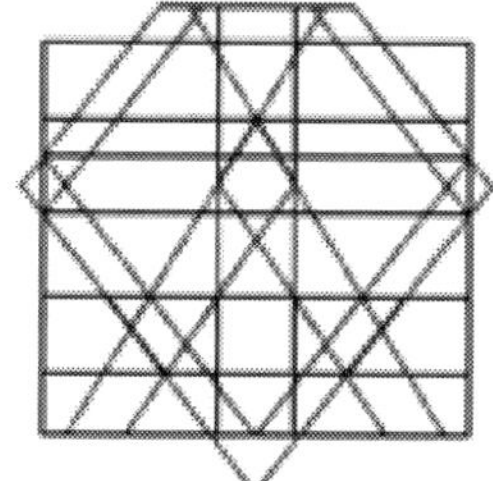

3. 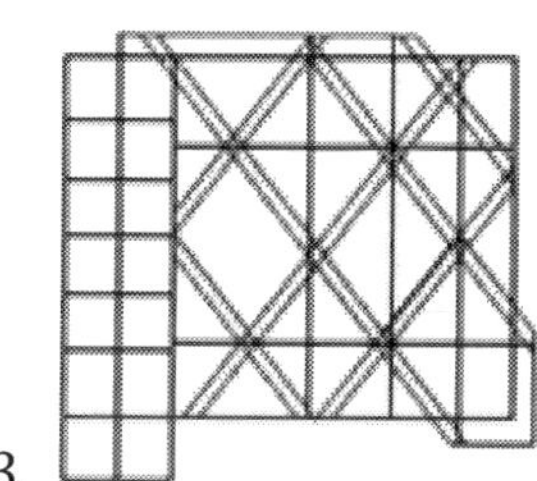

4. 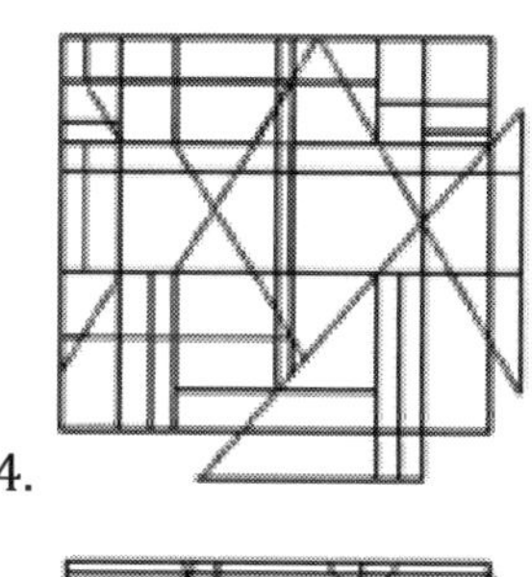

5. 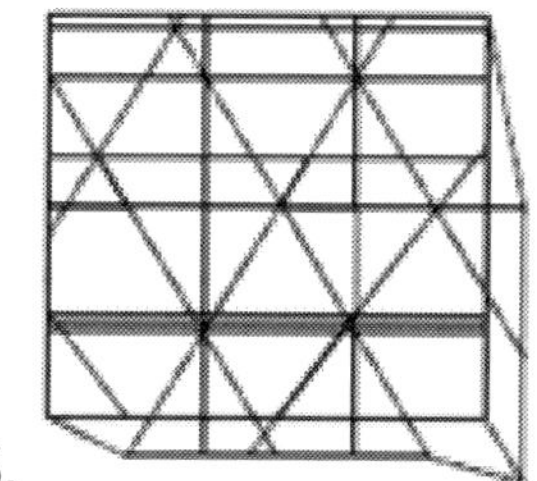

Answers:

1. A

2. D

3. E

4. C

5. B

Army Aviation Information Test

The Army Aviation Information section tests your knowledge of basic aviation information. Most of the information the questions are based on can be found in the FAA Helicopter Flying Handbook. In Army Aviation Information, you'll have 30 minutes to answer 40 questions. Since these are knowledge-based questions, you can improve your success rate here by reading up on the content that will be tested on the exam. In fact, since nearly all the rest of the SIFT subtests are testing for aptitude, this is one of the few sections where good old-fashioned studying can make a huge difference in your results. And unlike other sections, this section is not designed to be difficult for the average person to answer all the questions within the allotted time. With proper preparation, you should be able to finish all the questions in this section, and answer most of them correctly.

The section below consists primarily of brief excerpts from the FAA handbook on helicopter flight. The FAA helicopter handbook is a lengthy and thorough manual that covers everything you need to know to operate a helicopter. No matter what you read and retain from the excerpts we've included, you'll want to obtain a copy of the FAA helicopter manual for yourself. You can download it for free from the internet or if you like physical books, there are a variety of nominally priced options that can be purchased on Amazon. No matter which format you choose, make it a point to study this handbook thoroughly. Doing so is essential not only to your score on this section of the SIFT, but also to your attaining the necessary knowledge to become a skillful pilot. If you have time to read the whole manual, we recommend doing so, but if not, we advise that you focus your time on the following chapters:

Chapter 2: Aerodynamics of Flight

Chapter 3: Helicopter Flight Controls

Chapter 6: Weight and Balance

Chapter 9: Basic Flight Maneuvers

Chapter 10: Advanced Flight Maneuvers

Link for accessing the FAA Helicopter Handbook online or downloading it:

https://www.faa.gov/regulations_policies/handbooks_manuals/aviation/helicopter_flying_handbook/

If the link doesn't work (i.e., if the FAA decides to change the location), you can always access it by going to www.faa.gov and entering "helicopter flying handbook" in their search bar.

Aerodynamics

Forces Acting on the Aircraft

Once a helicopter leaves the ground, it is acted upon by four aerodynamic forces; thrust, drag, lift and weight. Understanding how these forces work and knowing how to control them with the use of power and flight controls are essential to flight. They are defined as follows:

- Thrust—the forward force produced by the power plant/propeller or rotor. It opposes or overcomes the force of drag. As a general rule, it acts parallel to the longitudinal axis. However, this is not always the case, as explained later.
- Drag—a rearward, retarding force caused by disruption of airflow by the wing, rotor, fuselage, and other protruding objects. Drag opposes thrust and acts rearward parallel to the relative wind.
- Weight—the combined load of the aircraft itself, the crew, the fuel, and the cargo or baggage. Weight pulls the aircraft downward because of the force of gravity. It opposes lift and acts vertically downward through the aircraft's center of gravity (CG).
- Lift—opposes the downward force of weight, is produced by the dynamic effect of the air acting on the airfoil, and acts perpendicular to the flightpath through the center of lift.

Lift

Lift is generated when an object changes the direction of flow of a fluid or when the fluid is forced to move by the object passing through it. When the object and fluid move relative to each other and the object turns the fluid flow in a direction perpendicular to that flow, the force required to do this work creates an equal and opposite force that is lift. The object may be moving through a stationary fluid, or the fluid may be flowing past a stationary object—these two are effectively identical as, in principle, it is only the frame of reference of the viewer which differs. The lift generated by an airfoil depends on such factors as:

- Speed of the airflow
- Density of the air
- Total area of the segment or airfoil
- Angle of attack (AOA) between the air and the airfoil

The AOA is the angle at which the airfoil meets the oncoming airflow (or vice versa). In the case of a helicopter, the object is the rotor blade (airfoil) and the fluid is the air. Lift is produced when a mass of air is deflected, and it always acts perpendicular to the resultant relative wind. A symmetric airfoil must have a positive AOA to generate positive lift. At a zero AOA, no lift is generated. At a negative AOA, negative lift is generated. A cambered or nonsymmetrical airfoil may produce positive lift at zero, or even small negative AOA.

The basic concept of lift is simple. However, the details of how the relative movement of air and airfoil interact to produce the turning action that generates lift are complex. In any case causing lift, an angled flat plate, revolving cylinder, airfoil, etc., the flow meeting the leading edge of the object is forced to split over and under the object. The sudden change in direction over the object causes an area of low pressure to form behind the leading edge on the upper surface of the object. In turn, due to this pressure gradient and the viscosity of the fluid, the flow over the object is accelerated down along the upper surface of the object. At the same time, the flow forced under the object is rapidly slowed or stagnated causing an area of high pressure. This also causes the flow to accelerate along the upper surface of the object. The two sections of the fluid each leave the trailing edge of the object with a downward component of momentum, producing lift.

Weight

Normally, weight is thought of as being a known, fixed value, such as the weight of the helicopter, fuel, and occupants. To lift the helicopter off the ground vertically, the rotor system must generate enough lift to overcome or offset the total weight of the helicopter and its occupants. Newton's First Law states: "Every object in a state of uniform motion tends to remain in that state of motion unless an external force is applied to it." In this case, the object is the helicopter whether at a hover or on the ground and the external force applied to it is lift, which is accomplished by increasing the pitch angle of the main rotor blades. This action forces the helicopter into a state of motion, without it the helicopter would either remain on the ground or at a hover.

The weight of the helicopter can also be influenced by aerodynamic loads. When you bank a helicopter while maintaining a constant altitude, the "G" load or load factor increases. The load factor is the actual load on the rotor blades at any time, divided by the normal load or gross weight (weight of the helicopter and its contents). Any time a helicopter flies in a constant altitude curved flightpath, the load supported by the rotor blades is greater than the total weight of the helicopter. The tighter the curved flightpath is, the steeper the bank is; the more rapid the flare or pullout from a dive is, the greater the load supported by the rotor. Therefore, the greater the load factor must be.

To overcome this additional load factor, the helicopter must be able to produce more lift. If excess engine power is not available, the helicopter either descends or has to decelerate in order to maintain the same altitude. The load factor and, hence, apparent gross weight increase is relatively small in banks up to 30°. Even so, under the right set of adverse circumstances, such as high-density altitude, turbulent air, high gross weight, and poor pilot technique, sufficient or excess power may not be available to maintain altitude and airspeed. Pilots must take all of these factors into consideration throughout the entire flight from the point of ascending to a hover to landing. Above 30° of bank, the apparent increase in gross weight soars. At 30° of bank, or pitch, the apparent increase is only 16 percent, but at 60°, it is twice the load on the wings and rotor system. For example, if the weight of the helicopter is 1,600 pounds, the weight supported by the rotor disk in a 30° bank at a constant altitude would be 1,856 pounds (1,600 + 16 percent (or 256)). In a 60° bank, it would be 3,200 pounds; in an 80° bank, it would be almost six times as much, or 8,000 pounds. It is important to note that each rotor blade must support a percentage of the gross weight. In a two bladed system, each blade of the 1,600-pound helicopter as stated above would have to lift 50 percent or 800 pounds. If this same helicopter had three rotor blades, each blade would have to lift only 33 percent, or 533 pounds. One additional cause of large load factors is rough or turbulent air. The severe vertical gusts produced by turbulence can cause a sudden increase in AOA, resulting in increased rotor blade loads that are resisted by the inertia of the helicopter.

Each type of helicopter has its own limitations which are based on the aircraft structure, size, and capabilities. Regardless of how much weight one can carry or the engine power that it may have, they are all susceptible to aerodynamic overloading. Unfortunately, if the pilot attempts to push the performance envelope the consequence can be fatal. Aerodynamic forces effect every movement in a helicopter, whether it is increasing the collective or a steep bank angle. Anticipating results from a particular maneuver or adjustment of a flight control is not good piloting technique. Instead pilots need to truly understand the capabilities of the helicopter under any and all circumstances and plan to never exceed the flight envelope for any situation.

Thrust

Thrust, like lift, is generated by the rotation of the main rotor system. In a helicopter, thrust can be forward, rearward, sideward, or vertical. The resultant lift and thrust determines the direction of movement of the helicopter.

The solidity ratio is the ratio of the total rotor blade area, which is the combined area of all the main rotor blades, to the total rotor disk area. This ratio provides a means to measure the potential for a rotor system to provide thrust and lift. The mathematical calculations needed to calculate the solidity ratio for each helicopter may not be of importance to most pilots but what should be are the capabilities of the rotor system to produce and maintain lift. Many helicopter accidents are caused from the rotor system being overloaded. Simply put, pilots attempt maneuvers that require more lift than the rotor system can produce or more power than the helicopter's powerplant can provide. Trying to land with a nose high attitude along with any other unfavorable condition (i.e., high gross weight or wind gusts) is most likely to end in disaster.

The tail rotor also produces thrust. The amount of thrust is variable through the use of the antitorque pedals and is used to control the helicopter's yaw.

Drag

The force that resists the movement of a helicopter through the air and is produced when lift is developed is called drag. Drag must be overcome by the engine to turn the rotor. Drag always acts parallel to the relative wind. Total drag is composed of three types of drag: profile, induced, and parasite.

Profile Drag

Profile drag develops from the frictional resistance of the blades passing through the air. It does not change significantly with the airfoil's AOA, but increases moderately when airspeed increases. Profile drag is composed of form drag and skin friction. Form drag results from the turbulent wake caused by the separation of airflow from the surface of a structure. The amount of drag is related to both the size and shape of the structure that protrudes into the relative wind. Skin friction is caused by surface roughness. Even though the surface appears smooth, it may be quite rough when viewed under a microscope. A thin layer of air clings to the rough surface and creates small eddies that contribute to drag.

Induced Drag

Induced drag is generated by the airflow circulation around the rotor blade as it creates lift. The high-pressure area beneath the blade joins the low-pressure area above the blade at the trailing edge and at the rotor tips. This causes a spiral, or vortex, which trails behind each blade whenever lift is being produced. These vortices deflect the airstream downward in the vicinity of the blade, creating an increase in downwash. Therefore, the blade operates in an average relative wind that is inclined downward and rearward near the blade. Because the lift produced by the blade is perpendicular to the relative wind, the lift is inclined aft by the same amount. The component of lift that is acting in a rearward direction is induced drag.

As the air pressure differential increases with an increase in AOA, stronger vortices form, and induced drag increases. Since the blade's AOA is usually lower at higher airspeeds, and higher at low speeds, induced drag decreases as airspeed increases and increases as airspeed decreases. Induced drag is the major cause of drag at lower airspeeds.

Parasite Drag

Parasite drag is present any time the helicopter is moving through the air. This type of drag increases with airspeed. Non-lifting components of the helicopter, such as the cabin, rotor mast, tail, and landing gear, contribute to parasite drag. Any loss of momentum by the airstream, due to such things as openings for engine cooling, creates additional parasite drag. Because of its rapid increase with increasing airspeed, parasite drag is the major cause of drag at higher airspeeds. Parasite drag varies with the square of the velocity; therefore, doubling the airspeed increases the parasite drag four times.

Total Drag

Total drag for a helicopter is the sum of all three drag forces. As airspeed increases, parasite drag increases, while induced drag decreases. Profile drag remains relatively constant throughout the speed range with some increase at higher airspeeds. Combining all drag forces results in a total drag curve. The low point on the total drag curve shows the airspeed at which drag is minimized. This is the point where the lift-to-drag ratio is greatest and is referred to as L/DMAX. At this speed, the total lift capacity of the helicopter, when compared to the total drag of the helicopter, is most favorable. This is an important factor in helicopter performance.

Flight Controls

Collective Pitch Control

The collective pitch control (or simply "collective" or "thrust lever") is located on the left side of the pilot's seat and is operated with the left hand. The collective is used to make changes to the pitch angle of the main rotor blades and does this simultaneously, or collectively, as the name implies. As the collective pitch control is raised, there is a simultaneous and equal increase in pitch angle of all main rotor blades; as it is lowered, there is a simultaneous and equal decrease in pitch angle. This is done through a series of mechanical linkages and the amount of movement in the collective lever determines the amount of blade pitch change. An adjustable friction control helps prevent inadvertent collective pitch movement.

Changing the pitch angle on the blades changes the angle of incidence on each blade. With a change in angle of incidence comes a change in drag, which affects the speed or revolutions per minute (rpm) of the main rotor. As the pitch angle increases, angle of incidence increases, drag increases, and rotor rpm decreases. Decreasing pitch angle decreases both angle of incidence and drag, while rotor rpm increases. In order to maintain a constant rotor rpm, which is essential in helicopter operations, a proportionate change in power is required to compensate for the change in drag. This is accomplished with the throttle control or governor, which automatically adjusts engine power.

Throttle Control

The function of the throttle is to regulate engine rpm. If the correlator or governor system does not maintain the desired rpm when the collective is raised or lowered, or if those systems are not installed, the throttle must be moved manually with the twist grip in order to maintain rpm. The throttle control is much like a motorcycle throttle, and works in virtually the same way. Twisting the throttle to the left increases rpm; twisting the throttle to the right decreases rpm.

Governor/Correlator

A governor is a sensing device that senses rotor and engine rpm and makes the necessary adjustments in order to keep rotor rpm constant. In normal operations, once the rotor rpm is set, the governor keeps the rpm constant, and there is no need to make any throttle adjustments. Governors are common on all turbine helicopters (as it is a function of the fuel control system of the turbine engine), and used on some piston powered helicopters.

A correlator is a mechanical connection between the collective lever and the engine throttle. When the collective lever is raised, power is automatically increased; when lowered, power is decreased. This system maintains rpm close to the desired value, but still requires adjustment of the throttle for fine tuning.

Some helicopters do not have correlators or governors and require coordination of all collective and throttle movements. When the collective is raised, the throttle must be increased; when the collective is lowered, the throttle must be decreased. As with any aircraft control, large adjustments of either collective pitch or throttle should be avoided. All corrections should be made through the use of smooth pressure.

In piston helicopters, the collective pitch is the primary control for manifold pressure, and the throttle is the primary control for rpm. However, the collective pitch control also influences rpm, and the throttle also influences manifold pressure; therefore, each is considered to be a secondary control of the other's function. Both the tachometer (rpm indicator) and the manifold pressure gauge must be analyzed to determine which control to use.

Cyclic Pitch Control

The cyclic pitch control is usually projected upward from the cockpit floor, between the pilot's legs or between the two pilot seats in some models. This primary flight control allows the pilot to fly the helicopter in any direction of travel: forward, rearward, left, and right. As discussed in Chapter 3, Aerodynamics of Flight, the total lift force is always perpendicular to the tip-path plane of the main rotor. The purpose of the cyclic pitch control is to tilt the tip-path plane in the direction of the desired horizontal direction. The cyclic controls the rotor disk tilt versus the horizon, which directs the rotor disk thrust to enable the pilot to control the direction of travel of the helicopter.

The rotor disk tilts in the same direction the cyclic pitch control is moved. If the cyclic is moved forward, the rotor disk tilts forward; if the cyclic is moved aft, the disk tilts aft, and so on. Because the rotor disk acts like a gyro, the mechanical linkages for the cyclic control rods are rigged in such a way that they decrease the pitch angle of the rotor blade approximately 90° before it reaches the direction of cyclic displacement, and increase the pitch angle of the rotor blade approximately 90° after it passes the direction of displacement. An increase in pitch angle increases AOA; a decrease in pitch angle decreases AOA. For example, if the cyclic is moved forward, the AOA decreases as the rotor blade passes the right side of the helicopter and increases on the left side. This results in maximum downward deflection of the rotor blade in front of the helicopter and maximum upward deflection behind it, causing the rotor disk to tilt forward.

Antitorque Pedals

The antitorque pedals, located on the cabin floor by the pilot's feet, control the pitch and therefore the thrust of the tail rotor blades or other antitorque system. Newton's Third Law applies to the helicopter fuselage and its rotation in the opposite direction of the main rotor blades unless counteracted and controlled. To make flight possible and to compensate for this torque, most helicopter designs incorporate an antitorque rotor or tail rotor. The antitorque pedals allow the pilot to control the pitch angle of the tail rotor blades, which in forward flight puts the helicopter in longitudinal trim and, while at a hover, enables the pilot to turn the helicopter 360°. The antitorque pedals are connected to the pitch change mechanism on the tail rotor gearbox and allow the pitch angle on the tail rotor blades to be increased or decreased.

Heading Control

The tail rotor is used to control the heading of the helicopter while hovering or when making hovering turns, as well as counteracting the torque of the main rotor. Hovering turns are commonly referred to as "pedal turns."

At speeds above translational lift, the pedals are used to compensate for torque to put the helicopter in longitudinal trim so that coordinated flight can be maintained. The cyclic control is used to change heading by making a turn to the desired direction.

The thrust of the tail rotor depends on the pitch angle of the tail rotor blades. This pitch angle can be positive, negative, or zero. A positive pitch angle tends to move the tail to the right. A negative pitch angle moves the tail to the left, while no thrust is produced with a zero-pitch angle. The maximum positive pitch angle of the tail rotor is generally greater than the maximum negative pitch angle available. This is because the primary purpose of the tail rotor is to counteract the torque of the main rotor. The capability for tail rotors to produce thrust to the left (negative pitch angle) is necessary, because during autorotation the drag of the transmission tends to yaw the nose to the left, or in the same direction the main rotor is turning.

From the neutral position, applying right pedal causes the nose of the helicopter to yaw right and the tail to swing to the left. Pressing on the left pedal has the opposite effect: the nose of the helicopter yaws to the left and the tail swings right.

With the antitorque pedals in the neutral position, the tail rotor has a medium positive pitch angle. In medium positive pitch, the tail rotor thrust approximately equals the torque of the main rotor during cruise flight, so the helicopter maintains a constant heading in level flight.

A vertical fin or stabilizer is used in many single-rotor helicopters to help aid in heading control. The fin is designed to optimize directional stability in flight with a zero-tail rotor thrust setting. The size of the fin is crucial to this design. If the surface is too large, the tail rotor thrust may be blocked. Heading control would be more difficult at slower airspeeds and at a hover and the vertical fin would then weathervane.

Helicopters that are designed with tandem rotors do not have an antitorque rotor. The helicopter is designed with both rotor systems rotating in opposite directions to counteract the torque rather than a tail rotor. Directional antitorque pedals are used for directional control of the aircraft while in flight, as well as while taxiing with the forward gear off the ground.

In intermeshing rotor systems, which are a set of two rotors turning in opposite directions with each rotor mast mounted on the helicopter with a slight angle to the other so that the blades intermesh without colliding, and a coaxial rotor systems, which are a pair of rotors mounted one above the other on the same shaft and turning in opposite directions, the heading pedals control the heading of the helicopter while at a hover by imbalancing torque between the rotors, allowing for the torque to turn the helicopter.

Weight and Balance

Weight

When determining if a helicopter is within the weight limits, consider the weight of the basic helicopter, crew, passengers, cargo, and fuel. Although the effective weight (load factor) varies during maneuvering flight, this chapter primarily considers the weight of the loaded helicopter while at rest.

It is critical to understand that the maximum allowable weight may change during the flight. When operations include OGE hovers and confined areas, planning must be done to ensure that the helicopter is capable of lifting the weight during all phases of flight. The weight may be acceptable during the early morning hours, but as the density altitude increases during the day, the maximum allowable weight may have to be reduced to keep the helicopter within its capability.

The following terms are used when computing a helicopter's weight:

Basic Empty Weight

The starting point for weight computations is the basic empty weight, which is the weight of the standard helicopter, optional equipment, unusable fuel, and all operating fluids including engine and transmission oil, and hydraulic fluid for those aircraft so equipped. Some helicopters might use the term "licensed empty weight," which is nearly the same as basic empty weight, except that it does not include full engine and transmission oil, just undrainable oil. If flying a helicopter that lists a licensed empty weight, be sure to add the weight of the oil to computations.

Maximum Gross Weight

The maximum weight of the helicopter. Most helicopters have an internal maximum gross weight, which refers to the weight within the helicopter structure and an external maximum gross weight, which refers to the weight of the helicopter with an external load. The external maximum weight may vary depending on where it is attached to the helicopter. Some large cargo helicopters may have several attachment points for sling load or winch operations. These helicopters can carry a tremendous amount of weight when the attachment point is directly under the CG of the aircraft.

Weight Limitations

Weight limitations are necessary to guarantee the structural integrity of the helicopter and enable pilots to predict helicopter performance accurately. Although aircraft manufacturers build in safety factors, a pilot should never intentionally exceed the load limits for which a helicopter is certificated. Operating below a minimum weight could adversely affect the handling characteristics of the helicopter. During single-pilot operations in some helicopters, a pilot needs to use a large amount of forward cyclic in order to maintain a hover. By adding ballast to the helicopter, the cyclic position is closer to the CG, which gives a greater range of control motion in every direction. When operating at or below the minimum weight of the helicopter, additional weight also improves autorotational characteristics since the autorotational descent can be established sooner. In addition, operating below minimum weight could prevent achieving the desirable rotor revolutions per minute (rpm) during autorotations.

Operating above a maximum weight could result in structural deformation or failure during flight, if encountering excessive load factors, strong wind gusts, or turbulence. Weight and maneuvering limitations also are factors considered for establishing fatigue life of components. Overweight, meaning overstressed, parts fail sooner than anticipated. Therefore, premature failure is a major consideration in determination of fatigue life and life cycles of parts.

Although a helicopter is certificated for a specified maximum gross weight, it is not safe to take off with this load under some conditions. Anything that adversely affects takeoff, climb, hovering, and landing performance may require off-loading of fuel, passengers, or baggage to some weight less than the published maximum. Factors that can affect performance include high altitude, high temperature, and high humidity conditions, which result in a high-density altitude. In-depth performance planning is critical when operating in these conditions.

Balance

Helicopter performance is not only affected by gross weight, but also by the position of that weight. It is essential to load the aircraft within the allowable CG range specified in the RFM's weight and balance limitations.

Center of Gravity

Ideally, a pilot should try to balance a helicopter perfectly so that the fuselage remains horizontal in hovering flight, with no cyclic pitch control needed except for wind correction. Since the fuselage acts as a pendulum suspended from the rotor, changing the CG changes the angle at which the aircraft hangs from the rotor. When the CG is directly under the rotor mast, the helicopter hangs horizontally; if the CG is too far forward of the mast, the helicopter hangs with its nose tilted down; if the CG is too far aft of the mast, the nose tilts up.

CG Forward of Forward Limit

A forward CG may occur when a heavy pilot and passenger take off without baggage or proper ballast located aft of the rotor mast. This situation becomes worse if the fuel tanks are located aft of the rotor mast because as fuel burns the CG continues to shift forward.

This condition is easily recognized when coming to a hover following a vertical takeoff. The helicopter has a nose-low attitude, and excessive rearward displacement of the cyclic control is needed to maintain a hover in a no-wind condition. Do not continue flight in this condition, since a pilot could rapidly lose rearward cyclic control as fuel is consumed. A pilot may also find it impossible to decelerate sufficiently to bring the helicopter to a stop. In the event of engine failure and the resulting autorotation, there may not be enough cyclic control to flare properly for the landing.

A forward CG is not as obvious when hovering into a strong wind, since less rearward cyclic displacement is required than when hovering with no wind. When determining whether a critical balance condition exists, it is essential to consider the wind velocity and its relation to the rearward displacement of the cyclic control.

CG Aft of Aft Limit

Without proper ballast in the cockpit, exceeding the aft CG may occur when:

- A lightweight pilot takes off solo with a full load of fuel located aft of the rotor mast.
- A lightweight pilot takes off with maximum baggage allowed in a baggage compartment located aft of the rotor mast.
- A lightweight pilot takes off with a combination of baggage and substantial fuel where both are aft of the rotor mast.

A pilot can recognize the aft CG condition when coming to a hover following a vertical takeoff. The helicopter will have a tail-low attitude, and will need excessive forward displacement of cyclic control to maintain a hover in a no-wind condition. If there is a wind, even greater forward cyclic is needed.

If flight is continued in this condition, it may be impossible to fly in the upper allowable airspeed range due to inadequate forward cyclic authority to maintain a nose-low attitude. In addition, with an extreme aft CG, gusty or rough air could accelerate the helicopter to a speed faster than that produced with full forward cyclic control. In this case, dissymmetry of lift and blade flapping could cause the rotor disk to tilt aft. With full forward cyclic control already applied, a pilot might not be able to lower the rotor disk, resulting in possible loss of control, or the rotor blades striking the tailboom.

Lateral Balance

For smaller helicopters, it is generally unnecessary to determine the lateral CG for normal flight instruction and passenger flights. This is because helicopter cabins are relatively narrow and most optional equipment is located near the centerline. However, some helicopter manuals specify the seat from which a pilot must conduct solo flight. In addition, if there is an unusual situation that could affect the lateral CG, such as a heavy pilot and a full load of fuel on one side of the helicopter, its position should be checked against the CG envelope. If carrying external loads in a position that requires large lateral cyclic control displacement to maintain level flight, fore and aft cyclic effectiveness could be limited dramatically. Manufacturers generally account for known lateral CG displacements by locating external attachment points opposite the lateral imbalance. Examples are placement of hoist systems attached to the side, and wing stores commonly used on military aircraft for external fuel pods or armament systems.

Basic Maneuvers

The Four Fundamentals

There are four fundamentals of flight upon which all maneuvers are based: straight-and-level flight, turns, climbs, and descents. All controlled flight maneuvers consist of one or more of the four fundamentals of flight. If a student pilot is able to perform these maneuvers well, and the student's proficiency is based on accurate "feel" and control analysis rather than mechanical movements, the ability to perform any assigned maneuver is only a matter of obtaining a clear visual and mental conception of it. The flight instructor must impart a good knowledge of these basic elements to the student, and must combine them and plan their practice so that perfect performance of each is instinctive without conscious effort. The importance of this to the success of flight training cannot be overemphasized. As the student progresses to more complex maneuvers, discounting any difficulties in visualizing the maneuvers, most student difficulties are caused by a lack of training, practice, or understanding of the principles of one or more of these fundamentals.

Guidelines

Good practices to follow during maneuvering flight include:

1. Move the cyclic only as fast as trim, torque, and rotor can be maintained. When entering a maneuver and the trim, rotor, or torque reacts quicker than anticipated, pilot limitations have been exceeded. If continued, an aircraft limitation will be exceeded. Perform the maneuver with less intensity until all aspects of the machine can be controlled. The pilot must be aware of the sensitivity of the flight controls due to the high speed of the main rotor.

2. Anticipate changes in aircraft performance due to loading or environmental condition. The normal collective increase to check rotor speed at sea level standard (SLS) may not be sufficient at 4,000 feet pressure altitude (PA) and 95 °F.
3. Anticipate the following characteristics during aggressive maneuvering flight, and adjust or lead with collective as necessary to maintain trim and torque:
    a. Left turns, torque increases (more antitorque). This applies to most helicopters, but not all.
    b. Right turns, torque decreases (less antitorque). This applies to most helicopters, but not all.
    c. Application of aft cyclic, torque decreases and rotor speed increases.
    d. Application of forward cyclic (especially when immediately following aft cyclic application), torque increases and rotor speed decreases.
    e. Always leave a way out.
    f. Know where the winds are.
    g. Engine failures occur during power changes and cruise flight.
    h. Crew coordination is critical. Everyone needs to be fully aware of what is going on, and each crewmember has a specific duty.
    i. In steep turns, the nose drops. In most cases, energy (airspeed) must be traded to maintain altitude as the required excess engine power may not be available (to maintain airspeed in a 2G/60° turn, rotor thrust/engine power must increase by 100 percent). Failure to anticipate this at low altitude endangers the crew and passengers. The rate of pitch change is proportional to gross weight and density altitude.
    j. Many overtorques during flight occur as the aircraft unloads from high G maneuvers. This is due to insufficient collective reduction following the increase to maintain consistent torque and rotor rpm as G-loading increased (dive recovery or recovery from high G-turn to the right).
    k. Normal helicopter landings usually require high power settings, with terminations to a hover requiring the highest power setting.
    l. The cyclic position relative to the horizon determines the helicopter's travel and attitude.

Vertical Takeoff to a Hover

A vertical takeoff to a hover involves flying the helicopter from the ground vertically to a skid height of two to three feet, while maintaining a constant heading. Once the desired skid height is achieved, the helicopter should remain nearly motionless over a reference point at a constant altitude and on a constant heading. The maneuver requires a high degree of concentration and coordination.

<u>Technique</u>

The pilot on the controls needs to clear the area left, right, and above to perform a vertical takeoff to a hover. The pilot should remain focused outside the aircraft and obtain clearance to take off from the controlling tower. If necessary, the pilot who is not on the controls assists in clearing the aircraft and provides adequate warning of any obstacles and any unannounced or unusual drift/altitude changes.

Heading control, direction of turn, and rate of turn at hover are all controlled by using the pedals. Hover height, rate of ascent, and the rate of descent are controlled by using the collective. Helicopter position and the direction of travel are controlled by the cyclic.

After receiving the proper clearance and ensuring that the area is clear of obstacles and traffic, begin the maneuver with the collective in the down position and the cyclic in a neutral position, or slightly into the wind. Very slowly increase the collective until the helicopter becomes light on the skids or wheels. At the same time apply pressure and counter pressure on the pedals to ensure the heading remains constant. Continue to apply pedals as necessary to maintain heading and coordinate the cyclic for a vertical ascent. As the helicopter slowly leaves the ground, check for proper attitude control response and helicopter center of gravity. A slow ascent will allow stopping if responses are outside the normal parameters indicating hung or entangled landing gear, center of gravity problems, or control issues. If a roll or tilt begin, decrease the collective and determine the cause of the roll or tilt. Upon reaching the desired hover altitude, adjust the flight controls as necessary to maintain position over the intended hover area. Student pilots should be reminded that while at a hover, the helicopter is rarely ever level. Helicopters usually hover left side low due to the tail rotor thrust being counteracted by the main rotor tilt. A nose low or high condition is generally caused by loading. Once stabilized, check the engine instruments and note the power required to hover.

Excessive movement of any flight control requires a change in the other flight controls. For example, if the helicopter drifts to one side while hovering, the pilot naturally moves the cyclic in the opposite direction. When this is done, part of the vertical thrust is diverted, resulting in a loss of altitude. To maintain altitude, increase the collective. This increases drag on the blades and tends to slow them down. To counteract the drag and maintain rpm, increase the throttle. Increased throttle means increased torque, so the pilot must add more pedal pressure to maintain the heading. This can easily lead to overcontrolling the helicopter. However, as level of proficiency increases, problems associated with overcontrolling decrease. Helicopter controls are usually more driven by pressure than by gross control movements.

Common Errors

1. Failing to ascend vertically as the helicopter becomes airborne.
2. Pulling excessive collective to become airborne, causing the helicopter to gain too much altitude.
3. Overcontrolling the antitorque pedals, which not only changes the heading of the helicopter, but also changes the rpm.
4. Reducing throttle rapidly in situations in which proper rpm has been exceeded, usually resulting in exaggerated heading changes and loss of lift, resulting in loss of altitude.
5. Failing to ascend slowly.

Hovering

Hovering is a maneuver in which the helicopter is maintained in nearly motionless flight over a reference point at a constant altitude and on a constant heading.

Technique

To maintain a hover over a point, use sideview and peripheral vision to look for small changes in the helicopter's attitude and altitude. When these changes are noted, make the necessary control inputs before the helicopter starts to move from the point. To detect small variations in altitude or position, the main area of visual attention needs to be some distance from the aircraft, using various points on the helicopter or the tip-path plane as a reference. Looking too closely or looking down leads to overcontrolling. Obviously, in order to remain over a certain point, know where the point is, but do not focus all attention there.

As with a takeoff, the pilot controls altitude with the collective and maintains a constant rpm with the throttle. The cyclic is used to maintain the helicopter's position; the pedals, to control heading. To maintain the helicopter in a stabilized hover, make small, smooth, coordinated corrections. As the desired effect occurs, remove the correction in order to stop the helicopter's movement. For example, if the helicopter begins to move rearward, apply a small amount of forward cyclic pressure. However, neutralize this pressure just before the helicopter comes to a stop, or it will begin to move forward.

After experience is gained, a pilot develops a certain "feel" for the helicopter. Small deviations can be felt and seen, so you can make the corrections before the helicopter actually moves. A certain relaxed looseness develops, and controlling the helicopter becomes second nature, rather than a mechanical response.

Common Errors

1. Tenseness and slow reactions to movements of the helicopter.
2. Failure to allow for lag in cyclic and collective pitch, which leads to overcontrolling. It is very common for a student to get ahead of the helicopter. Due to inertia, it requires some small time period for the helicopter to respond.
3. Confusing attitude changes for altitude changes, which results in improper use of the controls.
4. Hovering too high, creating a hazardous flight condition. The height velocity chart should be referenced to determine the maximum skid height to hover and safely recover the helicopter should a malfunction occur.
5. Hovering too low, resulting in occasional touchdown.
6. Becoming overly confident over prepared surfaces when taking off to a hover. Be aware that dynamic rollover accidents usually occur over a level surface.

Hovering Turn

A hovering turn is a maneuver performed at hovering altitude in which the nose of the helicopter is rotated either left or right while maintaining position over a reference point on the surface. Hovering turns can also be made around the mast or tail of the aircraft. The maneuver requires the coordination of all flight controls and demands precise control near the surface. A pilot should maintain a constant altitude, rate of turn, and rpm.

Technique

Initiate the turn in either direction by applying anti-torque pedal pressure toward the desired direction. It should be noted that during a turn to the left, more power is required because left pedal pressure increases the pitch angle of the tail rotor, which, in turn, requires additional power from the engine. A turn to the right requires less power. (On helicopters with a clockwise rotating main rotor, right pedal increases the pitch angle and, therefore, requires more power.)

As the turn begins, use the cyclic as necessary (usually into the wind) to keep the helicopter over the desired spot. To continue the turn, add more pedal pressure as the helicopter turns to the crosswind position. This is because the wind is striking the tail surface and tail rotor area, making it more difficult for the tail to turn into the wind. As pedal pressures increase due to crosswind forces, increase the cyclic pressure into the wind to maintain position. Use the collective with the throttle to maintain a constant altitude and rpm.

After the 90° portion of the turn, decrease pedal pressure slightly to maintain the same rate of turn. Approaching the 180°, or downwind portion, anticipate opposite pedal pressure due to the tail moving from an upwind position to a downwind position. At this point, the rate of turn has a tendency to increase at a rapid rate due to the tendency of the tail surfaces to weathervane. Because of the tailwind condition, hold rearward cyclic pressure to keep the helicopter over the same spot.

The horizontal stabilizer has a tendency to lift the tail during a tailwind condition. This is the most difficult portion of the hovering turn. Horizontal and vertical stabilizers have several different designs and locations, including the canted stabilizers used on some Hughes and Schweizer helicopters. The primary purpose of the vertical stabilizer is to unload the work of the antitorque system and to aid in trimming the helicopter in flight should the antitorque system fail. The horizontal stabilizer provides for a more usable CG range and aids in trimming the helicopter longitudinally.

Because of the helicopter's tendency to weathervane, maintaining the same rate of turn from the 180° position actually requires some pedal pressure opposite the direction of turn. If a pilot does not apply opposite pedal pressure, the helicopter tends to turn at a faster rate. The amount of pedal pressure and cyclic deflection throughout the turn depends on the wind velocity. As the turn is finished on the upwind heading, apply opposite pedal pressure to stop the turn. Gradually apply forward cyclic pressure to keep the helicopter from drifting.

Control pressures and direction of application change continuously throughout the turn. The most dramatic change is the pedal pressure (and corresponding power requirement) necessary to control the rate of turn as the helicopter moves through the downwind portion of the maneuver.

Turns can be made in either direction; however, in a high wind condition, the tail rotor may not be able to produce enough thrust, which means the pilot cannot control a turn to the right in a counterclockwise rotor system. Therefore, if control is ever questionable, first attempt to make a 90° turn to the left. If sufficient tail rotor thrust exists to turn the helicopter crosswind in a left turn, a right turn can be successfully controlled. The opposite applies to helicopters with clockwise rotor systems. In this case, start the turn to the right. Hovering turns should be avoided in winds strong enough to preclude sufficient aft cyclic control to maintain the helicopter on the selected surface reference point when headed downwind. Check the flight manual for the manufacturer's recommendations for this limitation.

Common Errors

1. Failing to maintain a slow, constant rate of turn.
2. Failing to maintain position over the reference point.
3. Failing to maintain rpm within normal range.
4. Failing to maintain constant altitude.
5. Failing to use the antitorque pedals properly

Hovering—Forward Flight

Forward hovering flight is normally used to move a helicopter to a specific location, and it may begin from a stationary hover. During the maneuver, constant groundspeed, altitude, and heading should be maintained.

Technique

Before starting, pick out two references directly in front and in line with the helicopter. These reference points should be kept in line throughout the maneuver.

Begin the maneuver from a normal hovering altitude by applying forward pressure on the cyclic. As movement begins, return the cyclic toward the neutral position to maintain low groundspeed—no faster than a brisk walk. Throughout the maneuver, maintain a constant groundspeed and path over the ground with the cyclic, a constant heading with the antitorque pedals, altitude with the collective, and the proper rpm with the throttle.

To stop the forward movement, apply rearward cyclic pressure until the helicopter stops. As forward motion stops, return the cyclic to the neutral position to prevent rearward movement. Forward movement can also be stopped by simply applying rearward pressure to level the helicopter and allowing it to drift to a stop.

Common Errors

1. Exaggerated movement of the cyclic, resulting in erratic movement over the surface.
2. Failure to use proper antitorque pedal control, resulting in excessive heading change.
3. Failure to maintain desired hovering altitude.
4. Failure to maintain proper rpm.
5. Failure to maintain alignment with direction of travel.

Hovering—Sideward Flight

Sideward hovering flight may be necessary to move the helicopter to a specific area when conditions make it impossible to use forward flight. During the maneuver, a constant groundspeed, altitude, and heading should be maintained.

Technique

Before starting sideward hovering flight, ensure the area for the hover is clear, especially at the tail rotor. Constantly monitor hover height and tail rotor clearance during all hovering maneuvers to prevent dynamic rollover or tail rotor strikes to the ground. Then, pick two points of in-line reference in the direction of sideward hovering flight to help maintain the proper ground track. These reference points should be kept in line throughout the maneuver.

Begin the maneuver from a normal hovering altitude by applying cyclic toward the side in which the movement is desired. As the movement begins, return the cyclic toward the neutral position to maintain low groundspeed—no faster than a brisk walk. Throughout the maneuver, maintain a constant groundspeed and ground track with cyclic. Maintain heading, which in this maneuver is perpendicular to the ground track, with the antitorque pedals, and a constant altitude with the collective. Use the throttle to maintain the proper operating rpm. Be aware that the nose tends to weathervane into the wind. Changes in the pedal position will change the rpm and must be corrected by collective and/or throttle changes to maintain altitude.

To stop the sideward movement, apply cyclic pressure in the direction opposite to that of movement and hold it until the helicopter stops. As motion stops, return the cyclic to the neutral position to prevent movement in the opposite direction. Applying sufficient opposite cyclic pressure to level the helicopter may also stop sideward movement. The helicopter then drifts to a stop.

Common Errors

1. Exaggerated movement of the cyclic, resulting in overcontrolling and erratic movement over the surface.
2. Failure to use proper antitorque pedal control, resulting in excessive heading change.
3. Failure to maintain desired hovering altitude.

4. Failure to maintain proper rpm.
5. Failure to make sure the area is clear prior to starting the maneuver.

Hovering—Rearward Flight

Rearward hovering flight may be necessary to move the helicopter to a specific area when the situation is such that forward or sideward hovering flight cannot be used. During the maneuver, maintain a constant groundspeed, altitude, and heading. Due to the limited visibility behind a helicopter, it is important that the area behind the helicopter be cleared before beginning the maneuver. Use of ground personnel is recommended.

Technique

Before starting rearward hovering flight, pick out two reference points in front of, and in line with the helicopter just like hovering forward. The movement of the helicopter should be such that these points remain in line. Begin the maneuver from a normal hovering altitude by applying rearward pressure on the cyclic. After the movement has begun, position the cyclic to maintain a slow groundspeed—no faster than a brisk walk. Throughout the maneuver, maintain constant groundspeed and ground track with the cyclic, a constant heading with the antitorque pedals, constant altitude with the collective, and the proper rpm with the throttle. To stop the rearward movement, apply forward cyclic and hold it until the helicopter stops. As the motion stops, return the cyclic to the neutral position. Also, as in the case of forward and sideward hovering flight, opposite cyclic can be used to level the helicopter and let it drift to a stop. Tail rotor clearance must be maintained. Generally, a higher-than-normal hover altitude is preferred.

Common Errors

1. Exaggerated movement of the cyclic resulting in overcontrolling and an uneven movement over the surface.
2. Failure to use proper antitorque pedal control, resulting in excessive heading change.
3. Failure to maintain desired hovering altitude.
4. Failure to maintain proper rpm.
5. Failure to make sure the area is clear prior to starting the maneuver.

Taxiing

Taxiing refers to operations on or near the surface of taxiways or other prescribed routes. Helicopters utilize three different types of taxiing.

Hover Taxi

A hover taxi is used when operating below 25 feet above ground level (AGL). Since hover taxi is just like forward, sideward, or rearward hovering flight, the technique to perform it is not presented here.

Air Taxi

An air taxi is preferred when movements require greater distances within an airport or heliport boundary. In this case, fly to the new location; however, it is expected that the helicopter will remain below 100 feet AGL with an appropriate airspeed and will avoid over flight of other aircraft, vehicles, and personnel.

Technique

Before starting, determine the appropriate airspeed and altitude combination to remain out of the cross-hatched or shaded areas of the height-velocity diagram. Additionally, be aware of crosswind conditions that could lead to loss of tail rotor effectiveness. Pick out two references directly in front of the helicopter for the ground path desired. These reference points should be kept in line throughout the maneuver.

Begin the maneuver from a normal hovering altitude by applying forward pressure on the cyclic. As movement begins, attain the desired airspeed with the cyclic. Control the desired altitude with the collective and rpm with the throttle. Throughout the maneuver, maintain a desired groundspeed and ground track with the cyclic, a constant heading with antitorque pedals, the desired altitude with the collective, and proper operating rpm with the throttle.

To stop the forward movement, apply aft cyclic pressure to reduce forward speed. Simultaneously lower the collective to initiate a descent to hover altitude. As forward motion stops, return the cyclic to the neutral position to prevent rearward movement. As approaching the proper hover altitude, increase the collective as necessary to stop descent at hover altitude (much like a quick stop maneuver).

Common Errors

1. Erratic movement of the cyclic, resulting in improper airspeed control and erratic movement over the surface.
2. Failure to use proper antitorque pedal control, resulting in excessive heading change.
3. Failure to maintain desired altitude.
4. Failure to maintain proper rpm.
5. Overflying parked aircraft causing possible damage from rotor downwash.
6. Flying in the cross-hatched or shaded area of the height-velocity diagram.
7. Flying in a crosswind that could lead to loss of tail rotor effectiveness.
8. Excessive tail-low attitudes.
9. Excessive power used or required to stop.
10. Failure to maintain alignment with direction of travel.

Surface Taxi

A surface taxi is used to minimize the effects of rotor downwash. Avoid excessive cyclic displacement while surface taxiing or on the ground which can lead to main rotor blades contacting the helicopter or rotor mast. This technique may be used with wheeled aircraft, or with those that have floats, skids or skis.

Technique

The helicopter should be in a stationary position on the surface with the collective full down and the rpm the same as that used for a hover. This rpm should be maintained throughout the maneuver. Then, move the cyclic slightly forward and apply gradual upward pressure on the collective to move the helicopter forward along the surface. Use the antitorque pedals to maintain heading and the cyclic to maintain ground track. The collective controls starting, stopping, and speed while taxiing. The higher the collective pitch, the faster the taxi speed; however, do not taxi faster than a brisk walk. If the helicopter is equipped with brakes, use them to help slow down. Do not use the cyclic to control groundspeed.

During a crosswind taxi, hold the cyclic into the wind a sufficient amount to eliminate any drifting movement.

Common Errors

1. Improper use of cyclic.
2. Failure to use antitorque pedals for heading control.
3. Improper use of the controls during crosswind operations.
4. Failure to maintain proper rpm.

Normal Takeoff from a Hover

A normal takeoff from a hover is an orderly transition to forward flight and is executed to increase altitude safely and expeditiously. During the takeoff, fly a profile that avoids the cross-hatched or shaded areas of the height-velocity diagram.

Technique

Bring the helicopter to a hover (position 1) and make a performance check, which includes power, balance, and flight controls. The power check should include an evaluation of the amount of excess power available; that is, the difference between the power being used to hover and the power available at the existing altitude and temperature conditions. The balance condition of the helicopter is indicated by the position of the cyclic when maintaining a stationary hover. Wind necessitates some cyclic deflection, but there should not be an extreme deviation from neutral. Flight controls must move freely, and the helicopter should respond normally. Then, visually clear the surrounding area.

Start the helicopter moving by smoothly and slowly easing the cyclic forward (position 2). As the helicopter starts to move forward, increase the collective, as necessary, to prevent the helicopter from sinking and adjust the throttle to maintain rpm. The increase in power requires an increase in the proper antitorque pedal to maintain heading. Maintain a straight takeoff path throughout the takeoff.

While accelerating through effective translational lift (position 3), the helicopter begins to climb and the nose tends to rise due to increased lift. At this point, adjust the collective to obtain normal climb power and apply enough forward cyclic to overcome the tendency of the nose to rise. At position 4, hold an attitude that allows a smooth acceleration toward climbing airspeed and a commensurate gain in altitude so that the takeoff profile does not take the helicopter through any of the cross-hatched or shaded areas of the height-velocity diagram. As airspeed increases (position 5), place the aircraft in trim and allow a crab to take place to maintain ground track and a more favorable climb configuration. As the helicopter continues to climb and accelerate to best rate-of-climb, apply aft cyclic pressure to raise the nose smoothly to the normal climb attitude.

Common Errors

1. Failing to use sufficient collective pitch to prevent loss of altitude prior to attaining translational lift.
2. Adding power too rapidly at the beginning of the transition from hovering to forward flight without forward cyclic compensation, causing the helicopter to gain excessive altitude before acquiring airspeed.
3. Assuming an extreme nose-down attitude near the surface in the transition from hovering to forward flight.
4. Failing to maintain a straight flightpath over the surface (ground track).
5. Failing to maintain proper airspeed during the climb.
6. Failing to adjust the throttle to maintain proper rpm.
7. Failing to transition to a level crab to maintain ground track.

Normal Takeoff from the Surface

Normal takeoff from the surface is used to move the helicopter from a position on the surface into effective translational lift and a normal climb using a minimum amount of power. If the surface is dusty or covered with loose snow, this technique provides the most favorable visibility conditions and reduces the possibility of debris being ingested by the engine.

Technique

Place the helicopter in a stationary position on the surface. Lower the collective to the full down position, and reduce the rpm below operating rpm. Visually clear the area and select terrain features or other objects to aid in maintaining the desired track during takeoff and climb out. Increase the throttle to the proper rpm, and raise the collective slowly until the helicopter is light on the skids. Hesitate momentarily and adjust the cyclic and antitorque pedals, as necessary, to prevent any surface movement. Continue to apply upward collective. As the helicopter leaves the ground, use the cyclic, as necessary, to begin forward movement as altitude is gained. Continue to accelerate, and as effective translational lift is attained, the helicopter begins to climb. Adjust attitude and power, if necessary, to climb in the same manner as a takeoff from a hover. A second less efficient but acceptable technique is to attempt a vertical takeoff to evaluate if power or lift is sufficient to clear obstructions. This allows the helicopter to be returned to the takeoff position if required.

Common Errors

1. Departing the surface in an attitude that is too nose-low. This situation requires the use of excessive power to initiate a climb.
2. Using excessive power combined with a level attitude, which causes a vertical climb, unless needed for obstructions and landing considerations.
3. Application of the collective that is too abrupt when departing the surface, causing rpm and heading control errors.

Crosswind Considerations During Takeoffs

If the takeoff is made during crosswind conditions, the helicopter is flown in a slip during the early stages of the maneuver. The cyclic is held into the wind a sufficient amount to maintain the desired ground track for the takeoff. The heading is maintained with the use of the antitorque pedals. In other words, the rotor is tilted into the wind so that the sideward movement of the helicopter is just enough to counteract the crosswind effect. To prevent the nose from turning in the direction of the rotor tilt, it is necessary to increase the antitorque pedal pressure on the side opposite the cyclic.

Straight-and-Level Flight

Straight-and-level flight is flight in which constant altitude and heading are maintained. The attitude of the rotor disk relative to the horizon determines the airspeed. The horizontal stabilizer design determines the helicopter's attitude when stabilized at an airspeed and altitude. Altitude is primarily controlled by use of the collective.

Technique

To maintain forward flight, the rotor tip-path plane must be tilted forward to obtain the necessary horizontal thrust component from the main rotor. By doing this, it causes the nose of the helicopter to lower which in turn will cause the airspeed to increase. In order to counteract this, the pilot must find the correct power setting to maintain level flight by adjusting the collective. The horizontal stabilizer aids in trimming the helicopter longitudinally and reduces the amount of nose tuck that would occur. On several helicopters, it is designed as a negative lift airfoil, which produces a lifting force in a downward direction.

When in straight-and-level flight, any increase in the collective, while holding airspeed constant, causes the helicopter to climb. A decrease in the collective, while holding airspeed constant, causes the helicopter to descend. A change in the collective requires a coordinated change of the throttle to maintain a constant rpm. Additionally, the antitorque pedals need to keep the helicopter in trim around the vertical axis.

To increase airspeed in straight-and-level flight, apply forward pressure on the cyclic and raise the collective as necessary to maintain altitude. To decrease airspeed, apply rearward pressure on the cyclic and lower the collective, as necessary, to maintain altitude.

Although the cyclic is sensitive, there is a slight delay in control reaction, and it is necessary to anticipate actual movement of the helicopter. When making cyclic inputs to control the altitude or airspeed of a helicopter, take care not to overcontrol. If the nose of the helicopter rises above the level-flight attitude, apply forward pressure to the cyclic to bring the nose down. If this correction is held too long, the nose drops too low. Since the helicopter continues to change attitude momentarily after the controls reach neutral, return the cyclic to neutral slightly before the desired attitude is reached. This principle holds true for any cyclic input.

Since helicopters are not very stable, but are inherently very controllable, if a gust or turbulence causes the nose to drop, the nose tends to continue to drop instead of returning to a straight-and-level attitude as it would on a fixed-wing aircraft. Therefore, a pilot must remain alert and fly the helicopter at all times.

Common Errors

1. Failure to trim the helicopter properly, tending to hold antitorque pedal pressure and opposite cyclic. This is commonly called cross-controlling.
2. Failure to maintain desired airspeed.
3. Failure to hold proper control position to maintain desired ground track.
4. Failure to allow helicopter to stabilize at new airspeed.

Turns

A turn is a maneuver used to change the heading of the helicopter.

Technique

Before beginning any turn, the area in the direction of the turn must be cleared not only at the helicopter's altitude, but also above and below. To enter a turn from straight-and-level flight, apply sideward pressure on the cyclic in the direction the turn is to be made. This is the only control movement needed to start the turn. Do not use the pedals to assist the turn. Use the pedals only to compensate for torque to keep the helicopter in trim around the vertical axis. Keeping the fuselage in the correct streamlined position around the vertical axis facilitates the helicopter flying forward with the least drag. Trim is indicated by a yaw string in the center, or a centered ball on a turn and slip indicator.

How fast the helicopter banks depends on how much lateral cyclic pressure is applied. How far the helicopter banks (the steepness of the bank) depends on how long the cyclic is displaced. After establishing the proper bank angle, return the cyclic toward the neutral position. When the bank is established, returning the cyclic to neutral or holding it inclined relative to the horizon will maintain the helicopter at that bank angle. Increase the collective and throttle to maintain altitude and rpm. As the torque increases, increase the proper antitorque pedal pressure to maintain longitudinal trim. Depending on the degree of bank, additional forward cyclic pressure may be required to maintain airspeed.

Rolling out of the turn to straight-and-level flight is the same as the entry into the turn except that pressure on the cyclic is applied in the opposite direction. Since the helicopter continues to turn as long as there is any bank, start the rollout before reaching the desired heading.

The discussion on level turns is equally applicable to making turns while climbing or descending. The only difference is that the helicopter is in a climbing or descending attitude rather than that of level flight. If a simultaneous entry is desired, merely combine the techniques of both maneuvers—climb or descent entry and turn entry. When recovering from a climbing or descending turn, the desired heading and altitude are rarely reached at the same time. If the heading is reached first, stop the turn and maintain the climb or descent until reaching the desired altitude. On the other hand, if the altitude is reached first, establish the level flight attitude and continue the turn to the desired heading.

Slips

A slip occurs when the helicopter slides sideways toward the center of the turn. It is caused by an insufficient amount of antitorque pedal in the direction of the turn, or too much in the direction opposite the turn, in relation to the amount of power used. In other words, if you hold improper antitorque pedal pressure, which keeps the nose from following the turn, the helicopter slips sideways toward the center of the turn.

Skids

A skid occurs when the helicopter slides sideways away from the center of the turn. It is caused by too much antitorque pedal pressure in the direction of the turn, or by too little in the direction opposite the turn in relation to the amount of power used. If the helicopter is forced to turn faster with increased pedal pressure instead of by increasing the degree of the bank, it skids sideways away from the center of the turn instead of flying in its normal curved path.

In summary, a skid occurs when the rate of turn is too great for the amount of bank being used, and a slip occurs when the rate of turn is too low for the amount of bank being used.

Normal Climb

The entry into a climb from a hover has already been described in the Normal Takeoff from a Hover subsection; therefore, this discussion is limited to a climb entry from cruising flight.

Technique

To enter a climb in a helicopter while maintaining airspeed, the first actions are increasing the collective and throttle, and adjusting the pedals as necessary to maintain a centered ball in the slip/skid indicator. Moving the collective up requires a slight aft movement of the cyclic to direct all of the increased power into lift and maintain the airspeed. Remember, a helicopter can climb with the nose down and descend with the nose up. Helicopter attitude changes mainly reflect acceleration or deceleration, not climb or descent. Therefore, the climb attitude is approximately the same as level flight in a stable climb, depending on the aircraft's horizontal stabilizer design.

If the pilot wishes to climb faster, with a decreased airspeed, then the climb can be initiated with aft cyclic. Depending on initial or entry airspeed for the climb, the climb can be accomplished without increasing the collective, if a much slower airspeed is acceptable. However, as the airspeed decreases, the airflow over the vertical fin decreases necessitating more antitorque (left) pedal application.

To level off from a climb, start adjusting the attitude to the level flight attitude a few feet prior to reaching the desired altitude. The amount of lead depends on the rate of climb at the time of level-off (the higher the rate of climb, the more the lead). Generally, the lead is 10 percent of the climb rate. For example, if the climb rate is 500 feet per minute (fpm), you should lead the level-off by 50 feet.

To begin the level-off, apply forward cyclic to adjust and maintain a level flight attitude, which can be slightly nose low. Maintain climb power until the airspeed approaches the desired cruising airspeed, then lower the collective to obtain cruising power and adjust the throttle to obtain and maintain cruising rpm. Throughout the level-off, maintain longitudinal trim with the antitorque pedals.

Common Errors

1. Failure to maintain proper power and airspeed.
2. Holding too much or too little antitorque pedal.
3. In the level-off, decreasing power before adjusting the nose to cruising attitude.

Normal Descent

A normal descent is a maneuver in which the helicopter loses altitude at a controlled rate in a controlled attitude.

Technique

To establish a normal descent from straight-and-level flight at cruising airspeed, lower the collective to obtain proper power, adjust the throttle to maintain rpm, and increase right antitorque pedal pressure to maintain heading in a counterclockwise rotor system, or left pedal pressure in a clockwise system. If cruising airspeed is the same as or slightly above descending airspeed, simultaneously apply the necessary cyclic pressure to obtain the approximate descending attitude. If the pilot wants to decelerate, the cyclic must be moved aft. If the pilot desires to descend with increased airspeed, then forward cyclic is all that is required if airspeed remains under the limit. As the helicopter stabilizes at any forward airspeed, the fuselage attitude will streamline due to the airflow over the horizontal stabilizer. As the airspeed changes, the airflow over the vertical stabilizer or fin changes, so the pedals must be adjusted for trim.

The pilot should always remember that the total lift and thrust vectoring is controlled by the cyclic. If a certain airspeed is desired, it will require a certain amount of cyclic and collective movement for level flight. If the cyclic is moved, the thrust-versus-lift ration is changed. Aft cyclic directs more power to lift, and altitude increases. Forward cyclic directs more power to thrust, and airspeed increases. If the collective is not changed and there is a change only in cyclic, the total thrust to lift ration does not change; aft cyclic results in a climb, and forward cyclic results in a descent with the corresponding airspeed changes.

To level off from the descent, lead the desired altitude by approximately 10 percent of the rate of descent. For example, a 500-fpm rate of descent would require a 50-foot lead. At this point, increase the collective to obtain cruising power, adjust the throttle to maintain rpm, and increase left antitorque pedal pressure to maintain heading (right pedal pressure in a clockwise rotor system).

Adjust the cyclic to obtain cruising airspeed and a level flight attitude as the desired altitude is reached.

Common Errors

1. Failure to maintain constant angle of descent during training.
2. Failure to level-off the aircraft sufficiently, which results in recovery below the desired altitude.
3. Failure to adjust antitorque pedal pressures for changes in power.

Conclusion

Once again, please note that these are merely excerpts from the FAA helicopter handbook. The full text of the handbook is freely available and you would do well to study it, both for improving your performance on the test and for augmenting your background knowledge should you be accepted into the Army's flight training program.

Spatial Apperception Test

The Spatial Apperception section of the SIFT lasts 10 minutes and features 25 questions. This is another test based on visual information rather than written text, or mathematical problems. The word *apperception* refers to the process by which you interpret some new information using the knowledge you already possess.

This section of the SIFT is measuring your ability to translate visual information from one perspective into an accurate mental representation of the same information from a completely different perspective. Military test developers have determined that this ability is critical to success in flight school and as a pilot, and they have also determined that the Spatial Apperception test is very accurate at measuring a person's aptitude and abilities in this area.

For each question, you'll first be shown a drawing of a terrain with a horizon, from the point of view of a pilot in the cockpit of an aircraft above the terrain. Then you'll be shown five more drawings of the aircraft from the perspective of someone on the ground observing the craft, each showing the aircraft in a different attitude. You will be required to determine which of the five drawings shows the aircraft in the attitude that would provide the view of the terrain shown in the first illustration to someone looking straight out of the cockpit of the aircraft.

The most important thing to keep in mind is that you're really only looking for three pieces of information. The three questions you'll need to answer for each drawing are:

- What is the vertical orientation of the aircraft? Is it climbing, diving, or flying straight ahead?
- Are the wings level, is the aircraft banking left, or is it banking right?
- In which direction is the aircraft heading?

Answering these three questions correctly will enable you to choose the right answer for any question in this section. Let's look at how to answer each of these questions a bit more in depth.

You should probably start in the same order, so first you want to determine the orientation of the plane. The key to answering this question is the placement of the horizon in the illustration. The horizon is where the sky meets one of the shaded areas, either land or sea. Is the horizon right in the middle of the drawing? Or in other words, is there about the same amount of space above the horizon as below it? If so, then the aircraft is flying straight ahead, or level. If most of the drawing is above the horizon, then the aircraft is climbing, and if most of the drawing is below the horizon, the aircraft is diving.

Next, is the plane flying level or is it banking to one side? If the horizon is level, then the plane's wings are level. If the horizon goes from the upper left to the lower right, the plane is banking left. If it goes from the lower left to the upper right, it's banking right. On whichever side of the picture the horizon is elevated, that's the direction that the plane is banking.

The final piece of the puzzle is determining which way the aircraft is headed. Is it headed toward the sea, toward the land, or flying along the coastline? Keep in mind that the plane doesn't have to be flying at a 90-degree angle to the coastline; if it's headed toward sea or land, it could be approaching at another angle.

One common mistake people make in the Spatial Apperception section of the SIFT is confusing the coastline with the horizon in some of the drawings. Always keep in mind the difference between these two, especially when looking at angled drawings. Another thing to keep in mind is that for every view out of the cockpit, there are two possible ways to view the aircraft: from coastline left and from coastline right. All of the answer choices on a given question will be from the same side, so before you start visualizing how you think the plane will appear, it would be useful to check the answer choices and see which side you need to picture it from.

Do not underestimate the difficulty of this section of the SIFT. The questions seem relatively simple in concept, and the steps for solving them are straightforward, but they require very close attention to detail. If you're not prepared or not focused, it is very easy to do poorly on this section without realizing it. The key is practice. Be sure to work through all the practice questions for this section.

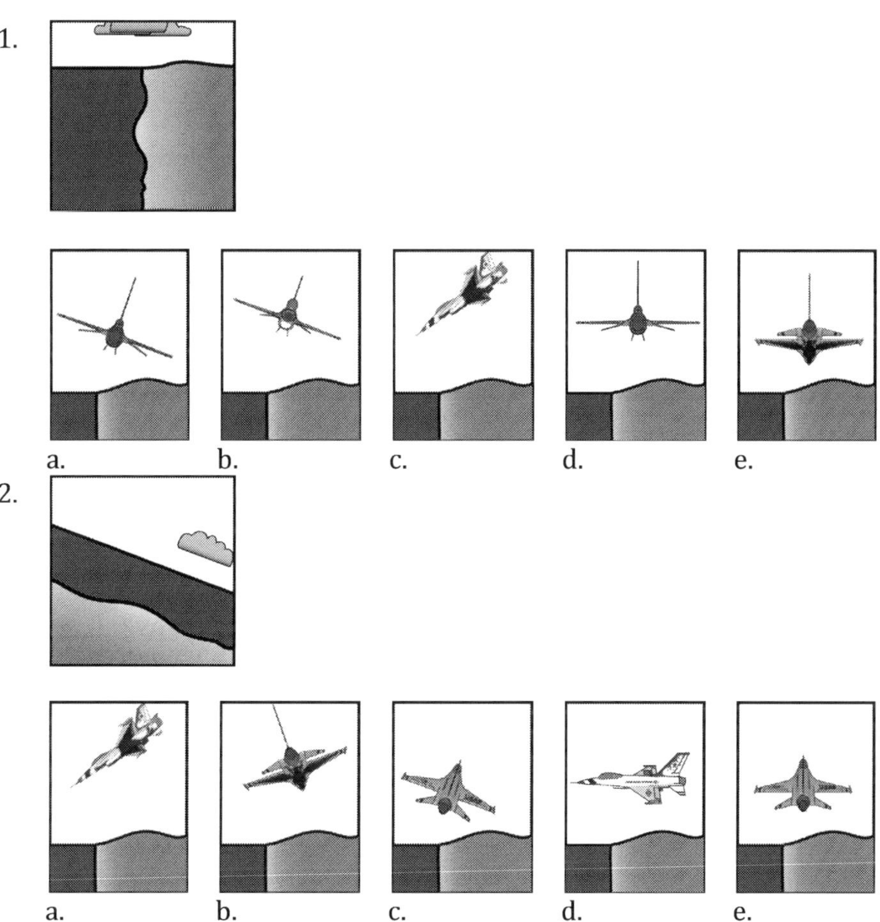

Answers: 1. E; 2. D

Reading Comprehension Test

Possessing excellent reading skills is a necessity for anyone hoping to become a military aviator. The Reading Comprehension section of the SIFT is designed to measure your abilities in this area.

This section tests your ability to read and understand written passages of the level of difficulty you can expect to encounter in your aviation training and career. Many of the passages used in our practice test were taken directly from helicopter operation instructional material.

You've probably taken numerous tests of reading comprehension in your educational career, and may have already identified the strategy that works best for you. If that's the case, you can go ahead and skip this next section. We're going to outline some of the strategies that we've found to be effective, but the key is finding the one or ones that work best for you.

Strategies

Read the Question(S) Before Reading the Passage

By identifying what you need to look for ahead of time, you can more quickly read the passage to find the information you need. In addition, reading the question will give you an idea of its complexity. If the question is simply asking you to find a detail in a passage, it probably won't take nearly as long as a question that requires you to make a conclusion about a hypothetical scenario. If it looks like the question will be very time-consuming, you can skip it and come back.

Systematically Eliminate Answers That Are Obviously Wrong

This will make it easier to focus on the remaining choices, and more importantly, you will improve your chances of correctly answering the question if you have to randomly guess.

Use Context Clues to Understand Difficult Words

You may encounter words and phrases that are new to you, and whose meanings you must decipher in order to answer a question correctly. If you don't know what they mean, you will have to use clues in the sentence to understand their meaning.

General Reading Comprehension Skills

Topics and Main Ideas

One of the most important skills in reading comprehension is the identification of **topics** and **main ideas.** There is a subtle difference between these two features. The topic is the subject of a text (i.e., what the text is all about). The main idea, on the other hand, is the most important point being made by the author. The topic is usually expressed in a few words at the most while the main idea often needs a full sentence to be completely defined. As an example, a short passage might have the topic of penguins and the main idea could be written as *Penguins are different from other birds in many ways*. In most nonfiction writing, the topic and the main idea will be stated directly and often appear in a sentence at the very beginning or end of the text. When being tested on an understanding of the author's topic, you may be able to skim the passage for the general idea, by reading only the first sentence of each paragraph. A body paragraph's first sentence is often--but not always--the main topic sentence which gives you a summary of the content in the paragraph.

However, there are cases in which the reader must figure out an unstated topic or main idea. In these instances, you must read every sentence of the text and try to come up with an overarching idea that is supported by each of those sentences.

Review Video: Topics and Main Ideas
Visit mometrix.com/academy and enter code: 407801

Supporting Details

Supporting details provide evidence and backing for the main point. In order to show that a main idea is correct, or valid, authors add details that help prove their point. All texts contain details, but they are only classified as supporting details when they serve to reinforce some larger point. Supporting details are most commonly found in informative and persuasive texts. In some cases, they will be clearly indicated with terms like *for example* or *for instance*, or they will be enumerated with terms like *first*, *second*, and *last*. However, you need to be prepared for texts that do not contain those indicators. As a reader, you should consider whether the author's supporting details really back up his or her main point. Supporting details can be factual and correct, yet they may not be relevant to the author's point. Conversely, supporting details can seem pertinent, but they can be ineffective because they are based on opinion or assertions that cannot be proven.

Topic and Summary Sentences

Topic and summary sentences are a convenient way to encapsulate the main idea of a text. In some textbooks and academic articles, the author will place a topic or summary sentence at the beginning of each section as a means of preparing the reader for what is to come. Research suggests that the brain is more receptive to new information when it has been prepared by the presentation of the main idea or some key words. The phenomenon is somewhat akin to the primer coat of paint that allows subsequent coats of paint to absorb more easily. A good topic sentence will be clear and not contain any jargon. When topic or summary sentences are not provided, good readers can jot down their own so that they can find their place in a text and refresh their memory.

Predictions Based on Prior Knowledge

A prediction is a guess about what will happen next. Readers constantly make predictions based on what they have read and what they already know. Consider the following sentence: *Staring at the computer screen in shock, Kim blindly reached over for the brimming glass of water on the shelf to her side.* The sentence suggests that Kim is agitated, and that she is not looking at the glass that she is going to pick up. So, a reader might predict that Kim is going to knock over the glass. Of course, not every prediction will be accurate: perhaps Kim will pick the glass up cleanly. Nevertheless, the author has certainly created the expectation that the water might be spilled. Predictions are always subject to revision as the reader acquires more information.

Making Inferences

Readers are often required to understand a text that claims and suggests ideas without stating them directly. An **inference** is a piece of information that is implied but not written outright by the author. For instance, consider the following sentence: *After the final out of the inning, the fans were filled with joy and rushed the field.* From this sentence, a reader can infer that the fans were watching a baseball game and their team won the game. Readers should take great care to avoid using information beyond the provided passage before making inferences. As you practice drawing inferences, you will find that they require concentration and attention.

Drawing Conclusions

In addition to inference and prediction, readers must often **draw conclusions** about the information they have read. When asked for a *conclusion* that may be drawn, look for critical "hedge" phrases, such as *likely, may, can, will often,* among many others. When you are being tested on this knowledge, remember the question that writers insert into these hedge phrases to cover every possibility. Often an answer will be wrong simply because there is no room for exception. Extreme positive or negative answers (such as always or never) are usually not correct. You **should not** rely on any outside knowledge that is not gathered from the passage to answer the related questions. Correct answers can be derived straight from the passage.

Sequence

Readers must be able to identify a text's **sequence**, or the order in which things happen. Often, when the sequence is very important to the author, the text is indicated with signal words like *first, then, next,* and *last.* However, a sequence can be merely implied and must be noted by the reader. Consider the sentence *He walked through the garden and gave water and fertilizer to the plants.* Clearly, the man did not walk through the garden before he collected water and fertilizer for the plants. So, the implied sequence is that he first collected water and fertilizer, next he walked through the garden, and last he gave water or fertilizer as necessary to the plants.

Texts do not always proceed in an orderly sequence from first to last. Sometimes they begin at the end and start over at the beginning. As a reader, you can enhance your understanding of the passage by taking brief notes to clarify the sequence.

Review Video: Sequence
Visit mometrix.com/academy and enter code: 489027

Comparison and Contrast

Authors will use different stylistic and writing devices to make their meaning clear for readers. One of those devices is comparison and contrast. As mentioned previously, when an author describes the ways in which two things are alike, he or she is comparing them. When the author describes the ways in which two things are different, he or she is contrasting them. The "compare and contrast" essay is one of the most common forms in nonfiction. These passages are often signaled with certain words: a comparison may have indicating terms such as *both, same, like, too,* and *as well*; while a contrast may have terms like *but, however, on the other hand, instead,* and *yet.* Of course, comparisons and contrasts may be implicit without using any such signaling language. A single sentence may both compare and contrast. Consider the sentence *Brian and Sheila love ice cream, but Brian prefers vanilla and Sheila prefers strawberry*. In one sentence, the author has described both a similarity (love of ice cream) and a difference (favorite flavor).

Review Video: Compare and Contrast
Visit mometrix.com/academy and enter code: 171799

Cause and Effect

One of the most common text structures is cause and effect. A cause is an act or event that makes something happen, and an effect is the thing that happens as a result of the cause. A cause-and-effect relationship is not always explicit, but there are some terms in English that signal causes, such as *since, because,* and *due to*. Furthermore, terms that signal effects include *consequently, therefore, this lead(s) to*. As an example, consider the sentence *Because the sky was clear, Ron did not bring an umbrella*. The cause is the clear sky, and the effect is that Ron did not bring an umbrella. However, readers may find that sometimes the cause-and-effect relationship will not be clearly noted. For instance, the sentence *He was late and missed the meeting* does not contain any signaling words, but the sentence still contains a cause (he was late) and an effect (he missed the meeting).

Review Video: Cause and Effect
Visit mometrix.com/academy and enter code: 428037

Identifying an Author's Position

In order to be an effective reader, one must pay attention to the author's **position** and purpose. Even those texts that seem objective and impartial, like textbooks, have a position and bias. Readers need to take these positions into account when considering the author's message. When an author uses emotional language or clearly favors one side of an argument, his or her position is clear. However, the author's position may be evident not only in what he or she writes, but also in what he or she doesn't write. In a normal setting, a reader would want to review some other texts on the same topic in order to develop a view of the author's position. If this was not possible, then you would want to acquire some background about the author. However, since you are in the middle of an exam and the only source of information is the text, you should look for language and argumentation that seems to indicate a particular stance on the subject.

Purpose

Usually, identifying the **purpose** of an author is easier than identifying his or her position. In most cases, the author has no interest in hiding his or her purpose. A text that is meant to entertain, for instance, should be written to please the reader. Most narratives, or stories, are written to entertain, though they may also inform or persuade. Informative texts are easy to identify, while the most difficult purpose of a text to identify is persuasion because the author has an interest in making this purpose hard to detect. When a reader discovers that the author is trying to persuade, he or she should be skeptical of the argument. For this reason, persuasive texts often try to establish an entertaining tone and hope to amuse the reader into agreement. On the other hand, an informative tone may be implemented to create an appearance of authority and objectivity.

An author's purpose is evident often in the organization of the text (e.g., section headings in bold font points to an informative text). However, you may not have such organization available to you in your exam. Instead, if the author makes his or her main idea clear from the beginning, then the likely purpose of the text is to inform. If the author begins by making a claim and provides various arguments to support that claim, then the purpose is probably to persuade. If the author tells a story or seems to want the attention of the reader more than to push a particular point or deliver information, then his or her purpose is most likely to entertain. As a reader, you must judge authors on how well they accomplish their purpose. In other words, you need to consider the type of passage (e.g., technical, persuasive, etc.) that the author has written and whether the author has followed the requirements of the passage type.

Word Meaning from Context

One of the benefits of reading is the expansion of one's vocabulary. In order to obtain this benefit, however, one needs to know how to identify the definition of a word from its context. This means defining a word based on the words around it and the way it is used in a sentence. Consider the following sentence: *The elderly scholar spent his evenings hunched over arcane texts that few other people even knew existed.* The adjective *arcane* is uncommon, but you can obtain significant information about it based on its use in the sentence. The fact that few other people know of their existence allows you to assume that "arcane texts" must be rare and be of interest to a few people. Also, the texts are being read by an elderly scholar. So, you can assume that they focus on difficult academic subjects. Sometimes, words can be defined by what they are not. Consider the following sentence: *Ron's fealty to his parents was not shared by Karen, who disobeyed their every command.* Someone who disobeys is not demonstrating *fealty*. So, you can infer that the word means something like *obedience* or *respect*.

Identifying the Logical Conclusion

Identifying a logical conclusion can help you determine whether you agree with the writer or not. Coming to this conclusion is much like making an inference: the approach requires you to combine the information given by the text with what you already know in order to make a logical conclusion. If the author intended the reader to draw a certain conclusion, then you can expect the author's argumentation and detail to be leading in that direction. One way to approach the task of drawing conclusions is to make brief notes of all the points made by the author. When the notes are arranged on paper, they may clarify the logical conclusion. Another way to approach conclusions is to consider whether the reasoning of the author raises any pertinent questions. Sometimes you will be able to draw several conclusions from a passage. On occasion these will be conclusions that were never imagined by the author. Therefore, be aware that these conclusions must be supported directly by the text.

Math Skills Test

On this section of the SIFT, you'll be tested for your knowledge, skill, and aptitude in math. Being highly skilled at math is very important for anyone seeking to become a pilot, for many reasons. In order to make it successfully through aviator training, and then to succeed as a pilot, a person will need to be able to solve basic math problems rapidly, and in their head, without having time to work them out on a calculator or with a pencil and paper. Beyond this, however, the highly developed analytical skills that enable a person to quickly solve math problems will be useful in all sorts of different ways and in all kinds of different situations. So, while this section of the SIFT does test knowledge and abilities, it's also testing for general learning aptitude.

To do well on this section, you'll need to have a solid mastery of some of the math subjects taught through all four years of high school, and some lower level college courses. This subtest lasts 40 minutes, and you are not allowed to use a calculator. It's very important to keep in mind that the MST section is adaptive, and factor this into your approach.

The math section will begin with a question of medium difficulty. If you answer it correctly, you will then be given a harder question. If you answer that question correctly, the next question will be even more difficult. This process will continue until you get an answer wrong, at which point you will be given an easier question. Answer it right, and the questions will start getting harder again, but if you answer it wrong, the computer will keep giving you easier questions until you get one right.

If you answer the first question incorrectly, the process works in reverse, giving you an easier question right off the bat. The computer will adapt to a test taker's answers in this manner after every question, so the next question that will be displayed is not determined until after an answer has been submitted for the previous question.

Because of this, it's important to take the time to do your best on every question. Don't skip a question just because it seems hard. If you're answering questions right, the questions are supposed to get harder. At the same time though, you want to make sure you answer enough questions so that the computer can accurately identify your skill level. Not answering enough questions can hurt you even more than answering some questions incorrectly. As with everything, there is a balance to be struck, but with computer adaptive testing, that balance leans more heavily toward answering correctly than answering as many questions as possible.

The following sections outline the basic math concepts needed to excel on the Math Skills subtest. As someone who is interested in flight training, you've probably taken a lot of math tests in your educational career, but just in case, here is one of the most important things to remember as you study math concepts:

More so than in almost any other subject, **practice matters**. Math concepts are explained in ways that make you think you understand them well, but until you can quickly work practice problems several days after you read about the underlying concepts without referring back to them, you haven't actually internalized them.

Numbers and Their Classifications

Numbers are the basic building blocks of mathematics. Specific features of numbers are identified by the following terms:

- Integers – The set of whole positive and negative numbers, including zero. Integers do not include fractions $\left(\frac{1}{3}\right)$, decimals (0.56), or mixed numbers $\left(7\frac{3}{4}\right)$.
- Prime number – A whole number greater than 1 that has only two factors, itself and 1; that is, a number that can be divided evenly only by 1 and itself.
- Composite number – A whole number greater than 1 that has more than two different factors; in other words, any whole number that is not a prime number. For example: The composite number 8 has the factors of 1, 2, 4, and 8.
- Even number – Any integer that can be divided by 2 without leaving a remainder. For example: 2, 4, 6, 8, and so on.
- Odd number – Any integer that cannot be divided evenly by 2. For example: 3, 5, 7, 9, and so on.
- Decimal number – a number that uses a decimal point to show the part of the number that is less than one. Example: 1.234.
- Decimal point – a symbol used to separate the ones place from the tenths place in decimals or dollars from cents in currency.
- Decimal place – the position of a number to the right of the decimal point. In the decimal 0.123, the 1 is in the first place to the right of the decimal point, indicating tenths; the 2 is in the second place, indicating hundredths; and the 3 is in the third place, indicating thousandths.

Review Video: Numbers and Their Classifications
Visit mometrix.com/academy and enter code: 461071

The decimal, or base 10, system is a number system that uses ten different digits $(0, 1, 2, 3, 4, 5, 6, 7, 8, 9)$. An example of a number system that uses something other than ten digits is the binary, or base 2, number system, used by computers, which uses only the numbers 0 and 1. It is thought that the decimal system originated because people had only their 10 fingers for counting.

Rational, irrational, and real numbers can be described as follows:

- Rational numbers include all integers, decimals, and fractions. Any terminating or repeating decimal number is a rational number.
- Irrational numbers cannot be written as fractions or decimals because the number of decimal places is infinite and there is no recurring pattern of digits within the number. For example, pi (π) begins with 3.141592 and continues without terminating or repeating, so pi is an irrational number.
- Real numbers are the set of all rational and irrational numbers.

Operations

There are four basic mathematical operations:

1. Addition increases the value of one quantity by the value of another quantity. *Example*: $2 + 4 = 6; 8 + 9 = 17$. The result is called the sum. With addition, the order does not matter. $4 + 2 = 2 + 4$.

2. Subtraction is the opposite operation to addition; it decreases the value of one quantity by the value of another quantity. *Example*: $6 - 4 = 2$; $17 - 8 = 9$. The result is called the difference. Note that with subtraction, the order does matter. $6 - 4 \neq 4 - 6$.
3. Multiplication can be thought of as repeated addition. One number tells how many times to add the other number to itself. *Example:* 3×2 (three times two) $= 2 + 2 + 2 = 6$. With multiplication, the order does not matter. $2 \times 3 = 3 \times 2$ or $3 + 3 = 2 + 2 + 2$.
4. Division is the opposite operation to multiplication; one number tells us how many parts to divide the other number into. *Example*: $20 \div 4 = 5$; if 20 is split into 4 equal parts, each part is 5. With division, the order of the numbers does matter. $20 \div 4 \neq 4 \div 20$.

An exponent is a superscript number placed next to another number at the top right. It indicates how many times the base number is to be multiplied by itself. Exponents provide a shorthand way to write what would be a longer mathematical expression. *Example*: $a^2 = a \times a$; $2^4 = 2 \times 2 \times 2 \times 2$. A number with an exponent of 2 is said to be "squared," while a number with an exponent of 3 is said to be "cubed."

The value of a number raised to an exponent is called its power. So, 8^4 is read as "8 to the 4th power," or "8 raised to the power of 4." A negative exponent is the same as the reciprocal of a positive exponent. *Example*: $a^{-2} = \frac{1}{a^2}$.

Review Video: Exponents
Visit mometrix.com/academy and enter code: 600998

Parentheses are used to designate which operations should be done first when there are multiple operations. *Example*: 4 – (2 + 1) = 1; the parentheses tell us that we must add 2 and 1, and then subtract the sum from 4, rather than subtracting 2 from 4 and then adding 1 (this would give us an answer of 3).

Order of Operations is a set of rules that dictates the order in which we must perform each operation in an expression so that we will evaluate it accurately. If we have an expression that includes multiple different operations, Order of Operations tells us which operations to do first. The most common mnemonic for Order of Operations is PEMDAS, or "Please Excuse My Dear Aunt Sally." PEMDAS stands for Parentheses, Exponents, Multiplication, Division, Addition, Subtraction. It is important to understand that multiplication and division have equal precedence, as do addition and subtraction, so those pairs of operations are simply worked from left to right in order.

Review Video: Order of Operations
Visit mometrix.com/academy and enter code: 259675

Example: Evaluate the expression $5 + 20 \div 4 \times (2 + 3)^2 - 6$ using the correct order of operations.

P: Perform the operations inside the parentheses, $(2 + 3) = 5$.

E: Simplify the exponents, $(5)^2 = 25$.

The equation now looks like this: $5 + 20 \div 4 \times 25 - 6$.

MD: Perform multiplication and division from left to right, $20 \div 4 = 5$; then $5 \times 25 = 125$.

The equation now looks like this: $5 + 125 - 6$.

AS: Perform addition and subtraction from left to right, $5 + 125 = 130$; then $130 - 6 = 124$.

The laws of exponents are as follows:

1. Any number to the power of 1 is equal to itself: $a^1 = a$.
2. The number 1 raised to any power is equal to 1: $1^n = 1$.
3. Any number raised to the power of 0 is equal to 1: $a^0 = 1$.
4. Add exponents to multiply powers of the same base number:$a^n \times a^m = a^{n+m}$.
5. Subtract exponents to divide powers of the same number; that is $a^n \div a^m = a^{n-m}$.
6. Multiply exponents to raise a power to a power: $(a^n)^m = a^{n \times m}$.
7. If multiplied or divided numbers inside parentheses are collectively raised to a power, this is the same as each individual term being raised to that power: $(a \times b)^n = a^n \times b^n$; $(a \div b)^n = a^n \div b^n$.

Note: Exponents do not have to be integers. Fractional or decimal exponents follow all the rules above as well.

Example: $5^{\frac{1}{4}} \times 5^{\frac{3}{4}} = 5^{\frac{1}{4}+\frac{3}{4}} = 5^1 = 5$.

A root, such as a square root, is another way of writing a fractional exponent. Instead of using a superscript, roots use the radical symbol ($\sqrt{}$) to indicate the operation. A radical will have a number underneath the bar, and may sometimes have a number in the upper left: $\sqrt[n]{a}$, read as "the nth root of *a*." The relationship between radical notation and exponent notation can be described by this equation: $\sqrt[n]{a} = a^{\frac{1}{n}}$. The two special cases of *n* = 2 and *n* = 3 are called square roots and cube roots. If there is no number to the upper left, it is understood to be a square root ($n = 2$). Nearly all of the roots you encounter will be square roots. A square root is the same as a number raised to the one-half power. When we say that *a* is the square root of *b* ($a = \sqrt{b}$), we mean that *a* multiplied by itself equals *b*: ($a \times a = b$).

Review Video: Square Root and Perfect Square
Visit mometrix.com/academy and enter code: 648063

A perfect square is a number that has an integer for its square root. There are 10 perfect squares from 1 to 100: 1, 4, 9, 16, 25, 36, 49, 64, 81, 100 (the squares of integers 1 through 10).

Scientific notation is a way of writing large numbers in a shorter form. The form $a \times 10^n$ is used in scientific notation, where *a* is greater than or equal to 1, but less than 10, and *n* is the number of places the decimal must move to get from the original number to *a*. *Example*: The number 230,400,000 is cumbersome to write. To write the value in scientific notation, place a decimal point between the first and second numbers, and include all digits through the last non-zero digit ($a = 2.304$). To find the appropriate power of 10, count the number of places the decimal point had to move ($n = 8$). The number is positive if the decimal moved to the left, and negative if it moved to the right. We can then write 230,400,000 as 2.304×10^8. If we look instead at the number 0.00002304, we have the same value for *a*, but this time the decimal moved 5 places to the right ($n = -5$). Thus, 0.00002304 can be written as 2.304×10^{-5}. Using this notation makes it simple to compare very large or very small numbers. By comparing exponents, it is easy to see that 3.28×10^4 is smaller than 1.51×10^5, because 4 is less than 5.

Review Video: Scientific Notation
Visit mometrix.com/academy and enter code: 976454

Positive and Negative Numbers

A precursor to working with negative numbers is understanding what absolute values are. A number's absolute value is simply the distance away from zero a number is on the number line. The absolute value of a number is always positive and is written $|x|$.

When adding signed numbers, if the signs are the same simply add the absolute values of the addends and apply the original sign to the sum. For example, $(+4) + (+8) = +12$ and $(-4) + (-8) = -12$. When the original signs are different, take the absolute values of the addends and subtract the smaller value from the larger value, then apply the original sign of the larger value to the difference. For instance, $(+4) + (-8) = -4$ and $(-4) + (+8) = +4$.

For subtracting signed numbers, change the sign of the number after the minus symbol and then follow the same rules used for addition. For example, $(+4) - (+8) = (+4) + (-8) = -4$.

If the signs are the same the product is positive when multiplying signed numbers. For example, $(+4) \times (+8) = +32$ and $(-4) \times (-8) = +32$. If the signs are opposite, the product is negative. For example, $(+4) \times (-8) = -32$ and $(-4) \times (+8) = -32$. When more than two factors are multiplied together, the sign of the product is determined by how many negative factors are present. If there are an odd number of negative factors then the product is negative, whereas an even number of negative factors indicates a positive product. For instance, $(+4) \times (-8) \times (-2) = +64$ and $(-4) \times (-8) \times (-2) = -64$.

The rules for dividing signed numbers are similar to multiplying signed numbers. If the dividend and divisor have the same sign, the quotient is positive. If the dividend and divisor have opposite signs, the quotient is negative. For example, $(-4) \div (+8) = -0.5$.

Factors and Multiples

Factors are numbers that are multiplied together to obtain a product. For example, in the equation $2 \times 3 = 6$, the numbers 2 and 3 are factors. A prime number has only two factors (1 and itself), but other numbers can have many factors.

A common factor is a number that divides exactly into two or more other numbers. For example, the factors of 12 are 1, 2, 3, 4, 6, and 12, while the factors of 15 are 1, 3, 5, and 15. The common factors of 12 and 15 are 1 and 3. A prime factor is also a prime number. Therefore, the prime factors of 12 are 2 and 3. For 15, the prime factors are 3 and 5.

The greatest common factor (GCF) is the largest number that is a factor of two or more numbers. For example, the factors of 15 are 1, 3, 5, and 15; the factors of 35 are 1, 5, 7, and 35. Therefore, the greatest common factor of 15 and 35 is 5.

Review Video: Greatest Common Factor (GCF)
Visit mometrix.com/academy and enter code: 838699

The least common multiple (LCM) is the smallest number that is a multiple of two or more numbers. For example, the multiples of 3 include 3, 6, 9, 12, 15, etc.; the multiples of 5 include 5, 10, 15, 20, etc. Therefore, the least common multiple of 3 and 5 is 15.

Fractions, Percentages, and Related Concepts

A fraction is a number that is expressed as one integer written above another integer, with a dividing line between them ($\frac{x}{y}$). It represents the quotient of the two numbers "x divided by y." It can also be thought of as x out of y equal parts.

The top number of a fraction is called the numerator, and it represents the number of parts under consideration. The 1 in $\frac{1}{4}$ means that 1 part out of the whole is being considered in the calculation. The bottom number of a fraction is called the denominator, and it represents the total number of equal parts. The 4 in $\frac{1}{4}$ means that the whole consists of 4 equal parts. A fraction cannot have a denominator of zero; this is referred to as "undefined."

Review Video: Fractions
Visit mometrix.com/academy and enter code: 262335

Fractions can be manipulated, without changing the value of the fraction, by multiplying or dividing (but not adding or subtracting) both the numerator and denominator by the same number. If you divide both numbers by a common factor, you are reducing or simplifying the fraction. Two fractions that have the same value, but are expressed differently are known as equivalent fractions. For example, $\frac{2}{10}, \frac{3}{15}, \frac{4}{20}$, and $\frac{5}{25}$ are all equivalent fractions. They can also all be reduced or simplified to $\frac{1}{5}$.

When two fractions are manipulated so that they have the same denominator, this is known as finding a common denominator. The number chosen to be that common denominator should be the least common multiple of the two original denominators. *Example*: $\frac{3}{4}$ and $\frac{5}{6}$; the least common multiple of 4 and 6 is 12. Manipulating to achieve the common denominator: $\frac{3}{4} = \frac{9}{12}; \frac{5}{6} = \frac{10}{12}$.

If two fractions have a common denominator, they can be added or subtracted simply by adding or subtracting the two numerators and retaining the same denominator. *Example*: $\frac{1}{2} + \frac{1}{4} = \frac{2}{4} + \frac{1}{4} = \frac{3}{4}$. If the two fractions do not already have the same denominator, one or both of them must be manipulated to achieve a common denominator before they can be added or subtracted.

Two fractions can be multiplied by multiplying the two numerators to find the new numerator and the two denominators to find the new denominator.

Example: $\frac{1}{3} \times \frac{2}{3} = \frac{1 \times 2}{3 \times 3} = \frac{2}{9}$.

Review Video: Multiplying Fractions
Visit mometrix.com/academy and enter code: 638849

Two fractions can be divided by flipping the numerator and denominator of the second fraction and then proceeding as though it were a multiplication. *Example*: $\frac{2}{3} \div \frac{3}{4} = \frac{2}{3} \times \frac{4}{3} = \frac{8}{9}$.

Review Video: Dividing Fractions
Visit mometrix.com/academy and enter code: 300874

A fraction whose denominator is greater than its numerator is known as a proper fraction, while a fraction whose numerator is greater than its denominator is known as an improper fraction. Proper fractions have values less than one and improper fractions have values greater than one.

A mixed number is a number that contains both an integer and a fraction. Any improper fraction can be rewritten as a mixed number. *Example*: $\frac{8}{3} = \frac{6}{3} + \frac{2}{3} = 2 + \frac{2}{3} = 2\frac{2}{3}$. Similarly, any mixed number can be rewritten as an improper fraction. *Example*: $1\frac{3}{5} = 1 + \frac{3}{5} = \frac{5}{5} + \frac{3}{5} = \frac{8}{5}$.

Review Video: Improper Fractions and Mixed Numbers
Visit mometrix.com/academy and enter code: 731507

Percentages can be thought of as fractions that are based on a whole of 100; that is, one whole is equal to 100%. The word percent means "per hundred." Fractions can be expressed as percents by finding equivalent fractions with a denomination of 100. *Example*: $\frac{7}{10} = \frac{70}{100} = 70\%$; $\frac{1}{4} = \frac{25}{100} = 25\%$.

To express a percentage as a fraction, divide the percentage number by 100 and reduce the fraction to its simplest possible terms. *Example*: $60\% = \frac{60}{100} = \frac{3}{5}$; $96\% = \frac{96}{100} = \frac{24}{25}$.

Converting decimals to percentages and percentages to decimals is as simple as moving the decimal point. To convert from a decimal to a percent, move the decimal point two places to the right. To convert from a percent to a decimal, move it two places to the left. *Example*: 0.23 = 23%; 5.34 = 534%; 0.007 = 0.7%; 700% = 7.00; 86% = 0.86; 0.15% = 0.0015.

It may be helpful to remember that the percentage number will always be larger than the equivalent decimal number.

A percentage problem can be presented three main ways: (1) Find what percentage of some number another number is. *Example*: What percentage of 40 is 8? (2) Find what number is some percentage of a given number. *Example*: What number is 20% of 40? (3) Find what number another number is a given percentage of. *Example*: What number is 8 20% of? The three components in all of these cases are the same: a whole (*W*), a part (*P*), and a percentage (%). These are related by the equation: $P = W \times \%$. This is the form of the equation you would use to solve problems of type (2). To solve types (1) and (3), you would use these two forms: $\% = \frac{P}{W}$ and $W = \frac{P}{\%}$.

Review Video: Percentages
Visit mometrix.com/academy and enter code: 141911

The thing that frequently makes percentage problems difficult is that they are most often also word problems, so a large part of solving them is figuring out which quantities are what. Here's an example: *In a school cafeteria, 7 students choose pizza, 9 choose hamburgers, and 4 choose tacos. Find the percentage that chooses tacos.* To find the whole, you must first add all of the parts: 7 + 9 + 4 = 20. The percentage can then be found by dividing the part by the whole

$(\% = \frac{P}{W})$: $\frac{4}{20} = \frac{20}{100} = 20\%$.

A ratio is a comparison of two quantities in a particular order. *Example*: If there are 14 computers in a lab, and the class has 20 students, there is a student to computer ratio of 20 to 14, commonly written as 20:14. Ratios are normally reduced to their smallest whole number representation, so 20:14 would be reduced to 10:7 by dividing both sides by 2.

A proportion is a relationship between two quantities that dictates how one changes when the other changes. A direct proportion describes a relationship in which a quantity increases by a set amount for every increase in the other quantity, or decreases by that same amount for every decrease in the other quantity. *Example*: Assuming a constant driving speed, the time required for a car trip increases as the distance of the trip increases. The distance to be traveled and the time required to travel are directly proportional.

Inverse proportion is a relationship in which an increase in one quantity is accompanied by a decrease in the other, or vice versa. *Example*: the time required for a car trip decreases as the speed increases, and increases as the speed decreases, so the time required is inversely proportional to the speed of the car.

Systems of Equations

Systems of Equations are a set of simultaneous equations that all use the same variables. A solution to a system of equations must be true for each equation in the system. *Consistent Systems* are those with at least one solution. *Inconsistent Systems* are systems of equations that have no solution.

Review Video: Systems of Equations
Visit mometrix.com/academy and enter code: 658153

To solve a system of linear equations by *substitution*, start with the easier equation and solve for one of the variables. Express this variable in terms of the other variable. Substitute this expression in the other equation, and solve for the other variable. The solution should be expressed in the form (x, y). Substitute the values into both of the original equations to check your answer. Consider the following problem.

Solve the system using substitution:

$$x + 6y = 15$$

$$3x - 12y = 18$$

Solve the first equation for x:

$$x = 15 - 6y$$

Substitute this value in place of x in the second equation, and solve for y:

$$3(15 - 6y) - 12y = 18$$

$$45 - 18y - 12y = 18$$

$$30y = 27$$

$$y = \frac{27}{30} = \frac{9}{10} = 0.9$$

Plug this value for y back into the first equation to solve for x:

$$x = 15 - 6(0.9) = 15 - 5.4 = 9.6$$

Check both equations if you have time:

$$9.6 + 6(0.9) = 9.6 + 5.4 = 15$$

$$3(9.6) - 12(0.9) = 28.8 - 10.8 = 18$$

Therefore, the solution is (9.6, 0.9).

To solve a system of equations using *elimination*, begin by rewriting both equations in standard form $Ax + By = C$. Check to see if the coefficients of one pair of like variables add to zero. If not, multiply one or both of the equations by a non-zero number to make one set of like variables add to zero. Add the two equations to solve for one of the variables. Substitute this value into one of the original equations to solve for the other variable. Check your work by substituting into the other equation. Next, we will solve the same problem as above, but using the addition method.

Solve the system using elimination:

$$x + 6y = 15$$

$$3x - 12y = 18$$

If we multiply the first equation by 2, we can eliminate the y terms:

$$2x + 12y = 30$$

$$3x - 12y = 18$$

Add the equations together and solve for x:

$5x = 48$

$$x = \frac{48}{5} = 9.6$$

Plug the value for x back into either of the original equations and solve for y:

$9.6 + 6y = 15$

$$y = \frac{15 - 9.6}{6} = 0.9$$

Check both equations if you have time:

$$9.6 + 6(0.9) = 9.6 + 5.4 = 15$$

$$3(9.6) - 12(0.9) = 28.8 - 10.8 = 18$$

Therefore, the solution is (9.6, 0.9).

Polynomial Algebra

To multiply two binomials, follow the *FOIL* method. FOIL stands for:

- **F**irst: Multiply the first term of each binomial
- **O**uter: Multiply the outer terms of each binomial

- **Inner**: Multiply the inner terms of each binomial
- **Last**: Multiply the last term of each binomial

Using FOIL, $(Ax + By)(Cx + Dy) = ACx^2 + ADxy + BCxy + BDy^2$.

Review Video: Multiplying Terms Using the FOIL Method
Visit mometrix.com/academy and enter code: 854792

To divide polynomials, begin by arranging the terms of each polynomial in order of one variable. You may arrange in ascending or descending order, but be consistent with both polynomials. To get the first term of the quotient, divide the first term of the dividend by the first term of the divisor. Multiply the first term of the quotient by the entire divisor and subtract that product from the dividend. Repeat for the second and successive terms until you either get a remainder of zero or a remainder whose degree is less than the degree of the divisor. If the quotient has a remainder, write the answer as a mixed expression in the form: quotient $+ \frac{\text{remainder}}{\text{divisor}}$.

Rational Expressions are fractions with polynomials in both the numerator and the denominator; the value of the polynomial in the denominator cannot be equal to zero. To add or subtract rational expressions, first find the common denominator, then rewrite each fraction as an equivalent fraction with the common denominator. Finally, add or subtract the numerators to get the numerator of the answer, and keep the common denominator as the denominator of the answer. When multiplying rational expressions, factor each polynomial and cancel like factors (a factor which appears in both the numerator and the denominator). Then, multiply all remaining factors in the numerator to get the numerator of the product, and multiply the remaining factors in the denominator to get the denominator of the product. Remember – cancel entire factors, not individual terms. To divide rational expressions, take the reciprocal of the divisor (the rational expression you are dividing by) and multiply by the dividend.

Below are patterns of some special products to remember: *perfect trinomial squares*, the *difference between two squares*, the *sum and difference of two cubes*, and *perfect cubes*.

- Perfect Trinomial Squares: $x^2 + 2xy + y^2 = (x + y)^2$ or $x^2 - 2xy + y^2 = (x - y)^2$
- Difference between Two Squares: $x^2 - y^2 = (x + y)(x - y)$
- Sum of Two Cubes: $x^3 + y^3 = (x + y)(x^2 - xy + y^2)$
  Note: the second factor is NOT the same as a perfect trinomial square, so do not try to factor it further.
- Difference between Two Cubes: $x^3 - y^3 = (x - y)(x^2 + xy + y^2)$
  Again, the second factor is NOT the same as a perfect trinomial square.
- Perfect Cubes: $x^3 + 3x^2y + 3xy^2 + y^3 = (x + y)^3$ and $x^3 - 3x^2y + 3xy^2 - y^3 = (x - y)^3$

In order to *factor* a polynomial, first check for a common monomial factor. When the greatest common monomial factor has been factored out, look for patterns of special products: differences of two squares, the sum or difference of two cubes for binomial factors, or perfect trinomial squares for trinomial factors. If the factor is a trinomial but not a perfect trinomial square, look for a factorable form, such as $x^2 + (a + b)x + ab = (x + a)(x + b)$ or $(ac)x^2 + (ad + bc)x + bd = (ax + b)(cx + d)$. For factors with four terms, look for groups to factor. Once you have found the factors, write the original polynomial as the product of all the factors. Make sure all of the polynomial factors are prime. Monomial factors may be prime or composite. Check your work by multiplying the factors to make sure you get the original polynomial.

Solving Quadratic Equations

The *Quadratic Formula* is used to solve quadratic equations when other methods are more difficult. To use the quadratic formula to solve a quadratic equation, begin by rewriting the equation in standard form $ax^2 + bx + c = 0$, where a, b, and c are coefficients. Once you have identified the values of the coefficients, substitute those values into the quadratic formula $= \frac{-b \pm \sqrt{b^2 - 4ac}}{2a}$. Evaluate the equation and simplify the expression. Again, check each root by substituting into the original equation. In the quadratic formula, the portion of the formula under the radical $(b^2 - 4ac)$ is called the *Discriminant*. If the discriminant is zero, there is only one root: zero. If the discriminant is positive, there are two different real roots. If the discriminant is negative, there are no real roots.

To solve a quadratic equation by *Factoring*, begin by rewriting the equation in standard form, if necessary. Factor the side with the variable then set each of the factors equal to zero and solve the resulting linear equations. Check your answers by substituting the roots you found into the original equation. If, when writing the equation in standard form, you have an equation in the form $x^2 + c = 0$ or $x^2 - c = 0$, set $x^2 = -c$ or $x^2 = c$ and take the square root of c. If $c = 0$, the only real root is zero. If c is positive, there are two real roots—the positive and negative square root values. If c is negative, there are no real roots because you cannot take the square root of a negative number.

Review Video: Factoring Quadratic Equations
Visit mometrix.com/academy and enter code: 336566

To solve a quadratic equation by *Completing the Square*, rewrite the equation so that all terms containing the variable are on the left side of the equal sign, and all the constants are on the right side of the equal sign. Make sure the coefficient of the squared term is 1. If there is a coefficient with the squared term, divide each term on both sides of the equal side by that number. Next, work with the coefficient of the single-variable term. Square half of this coefficient, and add that value to both sides. Now you can factor the left side (the side containing the variable) as the square of a binomial. $x^2 + 2ax + a^2 = C \Rightarrow (x + a)^2 = C$, where x is the variable, and a and C are constants. Take the square root of both sides and solve for the variable. Substitute the value of the variable in the original problem to check your work.

Basic Geometry

Angles

An angle is formed when two lines or line segments meet at a common point. It may be a common starting point for a pair of segments or rays, or it may be the intersection of lines. Angles are represented by the symbol $\angle$.

The vertex is the point at which two segments or rays meet to form an angle. If the angle is formed by intersecting rays, lines, and/or line segments, the vertex is the point at which four angles are formed. The pairs of angles opposite one another are called vertical angles, and their measures are equal. In the figure below, angles ABC and DBE are congruent, as are angles ABD and CBE.

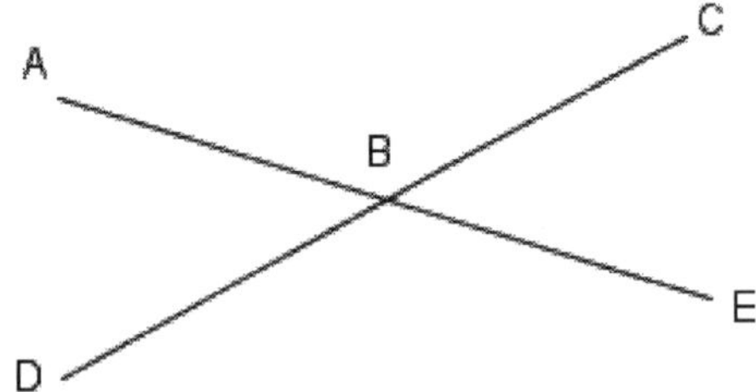

An acute angle is an angle with a degree measure less than 90°.

A right angle is an angle with a degree measure of exactly 90°.

An obtuse angle is an angle with a degree measure greater than 90° but less than 180°.

A straight angle is an angle with a degree measure of exactly 180°. This is also a semicircle.

A reflex angle is an angle with a degree measure greater than 180° but less than 360°.

A full angle is an angle with a degree measure of exactly 360°.

Two angles whose sum is exactly 90° are said to be complementary. The two angles may or may not be adjacent. In a right triangle, the two acute angles are complementary.

Two angles whose sum is exactly 180° are said to be supplementary. The two angles may or may not be adjacent. Two intersecting lines always form two pairs of supplementary angles. Adjacent supplementary angles will always form a straight line.

Circles

The center is the single point inside the circle that is equidistant from every point on the circle. (Point O in the diagram below.)

The radius is a line segment that joins the center of the circle and any one point on the circle. All radii of a circle are equal. (Segments OX, OY, and OZ in the diagram below.)

The diameter is a line segment that passes through the center of the circle and has both endpoints on the circle. The length of the diameter is exactly twice the length of the radius. (Segment XZ in the diagram below.)

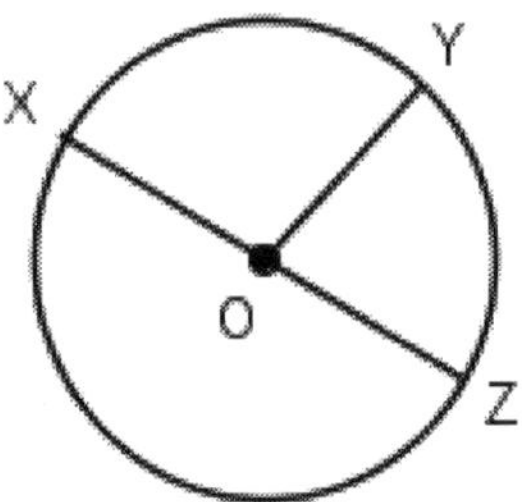

Triangles

A triangle is a polygon with three sides and three angles. Triangles can be classified according to the length of their sides or magnitude of their angles.

An acute triangle is a triangle whose three angles are all less than 90°. If two of the angles are equal, the acute triangle is also an isosceles triangle. If the three angles are all equal, the acute triangle is also an equilateral triangle.

A right triangle is a triangle with exactly one angle equal to 90°. All right triangles follow the Pythagorean Theorem. A right triangle can never be acute or obtuse.

An obtuse triangle is a triangle with exactly one angle greater than 90°. The other two angles may or may not be equal. If the two remaining angles are equal, the obtuse triangle is also an isosceles triangle.

An equilateral triangle is a triangle with three congruent sides. An equilateral triangle will also have three congruent angles, each 60°. All equilateral triangles are also acute triangles.

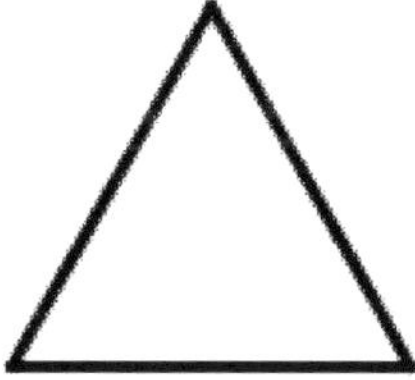

An isosceles triangle is a triangle with two congruent sides. An isosceles triangle will also have two congruent angles opposite the two congruent sides.

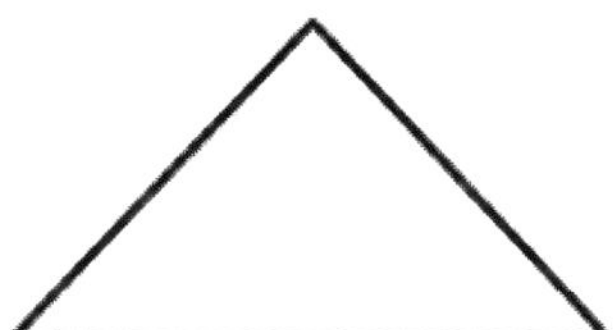

A scalene triangle is a triangle with no congruent sides. A scalene triangle will also have three angles of different measures. The angle with the largest measure is opposite the longest side, and the angle with the smallest measure is opposite the shortest side.

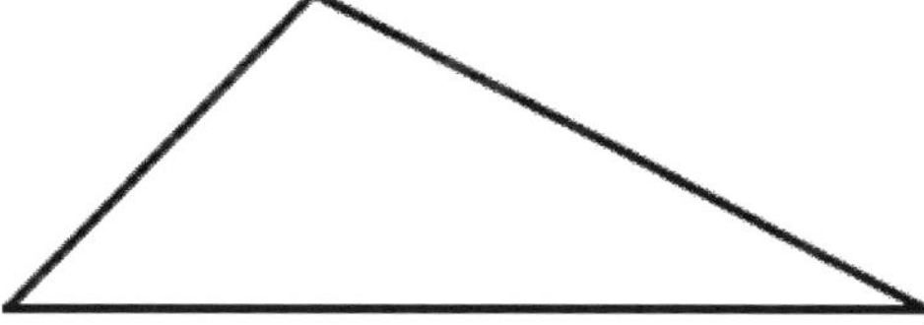

The Triangle Inequality Theorem states that the sum of the measures of any two sides of a triangle is always greater than the measure of the third side. If the sum of the measures of two sides were equal to the third side, a triangle would be impossible because the two sides would lie flat across the third side and there would be no vertex. If the sum of the measures of two of the sides was less than the third side, a closed figure would be impossible because the two shortest sides would never meet.

Similar triangles are triangles whose corresponding angles are congruent to one another. Their corresponding sides may or may not be equal, but they are proportional to one another. Since the angles in a triangle always sum to 180°, it is only necessary to determine that two pairs of corresponding angles are congruent, since the third will be also in that case.

Congruent triangles are similar triangles whose corresponding sides are all equal. Congruent triangles can be made to fit on top of one another by rotation, reflection, and/or translation. When trying to determine whether two triangles are congruent, there are several criteria that can be used.

Area Formulas

Rectangle: $A = wl$, where w is the width and l is the length

Square: $A = s^2$, where s is the length of a side.

Triangle: $A = \frac{1}{2}bh$, where b is the length of one side (base) and h is the distance from that side to the opposite vertex measured perpendicularly (height).

Circle: $A = \pi r^2$, where π is the mathematical constant approximately equal to 3.14 and r is the distance from the center of the circle to any point on the circle (radius).

Volume Formulas

Rectangular Prism – all 6 sides are rectangles. The volume can be calculated as $V = s_1 \times s_2 \times s_3$, or the lengths of the three different sides multiplied together.

Cube – a special type of prism in which all faces are squares. The volume can be calculated as $V = s^3$, where s is the length of any side.

Sphere – a round solid consisting of one continuous, uniformly-curved surface. The volume can be calculated as $V = \frac{4}{3}\pi r^3$, where r is the distance from the center of the sphere to any point on the surface (radius).

Mechanical Comprehension Test

The Mechanical Comprehension Test (MCT) isn't as long as the Math Skills or Reading Comprehension sections. It has a time limit of only 15 minutes. Keep in mind that this section is computer adaptive like the Math Skills subtest. Once again, this means that there is no fixed number of questions on the test. The questions get progressively harder each time you answer a question correctly, and progressively easier each time you answer a question incorrectly. This is an ongoing process throughout the test, and this format allows the computer software to tailor the questions to your current perceived skill level. Do not guess on this section unless you've exhausted all other options because incorrect answers will have a negative impact on your final score.

If you've ever taken the ASVAB, the Mechanical Comprehension subtest on the SIFT should not be all that foreign to you. The two tests cover a very similar breadth of concepts and in very similar ways. You'll see questions about gears, pulleys, levers, simple machines, mechanical advantage, and so on. Most questions in this section will be accompanied by a drawing to help illustrate the physical situation that is being asked about. None of the questions should baffle you, nor should any of them require knowledge of physics or mechanics beyond the high school level. The emphasis in Mechanical Comprehension is much more on aptitude and intuition than on acquired knowledge.

That is not to say that you shouldn't take an inventory of your knowledge and skills in physics and mechanics as part of your SIFT test preparation. On the contrary, developing a strong background in those areas is one of the best ways to make these concepts intuitive to you. If it has been a while since you've interacted with these topics on a regular basis, a refresher is probably in order. Since few applicants for military aviation training are engaged in the kind of jobs or academic studies which require them to rely on their knowledge of physics on a daily basis, we've included an extensive primer on all the basics that might show up on the SIFT.

Kinematics

To begin, we will look at the basics of physics. At its heart, physics is just a set of explanations for the ways in which matter and energy behave. There are three key concepts used to describe how matter moves:

1. Displacement
2. Velocity
3. Acceleration

Displacement

Concept: where and how far an object has gone

Calculation: final position – initial position

When something changes its location from one place to another, it is said to have undergone displacement. If a golf ball is hit across a sloped green into the hole, the displacement only takes into account the final and initial locations, not the path of the ball.

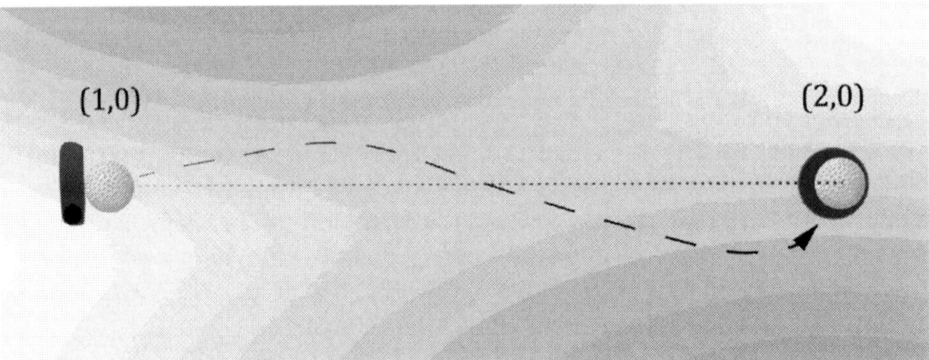

Displacement along a straight line is a very simple example of a vector quantity: that is, it has both a magnitude and a direction. Direction is as important as magnitude in many measurements. If we can determine the original and final position of the object, then we can determine the total displacement with this simple equation:

$$\text{Displacement} = \text{final position} - \text{original position}$$

The hole (final position) is at the Cartesian coordinate location (2, 0) and the ball is hit from the location (1, 0). The displacement is:

$$\text{Displacement} = (2,0) - (1,0)$$

$$\text{Displacement} = (1,0)$$

The displacement has a magnitude of 1 and a direction of the positive x direction.

Velocity

Concept: the rate of moving from one position to another

Calculation: change in position / change in time

Velocity answers the question, "How quickly is an object moving?" For example, if a car and a plane travel between two cities which are a hundred miles apart, but the car takes two hours and the plane takes one hour, the car has the same displacement as the plane, but a smaller velocity.

In order to solve some of the problems on the exam, you may need to assess the velocity of an object. If we want to calculate the average velocity of an object, we must know two things. First, we must know its displacement. Second, we must know the time it took to cover this distance. The formula for average velocity is quite simple:

$$\textbf{average velocity} = \frac{\textbf{displacement}}{\textbf{change in time}}$$

Or

$$\textbf{average velocity} = \frac{\textbf{final position} - \textbf{original position}}{\textbf{final time} - \textbf{original time}}$$

To complete the example, the velocity of the plane is calculated to be:

$$\text{plane average velocity} = \frac{100 \text{ miles}}{1 \text{ hour}} = 100 \text{ miles per hour}$$

The velocity of the car is less:

$$\text{car average velocity} = \frac{100 \text{ miles}}{2 \text{ hours}} = 50 \text{ miles per hour}$$

Often, people confuse the words *speed* and *velocity*. There is a significant difference. The average velocity is based on the amount of displacement, a vector. Alternately, the average speed is based on the distance covered or the path length. The equation for speed is:

$$\textbf{average speed} = \frac{\textbf{total distance traveled}}{\textbf{change in time}}$$

Notice that we used total distance and *not* change in position, because speed is path-dependent.

If the plane traveling between cities had needed to fly around a storm on its way, making the distance traveled 50 miles greater than the distance the car traveled, the plane would still have the same total displacement as the car.

The calculation for the speed: For this reason, average speed can be calculated:

$$\text{plane average speed} = \frac{150 \text{ miles}}{1 \text{ hour}} = 150 \text{ miles per hour}$$

$$\text{car average speed} = \frac{100 \text{ miles}}{2 \text{ hours}} = 50 \text{ miles per hour}$$

Acceleration

Concept: how quickly something changes from one velocity to another

Calculation: change in velocity / change in time

Acceleration is the rate of change of the velocity of an object. If a car accelerates from zero velocity to 60 miles per hour (88 feet per second) in two seconds, the car has an impressive acceleration. But if a car performs the same change in velocity in eight seconds, the acceleration is much lower and not as impressive.

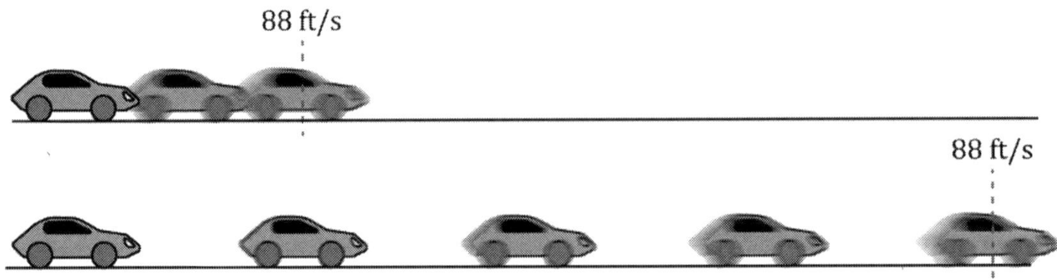

To calculate average acceleration, we may use the equation:

$$\textbf{average acceleration} = \frac{\textbf{change in velocity}}{\textbf{change in time}}$$

The acceleration of the cars is found to be:

$$\text{Car \#1 average acceleration} = \frac{\text{88 feet per second}}{\text{2 seconds}} = 44\ \frac{\text{feet}}{\text{second}^2}$$

$$\text{Car \#2 average acceleration} = \frac{\text{88 feet per second}}{\text{8 seconds}} = 11\ \frac{\text{feet}}{\text{second}^2}$$

Acceleration will be expressed in units of distance divided by time squared; for instance, meters per second squared or feet per second squared.

Projectile Motion

A specific application of the study of motion is projectile motion. Simple projectile motion occurs when an object is in the air and experiencing only the force of gravity. We will disregard drag for this topic. Some common examples of projectile motion are thrown balls, flying bullets, and falling rocks. The characteristics of projectile motion are:

1. The horizontal component of velocity doesn't change
2. The vertical acceleration due to gravity affects the vertical component of velocity

Because gravity only acts downwards, objects in projectile motion only experience acceleration in the y direction (vertical). The horizontal component of the object's velocity does not change in flight. This means that if a rock is thrown out off a cliff, the horizontal velocity, (think the shadow if the sun is directly overhead) will not change until the ball hits the ground.

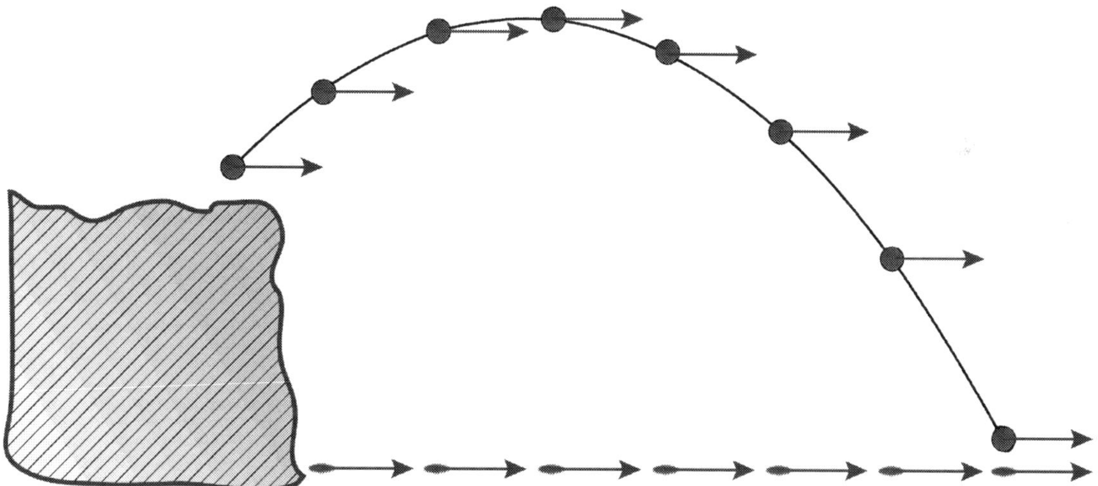

The velocity in the vertical direction is affected by gravity. Gravity imposes an acceleration of $g = 9.8\frac{m}{s^2}$ or $32\frac{ft}{s^2}$ downward on projectiles. The vertical component of velocity at any point is equal to:

$$\textbf{vertical velocity} = \textbf{original vertical velocity} - \textbf{g} \times \textbf{time}$$

When these characteristics are combined, there are three points of particular interest in a projectile's flight. At the beginning of a flight, the object has a horizontal component and a vertical component giving it a large speed. At the top of a projectile's flight, the vertical velocity equals zero, making the top the slowest part of travel. When the object passes the same height as the launch, the vertical velocity is opposite of the initial vertical velocity making the speed equal to the initial speed.

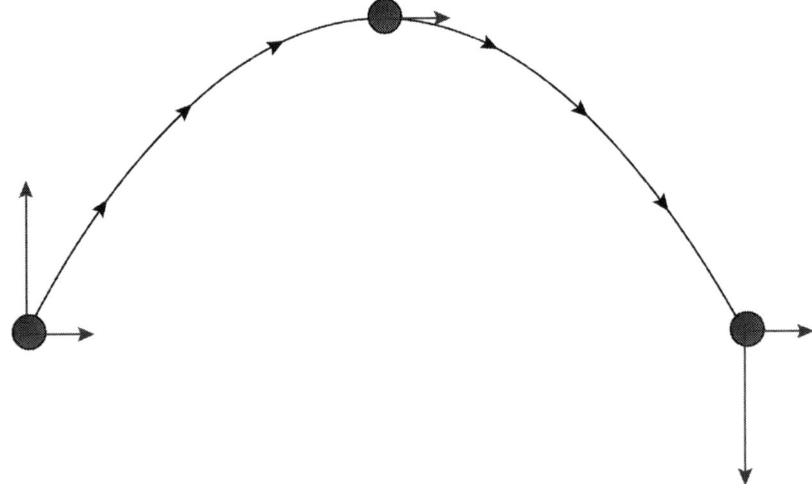

If the object continues falling below the initial height from which it was launched (e.g., it was launched from the edge of a cliff), it will have an even greater velocity than it did initially from that point until it hits the ground.

Rotational Kinematics

Concept: increasing the radius increases the linear speed

Calculation: linear speed = radius × rotational speed

Another interesting application of the study of motion is rotation. In practice, simple rotation is when an object rotates around a point at a constant speed. Most questions covering rotational kinematics will provide the distance from a rotating object to the center of rotation (radius) and ask about the linear speed of the object. A point will have a greater linear speed when it is farther from the center of rotation.

If a potter is spinning his wheel at a constant speed of one revolution per second, the clay six inches away from the center will be going faster than the clay three inches from the center. The clay directly in the center of the wheel will not have any linear velocity.

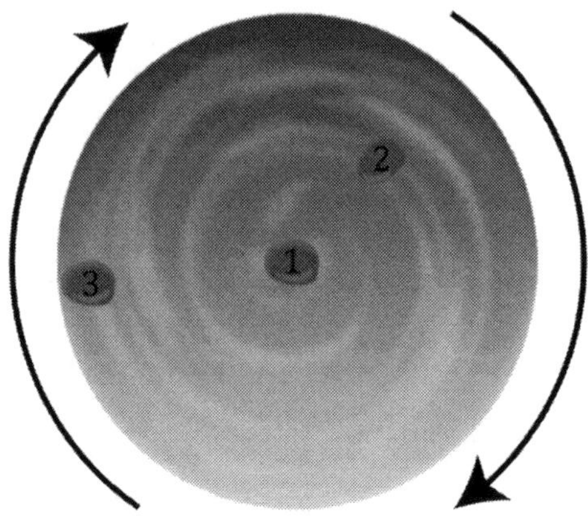

To find the linear speed of rotating objects using radians, we use the equation:

$$\textbf{linear speed} = (\textbf{rotational speed [in radians]}) \times (\textbf{radius})$$

Using degrees, the equation is:

$$\textbf{linear speed} = (\textbf{rotational speed [in degrees]}) \times \frac{\boldsymbol{\pi}\ \textbf{radians}}{\textbf{180 degrees}} \times (\textbf{radius})$$

To find the speed of the pieces of clay we use the known values (rotational speed of 1 revolution per second, radii of 0 inches, 3 inches, and 6 inches) and the knowledge that one revolution = 2 pi.

$$clay\ \#1\ speed = \left(2\pi \frac{rad}{s}\right) \times (0\ inches) = 0 \frac{inches}{second}$$

$$clay\ \#2\ speed = \left(2\pi \frac{rad}{s}\right) \times (3\ inches) = 18.8 \frac{inches}{second}$$

$$clay\ \#3\ speed = \left(2\pi \frac{rad}{s}\right) \times (6\ inches) = 37.7 \frac{inches}{second}$$

Cams

In the study of motion, a final application often tested is the cam. A cam and follower system allows mechanical systems to have timed, specified, and repeating motion. Although cams come in varied forms, tests focus on rotary cams. In engines, a cam shaft coordinates the valves for intake and exhaust. Cams are often used to convert rotational motion into repeating linear motion.

Cams rotate around one point. The follower sits on the edge of the cam and moves along with the edge. To understand simple cams, count the number of bumps on the cam. Each bump will cause the follower to move outwards.

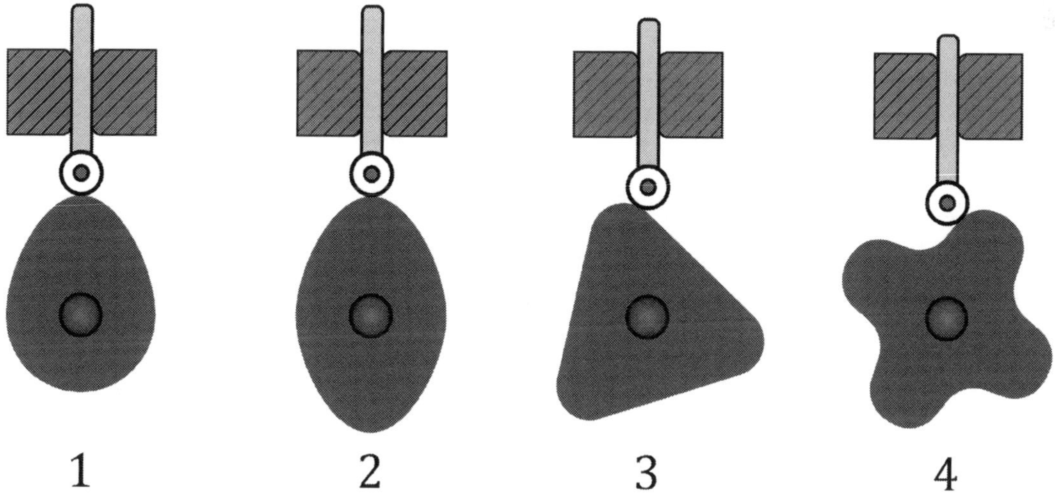

Another way to consider cams is to unravel the cam profile into a straight object. The follower will then follow the top of the profile.

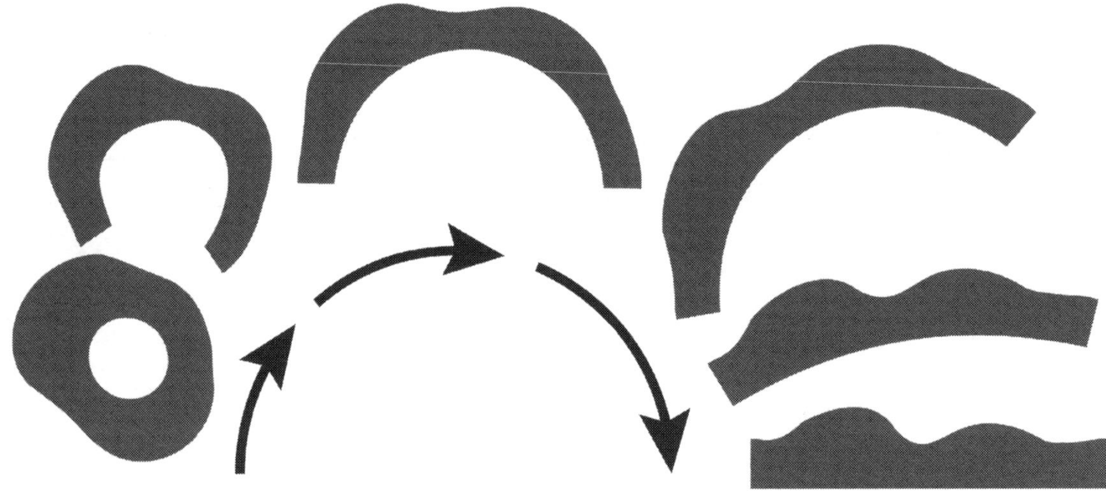

Kinetics

Newton's Three Laws of Mechanics

The questions on the exam may require you to demonstrate familiarity with the concepts expressed in Newton's three laws of motion which relate to the concept of force.

Newton's first law – A body at rest will tend to remain at rest, while a body in motion will tend to remain in motion, unless acted upon by an external force.

Newton's second law – The acceleration of an object is directly proportional to the force being exerted on it and inversely proportional to its mass.

Newton's third law – For every force, there is an equal and opposite force.

First Law

Concept: Unless something interferes, an object won't start or stop moving

Although intuition supports the idea that objects do not start moving until a force acts on them, the idea of an object continuing forever without any forces can seem odd. Before Newton formulated his laws of mechanics, general thought held that some force had to act on an object continuously in order for it to move at a constant velocity. This seems to make sense: when an object is briefly pushed, it will eventually come to a stop. Newton, however, determined that unless some other force acted on the object (most notably friction or air resistance), it would continue in the direction it was pushed at the same velocity forever.

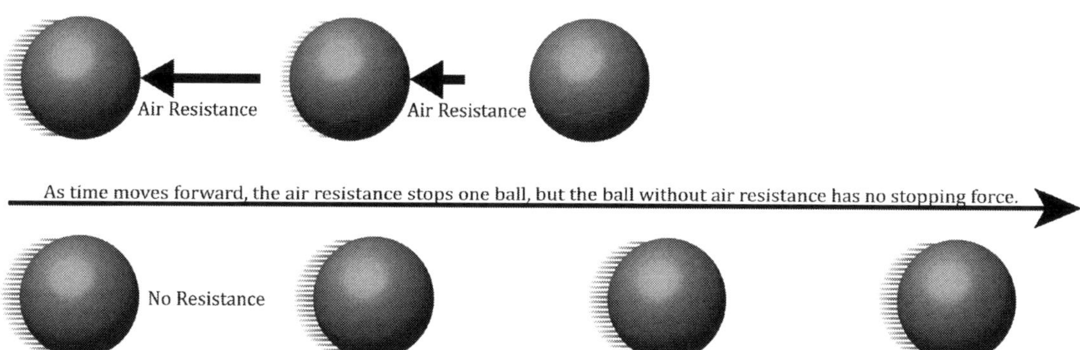

Second Law

Concept: Acceleration increases linearly with force.

Although Newton's second law can be conceptually understood as a series of relationships describing how an increase in one factor will decrease another factor, the law can be understood best in equation format:

$$\boldsymbol{Force = mass \times acceleration}$$

Or

$$\boldsymbol{Acceleration = \frac{force}{mass}}$$

Or

$$\boldsymbol{Mass = \frac{force}{acceleration}}$$

Each of the forms of the equation allows for a different look at the same relationships. To examine the relationships, change one factor and observe the result. If a steel ball, with a diameter of 6.3 cm, has a mass of 1 kg and an acceleration of 1 m/s^2, then the net force on the ball will be 1 Newton.

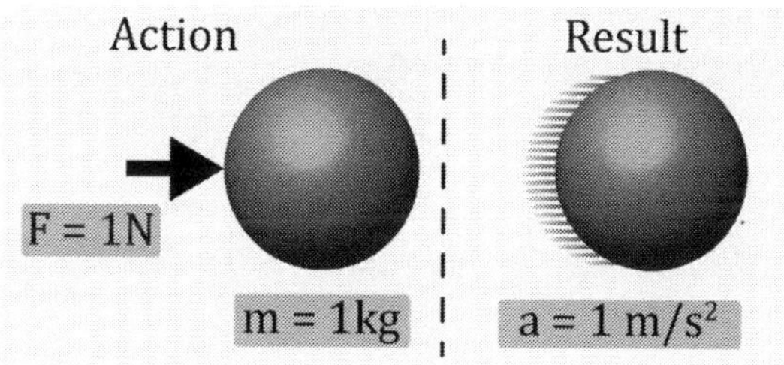

Third Law

Concept: Nothing can push or pull without being pushed or pulled in return.

When any object exerts a force on another object, the other object exerts the opposite force back on the original object. To observe this, consider two spring-based fruit scales, both tipped on their sides as shown with the weighing surfaces facing each other. If fruit scale #1 is pressing fruit scale #2 into the wall, it exerts a force on fruit scale #2, measurable by the reading on scale #2. However, because fruit scale #1 is exerting a force on scale #2, scale #2 is exerting a force on scale #1 with an opposite direction, but the same magnitude.

Force

Concept: a push or pull on an object

Calculation: $Force = mass \times acceleration$

A force is a vector which causes acceleration of a body. Force has both magnitude and direction. Furthermore, multiple forces acting on one object combine in vector addition. This can be demonstrated by considering an object placed at the origin of the coordinate plane. If it is pushed along the positive direction of the *x*-axis, it will move in this direction; if the force acting on it is in the positive direction of the *y*-axis, it will move in that direction. However, if both forces are applied at the same time, then the object will move at an angle to both the *x* and *y* axes, an angle determined by the relative amount of force exerted in each direction. In this way, we may see that the resulting force is a vector sum; that is, a net force that has both magnitude and direction.

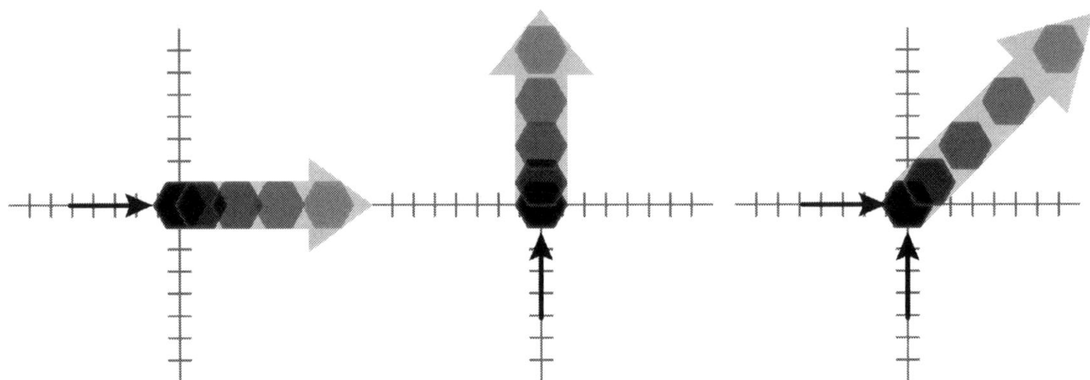

Mass

Concept: the amount of matter

Mass can be defined as the quantity of matter in an object. If we apply the same force to two objects of different mass, we will find that the resulting acceleration is different. Newton's Second Law of Motion describes the relationship between mass, force, and acceleration in the equation: ***Force =***

mass* x *acceleration. In other words, the acceleration of an object is directly proportional to the force being exerted on it and inversely proportional to its mass.

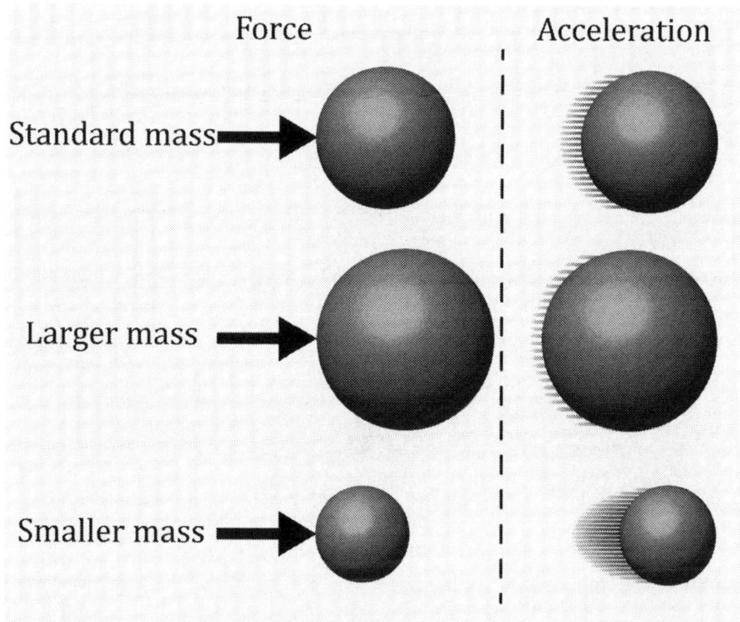

Gravity

Gravity is a force which exists between all objects with matter. Gravity is a pulling force between objects meaning that the forces on the objects point toward the opposite object. When Newton's third law is applied to gravity, the force pairs from gravity are shown to be equal in magnitude and opposite in direction.

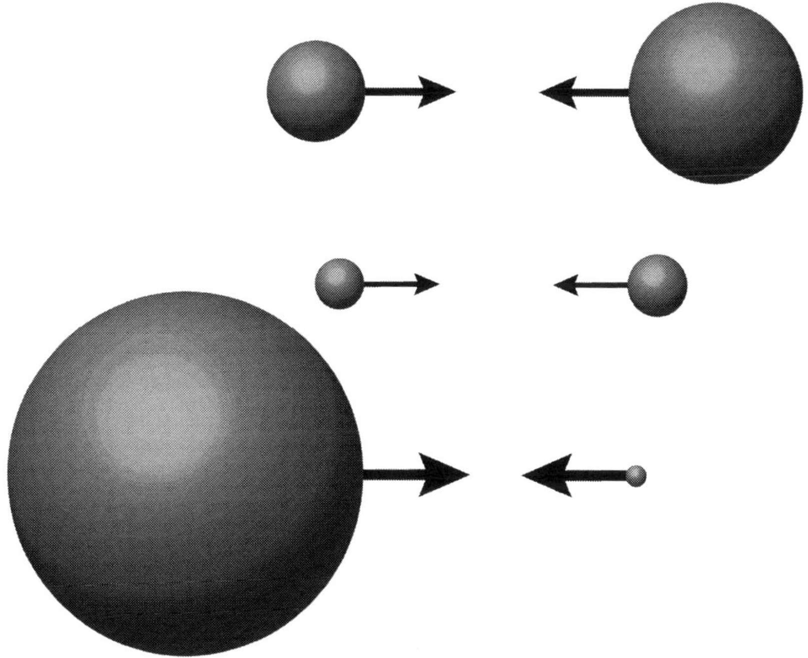

Weight

Weight is sometimes confused with mass. While mass is the amount of matter, weight is the force exerted by the earth on an object with matter by gravity. The earth pulls every object of mass toward its center while every object of mass pulls the earth toward its center. The object's pull on the earth is equal in magnitude to the pull which the earth exerts, but, because the mass of the earth is very large in comparison (5.97×10^{24} kg), only the object appears to be affected by the force.

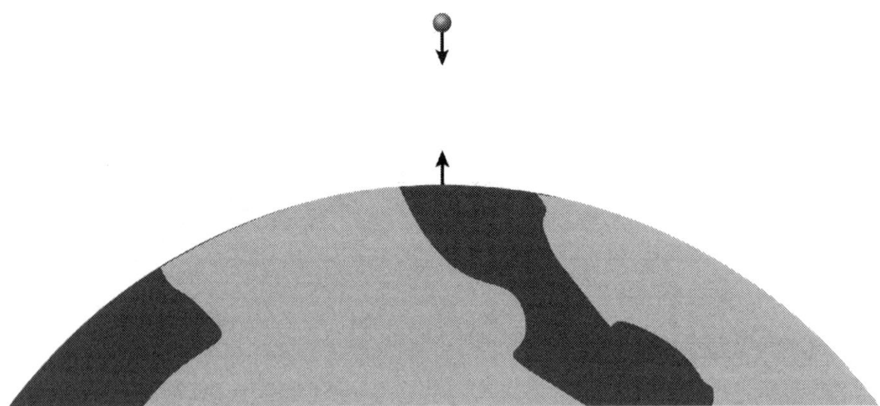

The gravity of earth causes a constant acceleration due to gravity (g) at a specific altitude. For most earthbound applications the acceleration due to gravity is 32.2 ft/s^2 or 9.8 m/s^2 in a downward direction. The equation for the force of gravity (weight) on an object is the equation from Newton's Second Law with the constant acceleration due to gravity (g).

$$\boldsymbol{Force = mass \times acceleration}$$

$$\boldsymbol{Weight = mass \times acceleration\ due\ to\ gravity}$$

$$\boldsymbol{W = m \times g}$$

The SI (International Standard of Units) unit for weight is the Newton $\left(\frac{kg \times m}{s^2}\right)$. The English Engineering unit system uses the pound, or lb, as the unit for weight and force $\left(\frac{slug \times ft}{s^2}\right)$. Thus, a 2 kg object under the influence of gravity would have a weight of:

$$\mathrm{W = m \times g}$$

$$\mathrm{W = 2\ kg \times 9.8\frac{m}{s^2} = 19.6\ N\ downwards}$$

Normal Force

Concept: the force perpendicular to a contact surface

The word "normal" is used in mathematics to mean perpendicular, and so the force known as normal force should be remembered as the perpendicular force exerted on an object that is resting on some other surface. For instance, if a box is resting on a horizontal surface, we may say that the normal force is directed upwards through the box (the opposite, downward force is the weight of the box). If the box is resting on a wedge, the normal force from the wedge is not vertical but is perpendicular to the wedge edge.

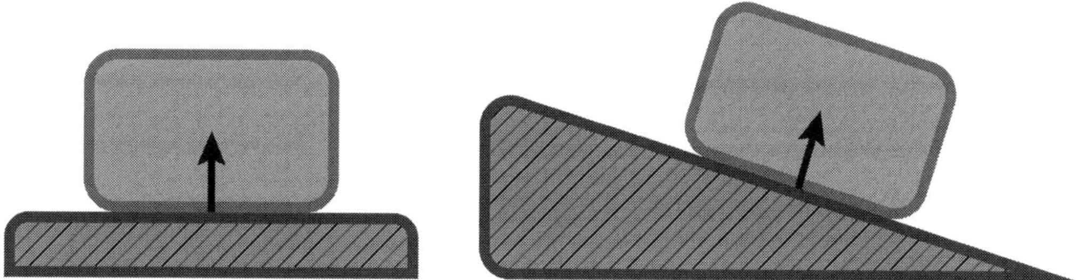

Tension

Concept: the pulling force from a cord

Another force that may come into play on the exam is called tension. Anytime a cord is attached to a body and pulled so that it is taut, we may say that the cord is under tension. The cord in tension applies a pulling tension force on the connected objects. This force is pointed away from the body and along the cord at the point of attachment. In simple considerations of tension, the cord is assumed to be both without mass and incapable of stretching. In other words, its only role is as the connector between two bodies. The cord is also assumed to pull on both ends with the same magnitude of tension force.

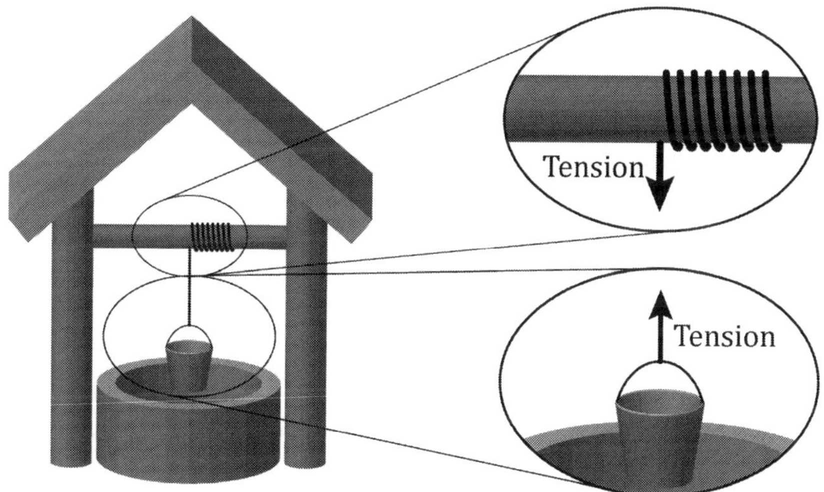

Friction

Concept: Friction is a resistance to motion between contacting surfaces

In order to illustrate the concept of friction, let us imagine a book resting on a table. As it sits, the force of its weight is equal to and opposite of the normal force. If, however, we were to exert a force on the book, attempting to push it to one side, a frictional force would arise, equal and opposite to our force. This kind of frictional force is known as static frictional force.

As we increase our force on the book, however, we will eventually cause it to accelerate in the direction of our force. At this point, the frictional force opposing us will be known as kinetic friction. For many combinations of surfaces, the magnitude of the kinetic frictional force is lower than that of the static frictional force, and consequently, the amount of force needed to maintain the movement of the book will be less than that needed to initiate the movement.

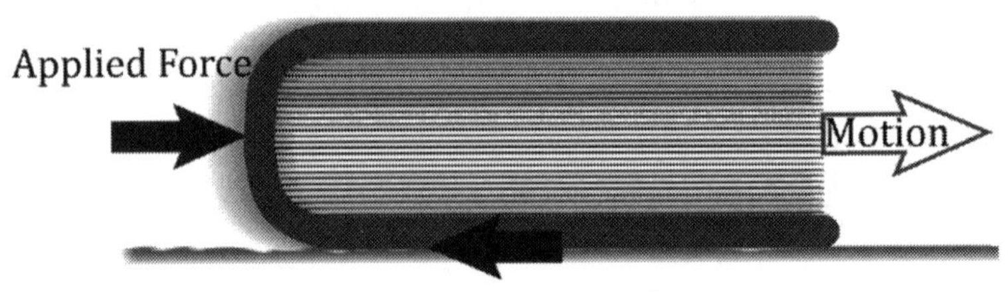

Rolling Friction

Occasionally, a question will ask you to consider the amount of friction generated by an object that is rolling. If a wheel is rolling at a constant speed, then the point at which it touches the ground will not slide, and there will be no friction between the ground and the wheel inhibiting movement. In fact, the friction at the point of contact between the wheel and the ground is static friction necessary to propulsion with wheels. When a vehicle accelerates, the static friction between the wheels and ground allows the vehicle to achieve acceleration. Without this friction, the vehicle would spin its wheels and go nowhere.

Although the static friction does not impede movement for the wheels, a combination of frictional forces can resist rolling motion. One such frictional force is bearing friction. Bearing friction is the kinetic friction between the wheel and an object it rotates around, such as a stationary axle.

Most questions will consider bearing friction the only force stopping a rotating wheel. There are many other factors that affect the efficiency of a rolling wheel such as deformation of the wheel, deformation of the surface, and force imbalances, but the net resulting friction can be modeled as a simple kinetic rolling friction. Rolling friction or rolling resistance is the catch-all friction for the combination of all the losses which impede wheels in real life.

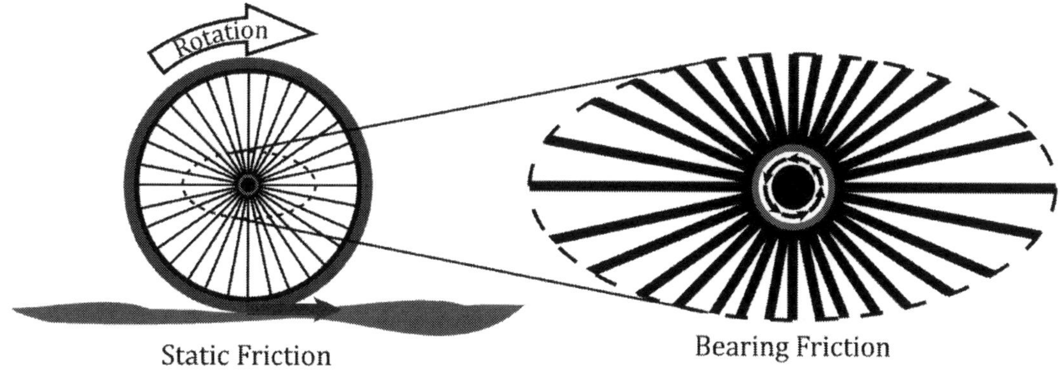

Drag Force

Friction can also be generated when an object is moving through air or liquid. A drag force occurs when a body moves through some fluid (either liquid or gas) and experiences a force that opposes the motion of the body. The drag force is greater if the air or fluid is thicker or is moving in the direction opposite to the object. Obviously, the higher the drag force, the greater amount of positive force required to keep the object moving forward.

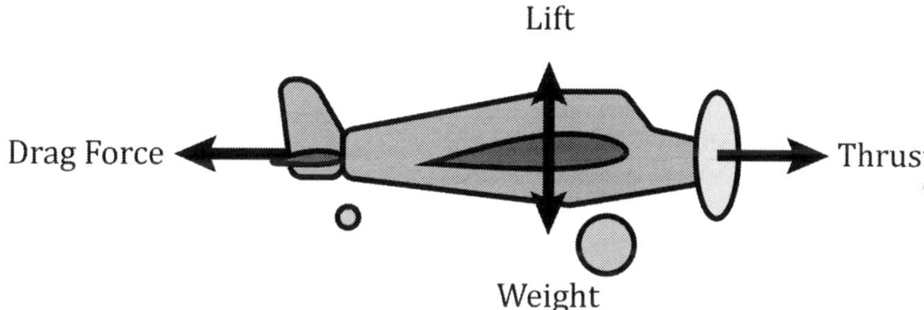

Balanced Forces

An object is in equilibrium when the sum of all forces acting on the object is zero. When the forces on an object sum to zero, the object does not accelerate. Equilibrium can be obtained when forces in the y-direction sum to zero, forces in the x-direction sum to zero, or forces in both directions sum to zero.

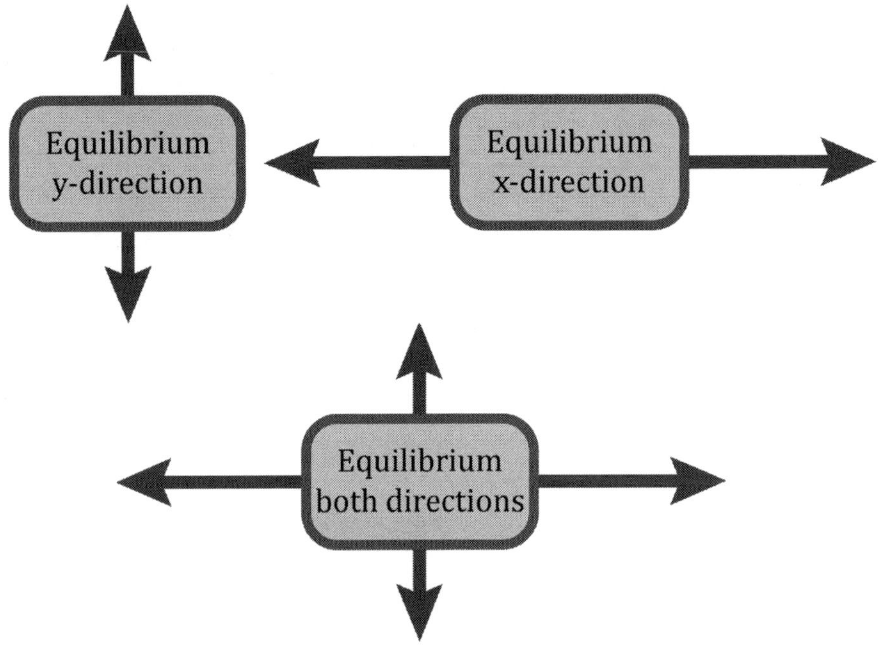

In most cases, a problem will provide one or more forces acting on object and ask for a force to balance the system. The force will be the opposite of the current force or sum of current forces.

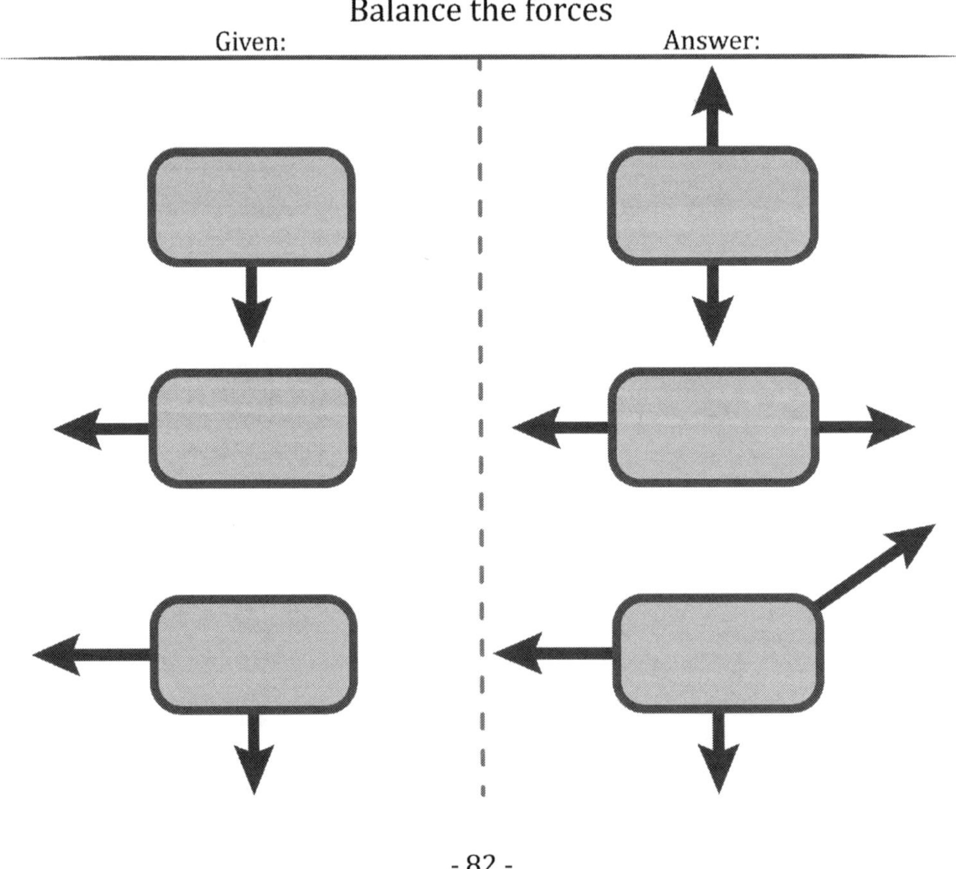

Rotational Kinetics

Many equations and concepts in linear kinematics and kinetics transfer to rotation. For example, angular position is an angle. Angular velocity, like linear velocity, is the change in the position (angle) divided by the time. Angular acceleration is the change in angular velocity divided by time. Although most tests will not require you to perform angular calculations, they will expect you to understand the angular version of force: torque.

Concept: Torque is a twisting force on an object

Calculation: $Torque = radius \times force$

Torque, like force, is a vector and has magnitude and direction. As with force, the sum of torques on an object will affect the angular acceleration of that object. The key to solving problems with torque is understanding the lever arm. A better description of the torque equation is:

Torque = force × the distance perpedicular to the force to the center of rotation

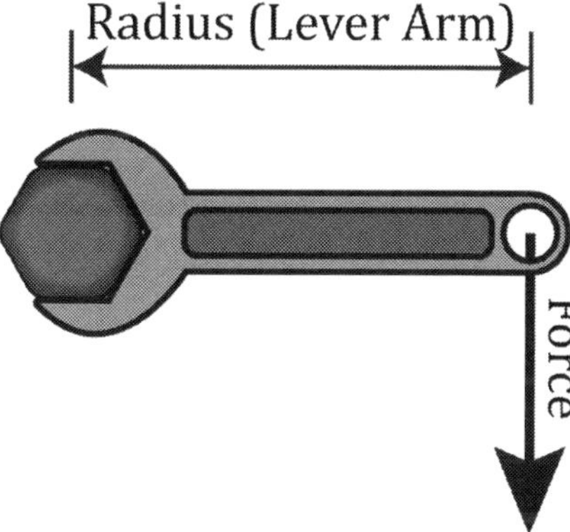

Because torque is directly proportional to the radius, or lever arm, a greater lever arm will result in a greater torque with the same amount of force. The wrench on the right has twice the radius and, as a result, twice the torque.

Alternatively, a greater force also increases torque. The wrench on the right has twice the force and twice the torque.

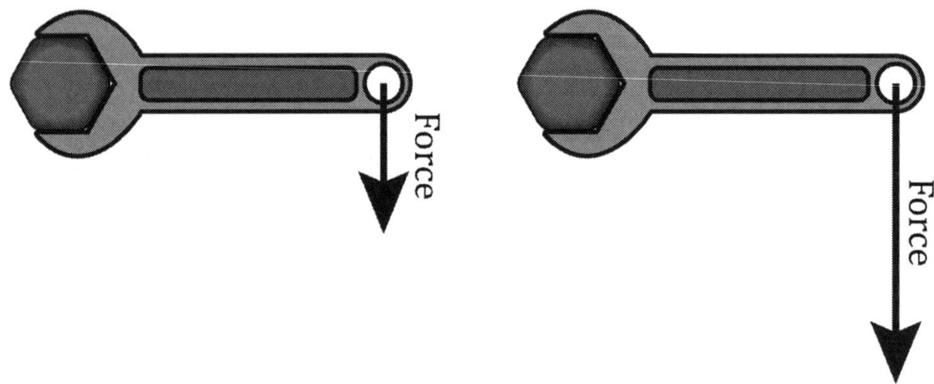

Work/Energy

Work

Concept: Work is the transfer of energy from one object to another

Calculation: Work = force × displacement

The equation for work in one dimension is fairly simple:

$$\boldsymbol{Work = Force \times displacement}$$

$$\boldsymbol{W = F \times d}$$

In the equation, the force and the displacement are the magnitude of the force exerted and the total change in position of the object on which the force is exerted, respectively. If force and displacement have the same direction, then the work is positive. If they are in opposite directions, however, the work is negative.

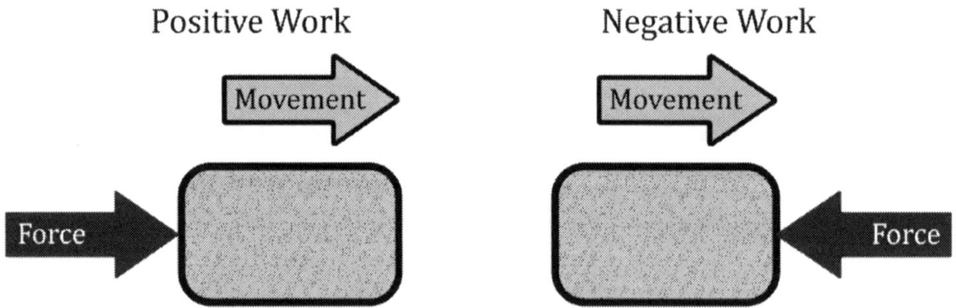

For two-dimensional work, the equation is a bit more complex:

$$\boldsymbol{Work = Force \times displacement \times cos(\theta \text{ between displacement and } force)}$$

$$\boldsymbol{W = F \times d \times cos(\theta)}$$

The angle in the equation is the angle between the direction of the force and the direction of the displacement. Thus, the work done when a box is pulled at a 20-degree angle with a force of 100 lb for 20 ft will be less than the work done when a differently weighted box is pulled horizontally with a force of 100 lb for 20 ft.

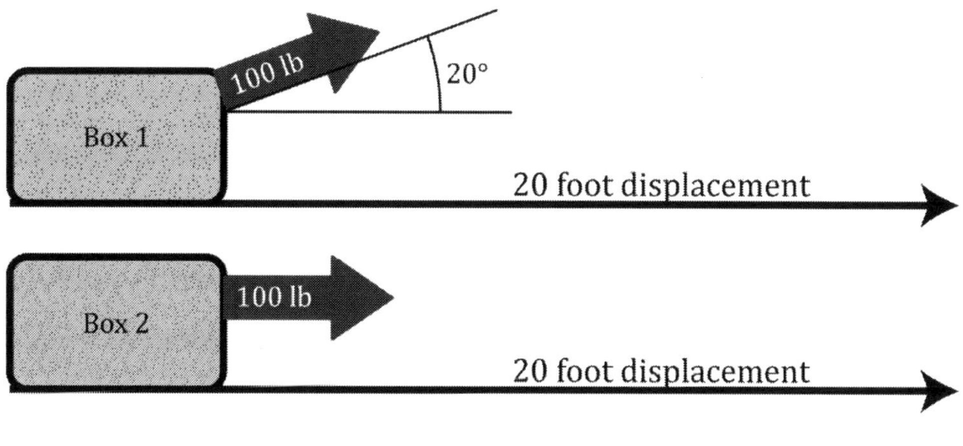

$$W_1 = 100\text{lb} \times 20\text{ft} \times \cos(20°) = 1880 \text{ ft} \cdot \text{lb}$$

$$W_2 = 100\text{lb} \times 20\text{ft} \times \cos(0°) = 2000 \text{ ft} \cdot \text{lb}$$

The unit ft · lb is the unit for both work and energy.

Energy

Concept: the ability of a body to do work on another object

Energy is a word that has found a million different uses in the English language, but in physics it refers to the measure of a body's ability to do work. In physics, energy may not have a million meanings, but it does have many forms. Each of these forms, such as chemical, electric, and nuclear, is the capability of an object to perform work. However, for the purpose of most tests, mechanical energy and mechanical work are the only forms of energy worth understanding in depth. Mechanical energy is the sum of an object's kinetic and potential energies. Although they will be introduced in greater detail, these are the forms of mechanical energy:

Kinetic Energy – energy an object has by virtue of its motion

Gravitational Potential Energy – energy by virtue of an object's height

Elastic Potential Energy – energy stored in compression or tension

Neglecting frictional forces, mechanical energy is conserved.

As an example, imagine a ball moving perpendicular to the surface of the earth, with its weight the only force acting on it. As the ball rises, the weight will be doing work on the ball, decreasing its speed and its kinetic energy, and slowing it down until it momentarily stops. During this ascent, the potential energy of the ball will be rising. Once the ball begins to fall back down, it will lose potential energy as it gains kinetic energy. Mechanical energy is conserved throughout; the potential energy of the ball at its highest point is equal to the kinetic energy of the ball at its lowest point prior to impact.

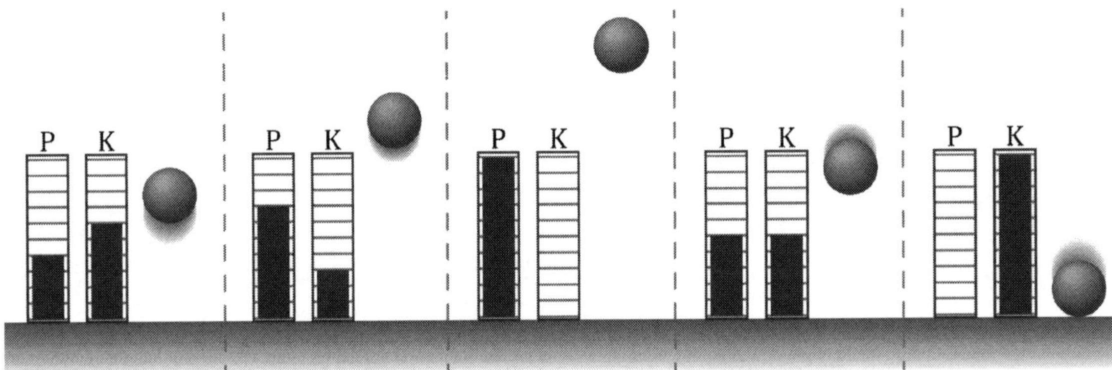

In systems where friction and air resistance are not negligible, we observe a different sort of result. For example, imagine a block sliding across the floor until it comes to a stop due to friction. Unlike a compressed spring or a ball flung into the air, there is no way for this block to regain its energy with a return trip. Therefore, we cannot say that the lost kinetic energy is being stored as potential energy. Instead, it has been dissipated and cannot be recovered. The total mechanical energy of the block-floor system has been not conserved in this case but rather reduced. The total energy of the system has not decreased, since the kinetic energy has been converted into thermal energy, but that energy is no longer useful for work.

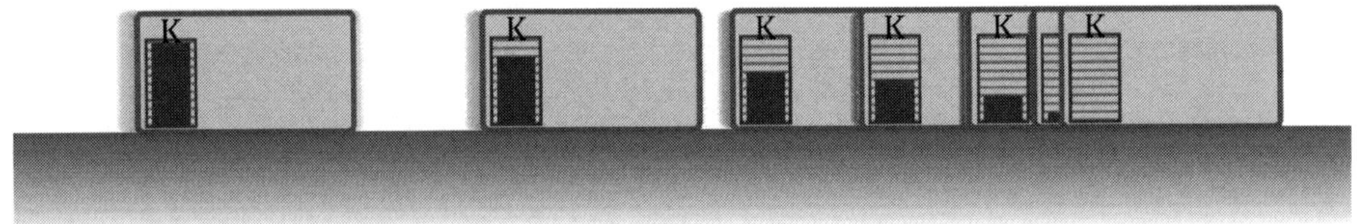

Energy, though it may change form, will be neither created nor destroyed during physical processes. However, if we construct a system and some external force performs work on it, the result may be slightly different. If the work is positive, then the overall store of energy is increased; if it is negative, however, we can say that the overall energy of the system has decreased.

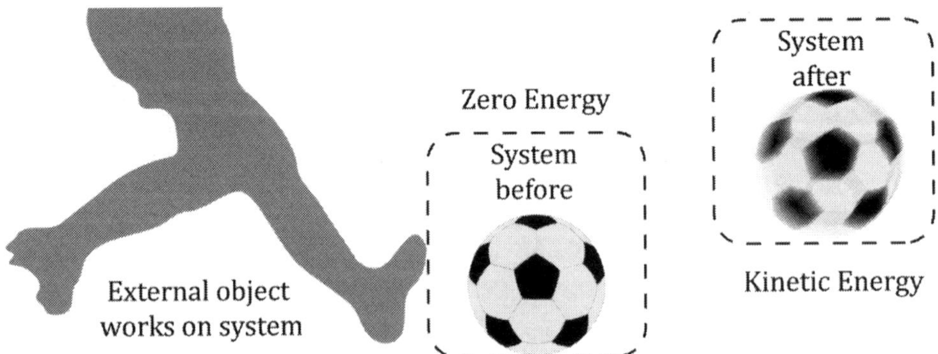

Kinetic Energy

The kinetic energy of an object is the amount of energy it possesses by reason of being in motion. Kinetic energy cannot be negative. Changes in kinetic energy will occur when a force does work on an object, such that the motion of the object is altered. This change in kinetic energy is equal to the amount of work that is done. This relationship is commonly referred to as the work-energy theorem.

One interesting application of the work-energy theorem is that of objects in a free fall. To begin with, let us assert that the force acting on such an object is its weight, equal to its mass times g (the force of gravity). The work done by this force will be positive, as the force is exerted in the direction in which the object is traveling. Kinetic energy will, therefore, increase, according to the work-kinetic energy theorem.

If the object is dropped from a great enough height, it eventually reaches its terminal velocity, where the drag force is equal to the weight, so the object is no longer accelerating and its kinetic energy remains constant.

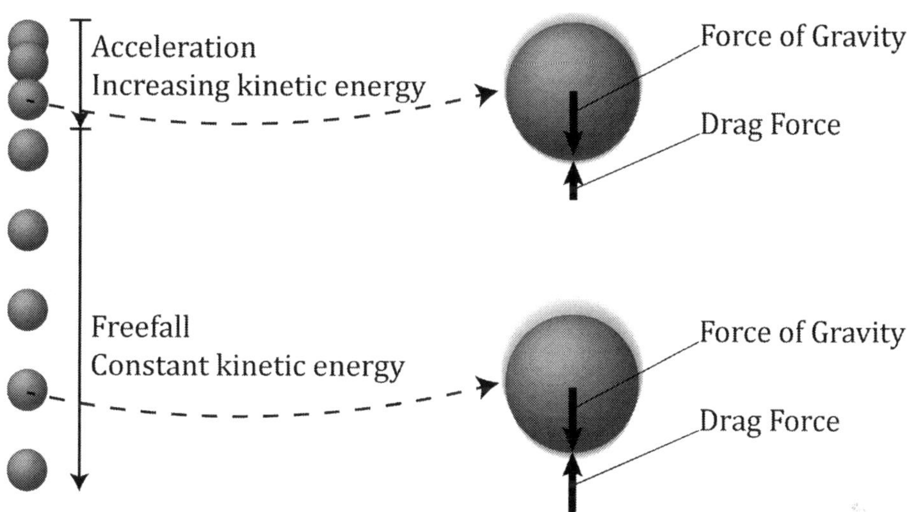

Gravitational Potential Energy

Gravitational potential energy is simply the potential for a certain amount of work to be done by one object on another using gravity. For objects on earth, the gravitational potential energy is equal to the amount of work which the earth can act on the object. The work which gravity performs on objects moving entirely or partially in the vertical direction is equal to the force exerted by the earth (weight) times the distance traveled in the direction of the force (height above the ground or reference point):

$$\textbf{Work from gravity} = \textbf{weight} \times \textbf{height above the ground}$$

Thus, the gravitational potential energy is the same as the potential work.

Gravitational Potential Energy = weight × height

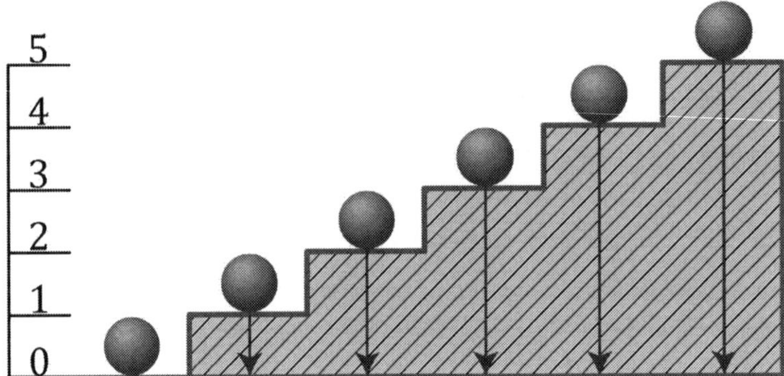

Elastic Potential Energy

Elastic potential energy is the potential for a certain amount of work to be done by one object on another using elastic compression or tension. The most common example is the spring. A spring will resist any compression or tension away from its equilibrium position (natural position). A small buggy is pressed into a large spring. The spring contains a large amount of elastic potential energy. If the buggy and spring are released, the spring will push exert a force on the buggy for a distance. This work will put kinetic energy into the buggy. The energy can be imagined as a liquid poured from one container into another. The spring pours its elastic energy into the buggy, which receives the energy as kinetic energy.

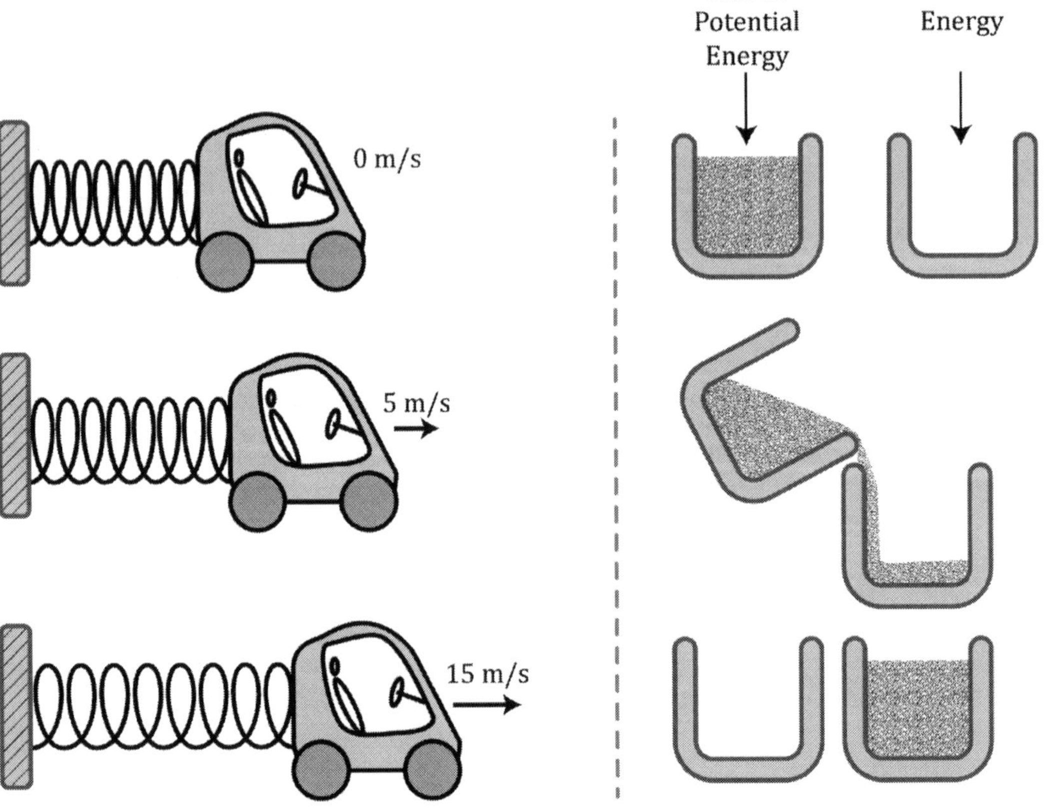

Power

Concept: the rate of work

Calculation: work/time

On occasion, you may need to demonstrate an understanding of power, as it is defined in applied physics. Power is the rate at which work is done. Power, like work and energy, is a scalar quantity. Power can be calculated by dividing the amount of work performed by the amount of time in which the work was performed.

$$\textbf{Power} = \frac{\textbf{work}}{\textbf{time}}$$

If more work is performed in a shorter amount of time, more power has been exerted. Power can be expressed in a variety of units. The preferred metric expression is one of watts or joules per seconds. For engine power, it is often expressed in horsepower.

Machines

Simple Machines

Concept: Tools which transform forces to make tasks easier.

As their job is to transform forces, simple machines have an input force and an output force or forces. Simple machines transform forces in two ways: direction and magnitude. A machine can change the direction of a force, with respect to the input force, like a single stationary pulley which only changes the direction of the output force. A machine can also change the magnitude of the force like a lever.

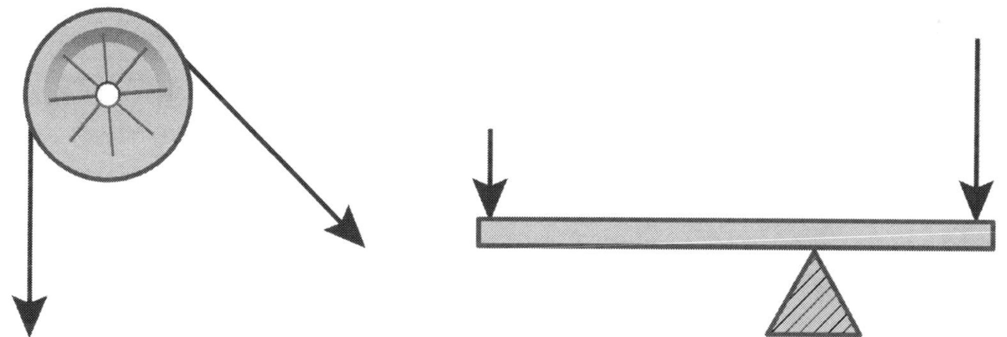

Simple machines include the inclined plane, the wedge, the screw, the pulley, the lever, and the wheel.

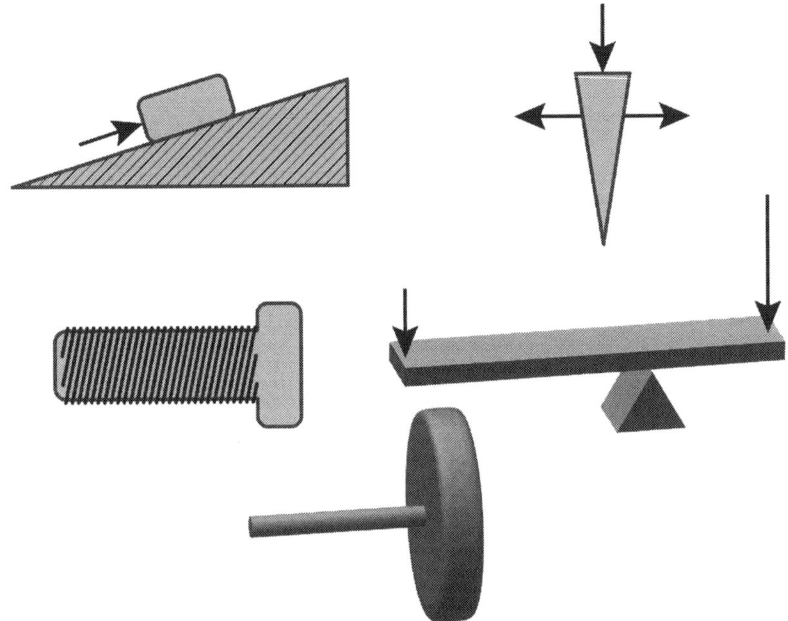

Mechanical Advantage

Concept: the amount of change a simple machine provides to the magnitude of a force

Calculation: output force/input force

Mechanical advantage is the measure of the output force divided by the input force. Thus, mechanical advantage measures the change performed by a machine. Machines cannot create energy, only transform it. Thus, in frictionless, ideal machines, the input work equals the output work.

$$Work_{input} = Work_{output}$$

$$force_{input} \times distance_{input} = force_{output} \times distance_{output}$$

This means that a simple machine can increase the force of the output by decreasing the distance which the output travels or it can increase the distance of the output by decreasing the force at the output.

By moving parts of the equation for work, we can arrive at the equation for mechanical advantage.

$$\textbf{Mechanical Advantage} = \frac{\textbf{force}_{\textbf{output}}}{\textbf{force}_{\textbf{input}}} = \frac{\textbf{distance}_{\textbf{input}}}{\textbf{distance}_{\textbf{output}}}$$

If the mechanical advantage is greater than one, the output force is greater than the input force and the input distance is greater than the output distance. Conversely, if the mechanical advantage is less than one, the input force is greater than the output force and the output distance is greater than the input distance. In equation form this is:

If Mechanical Advantage > 1:

$$force_{input} < force_{output} \text{ and } distance_{output} < distance_{input}$$

If Mechanical Advantage < 1:

$$force_{input} > force_{output} \text{ and } distance_{output} > distance_{input}$$

Inclined Plane

The inclined plane is perhaps the most common of the simple machines. It is simply a flat surface that elevates as you move from one end to the other; a ramp is an easy example of an inclined plane. Consider how much easier it is for an elderly person to walk up a long ramp than to climb a shorter but steeper flight of stairs; this is because the force required is diminished as the distance increases. Indeed, the longer the ramp, the easier it is to ascend.

On the exam, this simple fact will most often be applied to moving heavy objects. For instance, if you have to move a heavy box onto the back of a truck, it is much easier to push it up a ramp than to lift it directly onto the truck bed. The longer the ramp, the greater the mechanical advantage, and the easier it will be to move the box. The mechanical advantage of an inclined plane is equal to the slant length divided by the rise of the plane.

$$\textbf{Mechanical Advantage} = \frac{\textbf{slant length}}{\textbf{rise}}$$

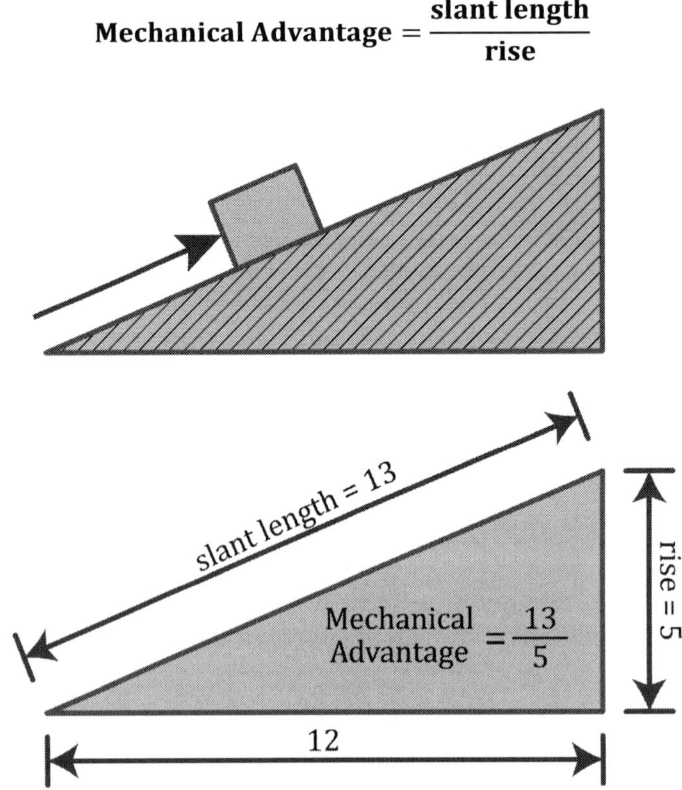

As you solve this kind of problem, however, remember that the same amount of work is being performed whether the box is lifted directly or pushed up a twenty-foot ramp; a simple machine only changes the force and the distance.

Wedge

A wedge is a variation on the inclined plane, in which the wedge moves between objects or parts and forces them apart. The unique characteristic of a wedge is that, unlike an inclined plane, it is designed to move. Perhaps the most familiar use of the wedge is in splitting wood. A wedge is driven into the wood by hitting the flat back end. The thin end of a wedge is easier to drive into the wood since it has less surface area and, therefore, transmits more force per area. As the wedge is driven in, the increased width helps to split the wood.

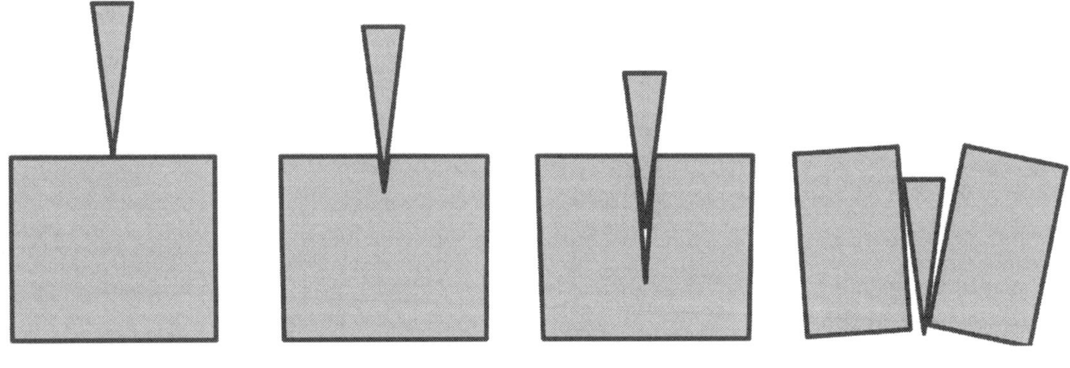

The exam may require you to select the wedge that has the highest mechanical advantage. This should be easy: the longer and thinner the wedge, the greater the mechanical advantage. The equation for mechanical advantage is:

$$\textbf{Mechanical Advantage} = \frac{\textbf{Length}}{\textbf{Width}}$$

Screw

A screw is simply an inclined plane that has been wound around a cylinder so that it forms a sort of spiral.

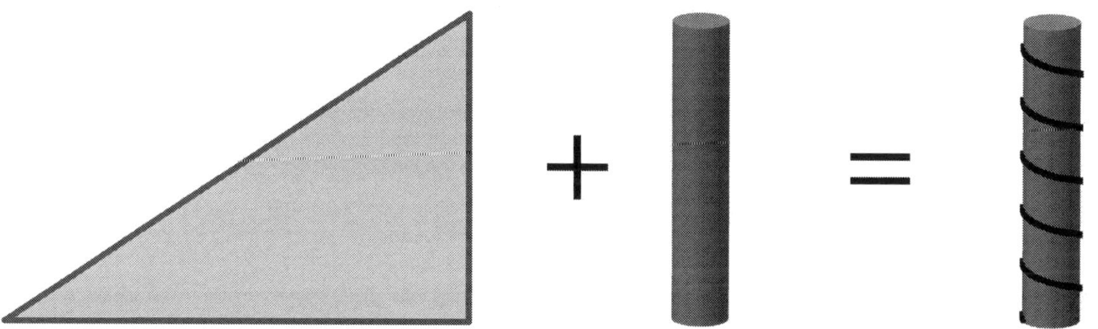

When it is placed into some medium, as for instance wood, the screw will move either forward or backward when it is rotated. The principle of the screw is used in a number of different objects, from jar lids to flashlights. On the exam, you are unlikely to see many questions regarding screws, though you may be presented with a given screw rotation and asked in which direction the screw will move. However, for consistency's sake, the equation for the mechanical advantage is a modification of the inclined plane's equation. Again, the formula for an inclined plane is:

$$Mechanical\ Advantage = \frac{slant\ length}{rise}$$

Because the rise of the inclined plane is the length along a screw, length between rotations = rise. Also, the slant length will equal the circumference of one rotation = 2πr.

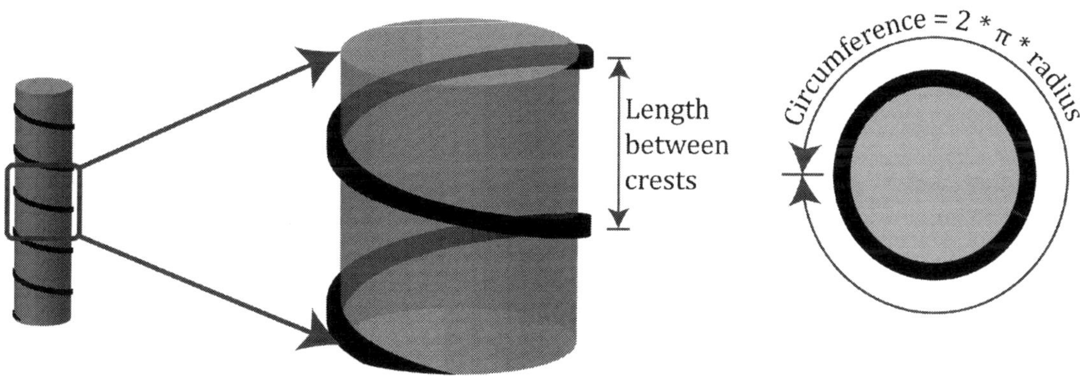

$$\textbf{Mechanical Advantage} = \frac{\mathbf{2 \times \pi \times radius}}{\textbf{length between crests}}$$

Lever

The lever is the most common kind of simple machine. See-saws, shovels, and baseball bats are all examples of levers. There are three classes of levers which are differentiated by the relative orientations of the fulcrum, resistance, and effort. The fulcrum is the point at which the lever rotates; the effort is the point on the lever where force is applied; the resistance is the part of the lever that acts in response to the effort.

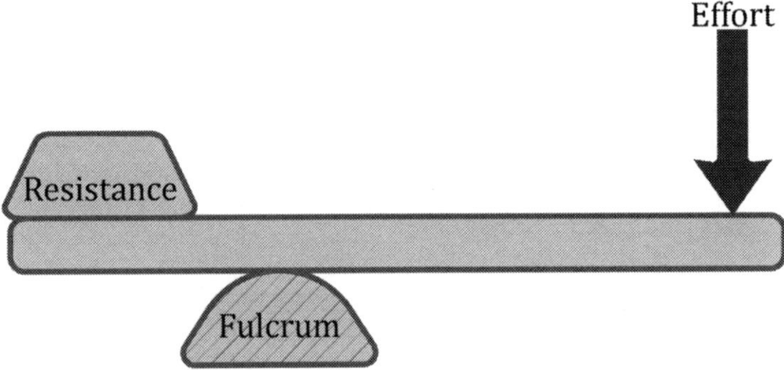

The mechanical advantage of a lever depends on the distances of the effort and resistance from the fulcrum. Mechanical advantage equals:

$$\textbf{Mechanical Advantage} = \frac{\textbf{effort distance}}{\textbf{resistance distance}}$$

For each class of lever, the location of the important distances changes:

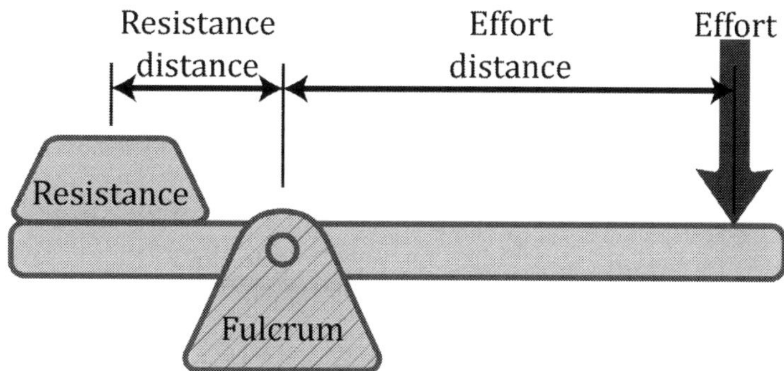

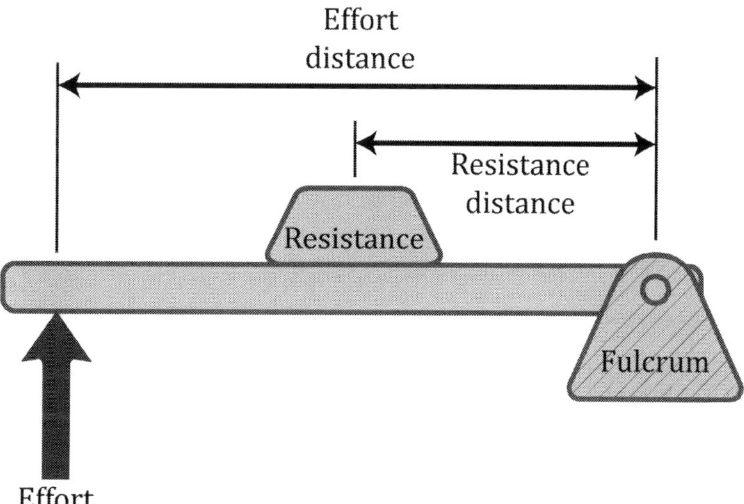

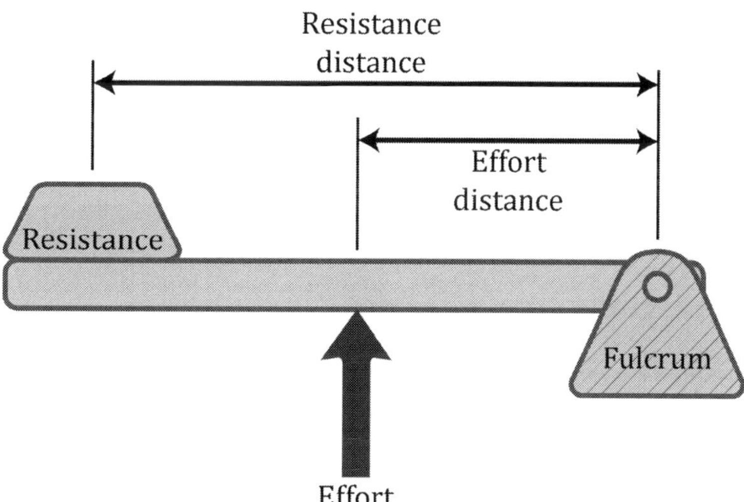

In a first-class lever, the fulcrum is between the effort and the resistance. A seesaw is a good example of a first-class lever: when effort is applied to force one end up, the other end goes down, and vice versa. The shorter the distance between the fulcrum and the resistance, the easier it will be to move the resistance. As an example, consider whether it is easier to lift another person on a see-saw when they are sitting close to the middle or all the way at the end. A little practice will show you that it is much more difficult to lift a person the farther away he or she is on the see-saw.

In a second-class lever, the resistance is in-between the fulcrum and the effort. While a first-class lever is able to increase force and distance through mechanical advantage, a second-class lever is only able to increase force. A common example of a second-class lever is the wheelbarrow: the force exerted by your hand at one end of the wheelbarrow is magnified at the load. Basically, with a second class lever you are trading distance for force; by moving your end of the wheelbarrow a bit farther, you produce greater force at the load.

Third class levers are used to produce greater distance. In a third-class lever, the force is applied in between the fulcrum and the resistance. A baseball bat is a classic example of a third-class lever; the bottom of the bat, below where you grip it, is considered the fulcrum. The end of the bat, where the ball is struck, is the resistance. By exerting effort at the base of the bat, close to the fulcrum, you are able to make the end of the bat fly quickly through the air. The closer your hands are to the base of the bat, the faster you will be able to make the other end of the bat travel.

Pulley

The pulley is a simple machine in which a rope is carried by the rotation of a wheel. Another name for a pulley is a block. Pulleys are typically used to allow the force to be directed from a convenient location. For instance, imagine you are given the task of lifting a heavy and tall bookcase. Rather than tying a rope to the bookcase and trying to lift it up, it would make sense to tie a pulley system to a rafter above the bookcase and run the rope through it, so that you could pull down on the rope and lift the bookcase. Pulling down allows you to incorporate your weight (normal force) into the act of lifting, thereby making it easier.

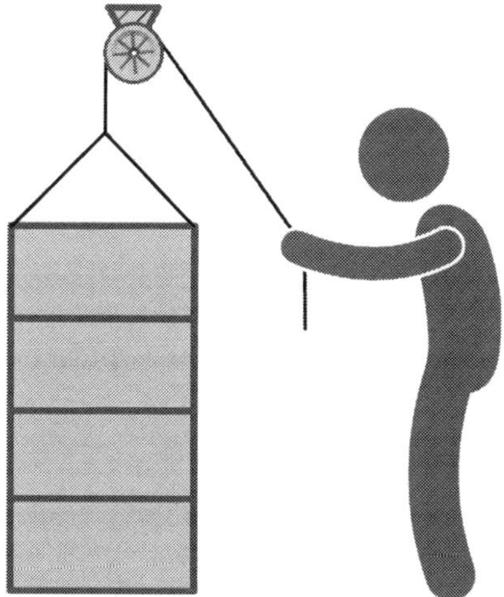

If there is just one pulley above the bookcase, you have created a first-class lever which will not diminish the amount of force that needs to be applied to lift the bookcase. There is another way to use a pulley, however, that can make the job of lifting a heavy object considerably easier. First, tie the rope directly to the rafter. Then, attach a pulley to the top of the bookcase and run the rope through it. If you can then stand so that you are above the bookcase, you will have a much easier time lifting this heavy object. Why? Because the weight of the bookcase is now being distributed: half of it is acting on the rafter, and half of it is acting on you. In other words, this arrangement allows you to lift an object with half the force. This simple pulley system, therefore, has a mechanical advantage of 2. Note that in this arrangement, the unfixed pulley is acting like a second-class lever. The price you pay for your mechanical advantage is that whatever distance you raise your end of the rope, the bookcase will only be lifted half as much.

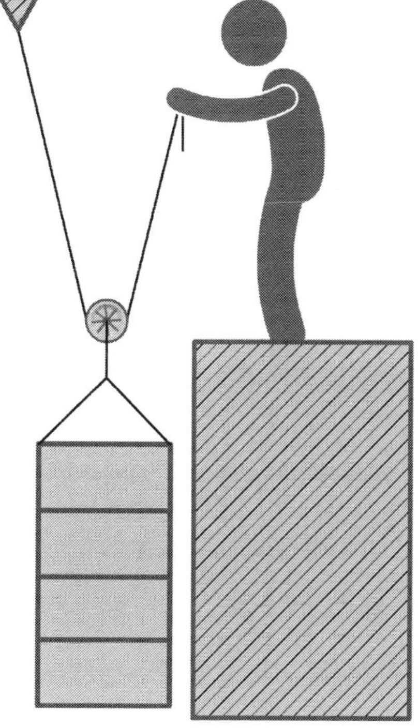

Of course, it might be difficult for you to find a place high enough to enact this system. If this is the case, you can always tie another pulley to the rafter and run the rope through it and back down to the floor. Since this second pulley is fixed, the mechanical advantage will remain the same.

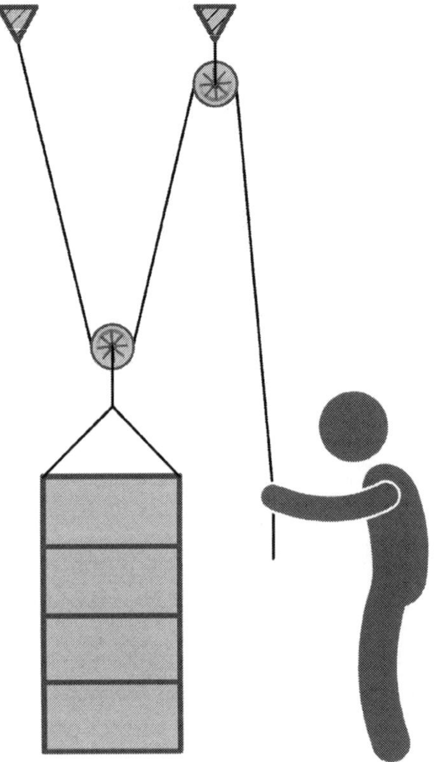

There are other, slightly more complex ways to obtain an even greater mechanical advantage with a system of pulleys. On the exam, you may be required to determine the pulley and tackle (rope) arrangement that creates the greatest mechanical advantage. The easiest way to determine the answer is to count the number of ropes that are going to and from the unfixed pulley; the more ropes coming and going, the greater the mechanical advantage.

Wheel and Axle

Another basic arrangement that makes use of simple machines is called the wheel and axle. When most people think of a wheel and axle, they immediately envision an automobile tire. The steering wheel of the car, however, operates on the same mechanical principle, namely that the force required to move the center of a circle is much greater than the force require to move the outer rim of a circle. When you turn the steering wheel, you are essentially using a second-class lever by increasing the output force by increasing the input distance. The force required to turn the wheel from the outer rim is much less than would be required to turn the wheel from its center. Just imagine how difficult it would be to drive a car if the steering wheel was the size of a saucer!

Conceptually, the mechanical advantage of a wheel is easy to understand. For instance, all other things being equal, the mechanical advantage created by a system will increase along with the radius. In other words, a steering wheel with a radius of 12 inches has a greater mechanical advantage than a steering wheel with a radius of ten inches; the same amount of force exerted on the rim of each wheel will produce greater force at the axis of the larger wheel.

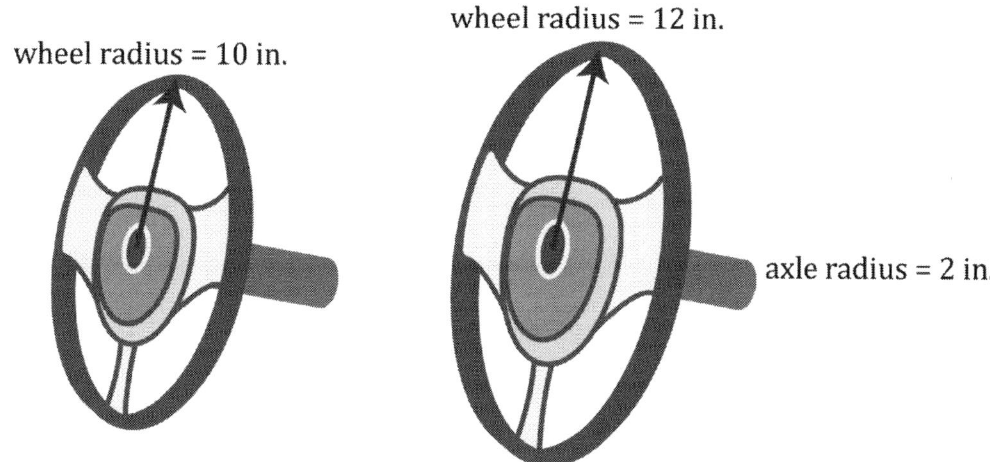

The equation for the mechanical advantage of a wheel and axle is:

$$\textbf{Mechanical Advantage} = \frac{\textbf{radius}_{\textbf{wheel}}}{\textbf{radius}_{\textbf{axle}}}$$

Thus, the mechanical advantage of the steering wheel with a larger radius will be:

$$Mechanical\ Advantage = \frac{12\ inches}{2\ inches} = 6$$

Gears

The exam may ask you questions involving some slightly more complex mechanisms. It is very common, for instance, for there to be a couple of questions concerning gears. Gears are a system of interlocking wheels that can create immense mechanical advantages. The amount of mechanical advantage, however, will depend on the gear ratio; that is, on the relation in size between the gears.

When a small gear is driving a big gear, the speed of the big gear is relatively slow; when a big gear is driving a small gear, the speed of the small gear is relatively fast.

The equation for the mechanical advantage is:

$$\textbf{Mechanical Advantage} = \frac{\textbf{Torque}_{\textbf{output}}}{\textbf{Torque}_{\textbf{input}}} = \frac{\mathbf{r}_{\textbf{output}}}{\mathbf{r}_{\textbf{input}}} = \frac{\textbf{\# of teeth}_{\textbf{output}}}{\textbf{\# of teeth}_{\textbf{input}}}$$

Note that mechanical advantage is greater than 1 when the output gear is larger. In these cases, the output velocity ($\boldsymbol{\omega}$) will be lower. The equation for the relative speed of a gear system is:

$$\frac{\boldsymbol{\omega}_{\textbf{input}}}{\boldsymbol{\omega}_{\textbf{output}}} = \frac{\mathbf{r}_{\textbf{output}}}{\mathbf{r}_{\textbf{input}}}$$

$$Mechanical\ Advantage = \frac{teeth_{output}}{teeth_{input}} = \frac{20}{10} = 2$$

$$Mechanical\ Advantage = \frac{teeth_{output}}{teeth_{input}} = \frac{16}{8} = 2$$

Uses of Gears

Gears are used to change direction of output torque, change location of output torque, change amount of output torque, and change angular velocity of output.

Change output direction

Change torque location

Change torque amount

Change output velocity

Gear Ratios

A gear ratio is a measure of how much the speed and torque are changing in a gear system. It is the ratio of output speed to input speed. Because the number of teeth is directly proportional to the speed in meshing gears, a gear ratio can also be calculated using the number of teeth on the gears. When the driving gear has 30 teeth and the driven gear has 10 teeth, the gear ratio is 3:1.

$$Gear\ Ratio = \frac{\#\ of\ teeth_{driving}}{\#\ of\ teeth_{driven}} = \frac{30}{10} = \frac{3}{1} = 3:1$$

This means that the smaller, driven gear rotates 3 times for every 1 rotation of the driving gear.

The Hydraulic Jack

The hydraulic jack is a simple machine using two tanks and two pistons to change the amount of an output force.

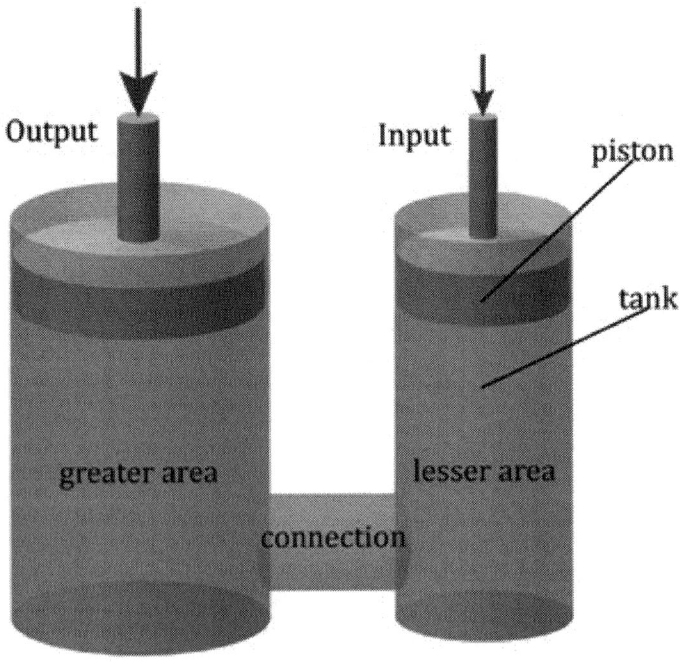

Since fluids are effectively incompressible, when you apply pressure to one part of a contained fluid, that pressure will have to be relieved in equal measure elsewhere in the container. Supposed the input piston has half the surface area of the output piston (10 in^2 compared to 20 in^2), and it is being pushed downward with 50 pounds of force. The pressure being applied to the fluid is $50\ lb \div 10\ in^2 = 5\frac{lb}{in^2}$ or 5 psi. When that 5 psi of pressure is applied to the output piston, it pushes that piston upward with a force of $5\frac{lb}{in^2} \times 20\ in^2 = 100\ lb$.

The hydraulic jack functions similarly to a first-class lever, but with the important factor being the area of the pistons rather than the length of the lever arms. Note that the mechanical advantage is based on the relative areas, not the relative radii, of the pistons. The radii must be squared to compute the relative areas.

$$\textbf{Mechanical Advantage} = \frac{\textbf{Force}_{\textbf{output}}}{\textbf{Force}_{\textbf{input}}} = \frac{\textbf{area}_{\textbf{output}}}{\textbf{area}_{\textbf{input}}} = \frac{\textbf{radius}_{\textbf{output}}^{2}}{\textbf{radius}_{\textbf{input}}^{2}}$$

Pulleys and Belts

Another system involves two pulleys connected by a drive belt (a looped band that goes around both pulleys). The operation of this system is similar to that of gears, with the exception that the pulleys will rotate in the same direction, while interlocking gears will rotate in opposite directions.

A smaller pulley will always spin faster than a larger pulley, though the larger pulley will generate more torque.

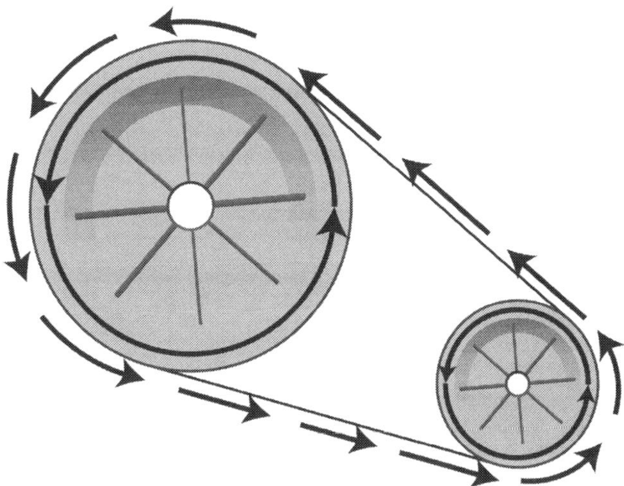

The speed ratio between the pulleys can be determined by comparing their radii; for instance, a 4-inch pulley and a 12-inch pulley will have a speed ratio of 3:1.

Momentum/Impulse

Linear Momentum

Concept: how much a body will resist stopping

Calculation: $momentum = mass \times velocity$

In physics, linear momentum can be found by multiplying the mass and velocity of an object:

$$\textbf{Momentum} = \textbf{mass} \times \textbf{velocity}$$

Momentum and velocity will always be in the same direction. Newton's second law describes momentum, stating that the rate of change of momentum is proportional to the force exerted and is in the direction of the force. If we assume a closed and isolated system (one in which no objects leave or enter, and upon which the sum of external forces is zero), then we can assume that the momentum of the system will neither increase nor decrease. That is, we will find that the momentum is a constant. The law of conservation of linear momentum applies universally in physics, even in situations of extremely high velocity or with subatomic particles.

Collisions

This concept of momentum takes on new importance when we consider collisions. A collision is an isolated event in which a strong force acts between each of two or more colliding bodies for a brief period of time. However, a collision is more intuitively defined as one or more objects hitting each other.

When two bodies collide, each object exerts a force on the opposite member. These equal and opposite forces change the linear momentum of the objects. However, when both bodies are considered, the net momentum in collisions is conserved.

There are two types of collisions: elastic and inelastic. The difference between the two lies in whether kinetic energy is conserved. If the total kinetic energy of the system is conserved, the collision is elastic. Visually, elastic collisions are collisions in which objects bounce perfectly. If some of the kinetic energy is transformed into heat or another form of energy, the collision is inelastic. Visually, inelastic collisions are collisions in which the objects do not bounce perfectly or even stick to each other.

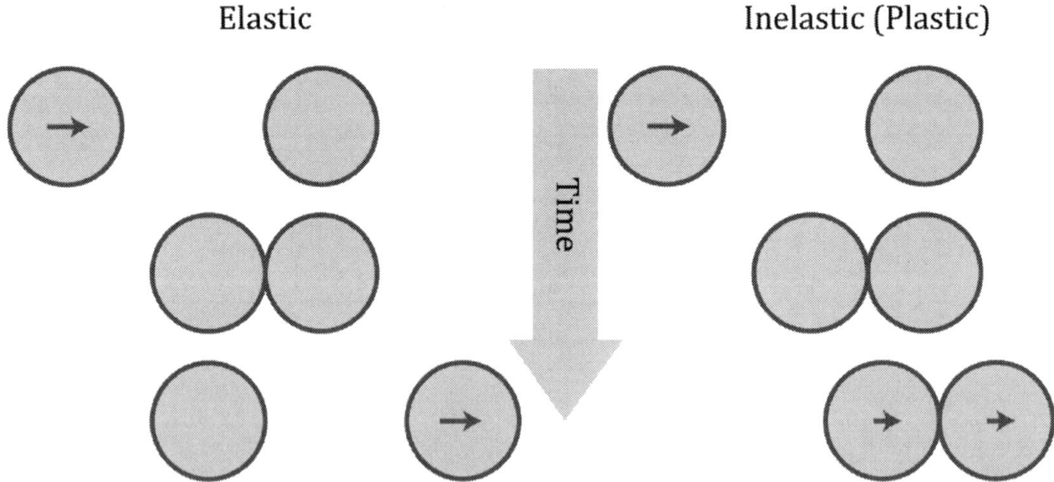

If the two bodies involved in an elastic collision have the same mass, then the body that was moving will stop completely, and the body that was at rest will begin moving at the same velocity as the projectile was moving before the collision.

Fluids

Fluids

Concept: liquids and gasses

A few of the questions on the exam will probably require you to consider the behavior of fluids. It sounds obvious, perhaps, but fluids can best be defined as substances that flow. A fluid will conform, slowly or quickly, to any container in which it is placed. Both liquids and gasses are considered to be fluids. Fluids are essentially those substances in which the atoms are not arranged in any permanent, rigid way. In ice, for instance, atoms are all lined up in what is known as a crystalline lattice, while in water and steam the only intermolecular arrangements are haphazard connections between neighboring molecules.

Flow Rates

When liquids flow in and out of containers with certain rates, the change in volume is the volumetric flow in minus the volumetric flow out. Volumetric flow is essentially the amount of volume moved past some point divided by the time it took for the volume to pass.

$$\textbf{Volumetric flow rate} = \frac{\textbf{volume moved}}{\textbf{time for the movement}}$$

If the flow into a container is greater than the flow out, the container will fill with the fluid. However, if the flow out of a container is greater than the flow into a container, the container will drain of the fluid.

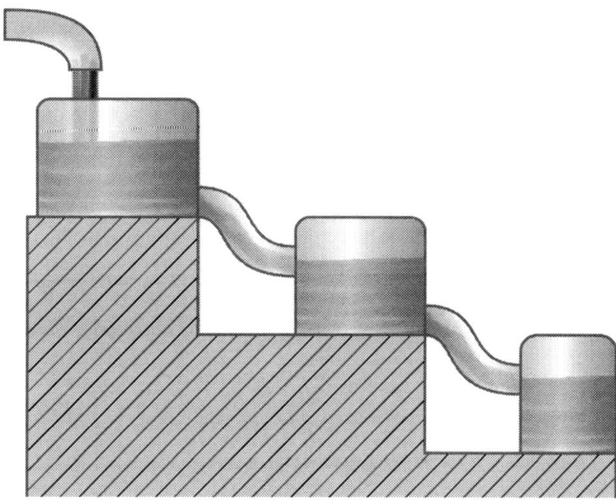

Density

Concept: how much mass is in a specific volume of a substance

Calculation: $density = \rho = \frac{mass}{volume}$

Density is essentially how much stuff there is in a volume or space. The density of a fluid is generally expressed with the symbol ρ (the Greek letter rho.) The density may be found with the simple equation:

$$\textbf{density} = \boldsymbol{\rho} = \frac{\textbf{mass}}{\textbf{volume}}$$

Density is a scalar property, meaning that it has no direction component.

Pressure

Concept: The amount of force applied per area

Calculation: $Pressure = \frac{force}{area}$

Pressure, like fluid density, is a scalar and does not have a direction. The equation for pressure is concerned only with the magnitude of that force, not with the direction in which it is pointing. The SI unit of pressure is the Newton per square meter, or Pascal.

$$\textbf{Pressure} = \frac{\textbf{force}}{\textbf{area}}$$

As every deep-sea diver knows, the pressure of water becomes greater the deeper you go below the surface; conversely, experienced mountain climbers know that air pressure decreases as they gain a higher altitude. These pressures are typically referred to as hydrostatic pressures because they involve fluids at rest.

Pascal's Principle

The exam may also require you to demonstrate some knowledge of how fluids move. Anytime you squeeze a tube of toothpaste, you are demonstrating the idea known as Pascal's principle. This principle states that a change in the pressure applied to an enclosed fluid is transmitted undiminished to every portion of the fluid as well as to the walls of the containing vessel.

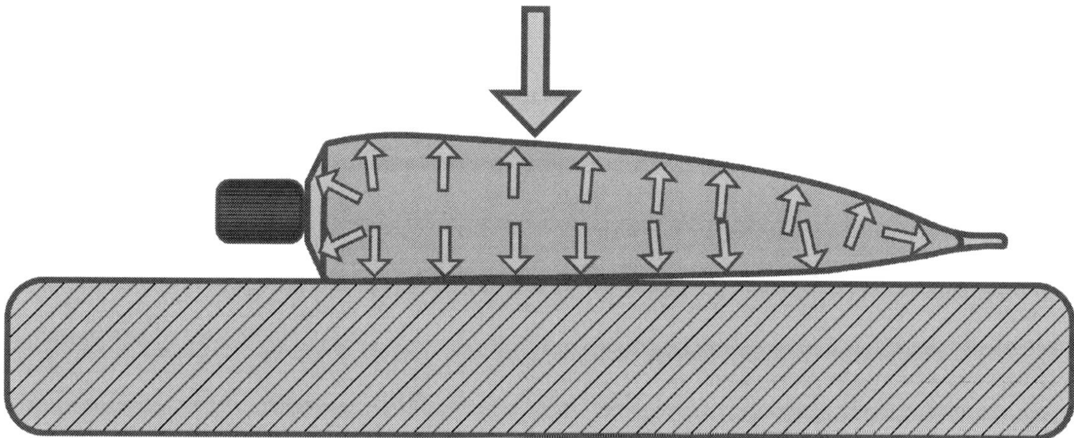

Buoyant Force

If an object is submerged in water, it will have a buoyant force exerted on it in the upward direction. Often, of course, this buoyant force is much too small to keep an object from sinking to the bottom. Buoyancy is summarized in Archimedes' principle; a body wholly or partially submerged in a fluid will be buoyed up by a force equal to the weight of the fluid that the body displaces.

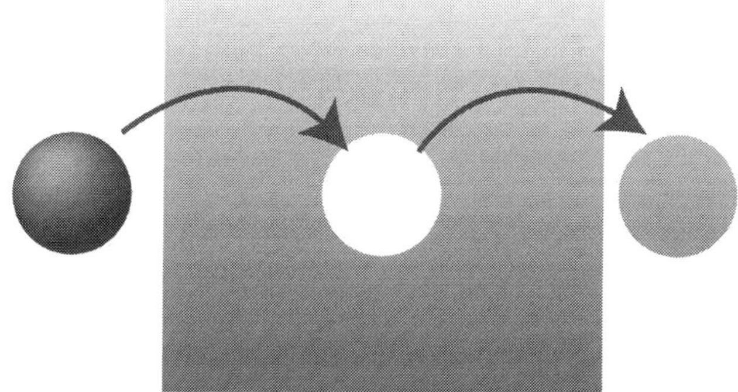

If the buoyant force is greater than the weight of an object, the object will go upward. If the weight of the object is greater than the buoyant force, the object will sink. When an object is floating on the surface, the buoyant force has the same magnitude as the weight.

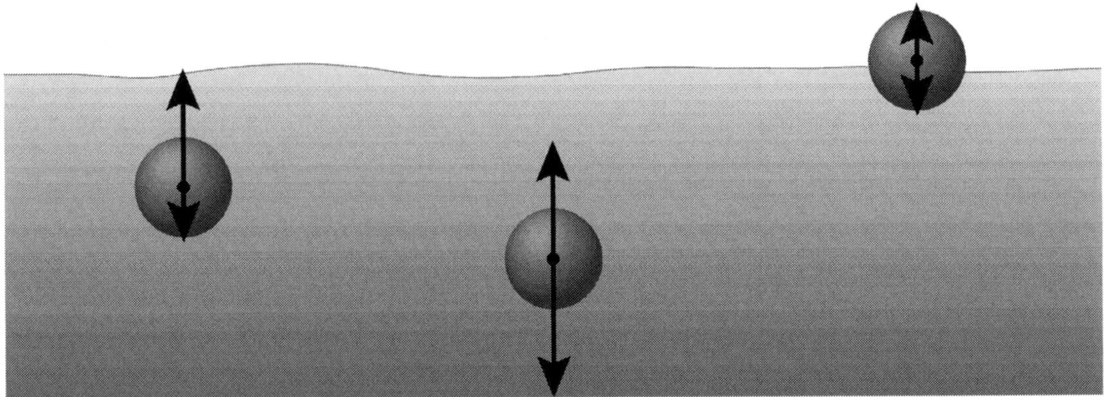

Even though the weight of a floating object is precisely balanced by a buoyant force, these forces will not necessarily act at the same point. The weight will act from the center of mass of the object, while the buoyancy will act from the center of mass of the hole in the water made by the object (known as the center of buoyancy). If the floating object is tilted, then the center of buoyancy will shift and the object may be unstable. In order to remain in equilibrium, the center of buoyancy must always shift in such a way that the buoyant force and weight provide a restoring torque, one that will restore the body to its upright position. This concept is, of course, crucial to the construction of boats which must always be made to encourage restoring torque.

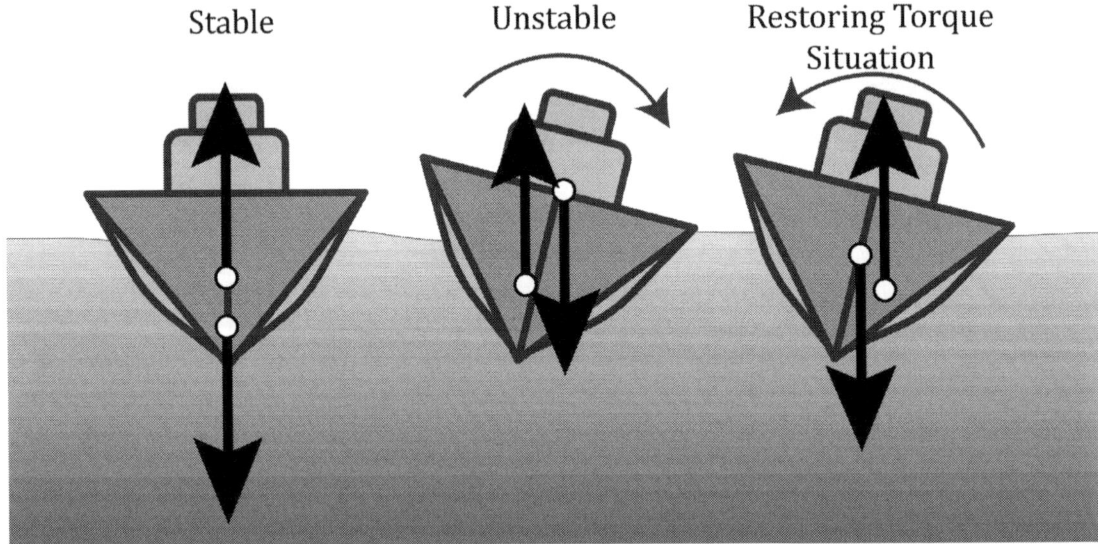

Ideal Fluids

Because the motion of actual fluids is extremely complex, the exam usually assumes ideal fluids when they set up their problems. Using ideal fluids in fluid dynamics problems is like discounting friction in other problems. Therefore, when we deal with ideal fluids, we are making four assumptions. It is important to keep these in mind when considering the behavior of fluids on the exam. First, we are assuming that the flow is steady; in other words, the velocity of every part of the fluid is the same. Second, we assume that fluids are incompressible, and, therefore, have a consistent density. Third, we assume that fluids are nonviscous, meaning that they flow easily and without resistance. Fourth, we assume that the flow of ideal fluids is irrotational: that is, particles in the fluid will not rotate around a center of mass.

Bernoulli's Principle

When fluids move, they do not create or destroy energy; this modification of Newton's second law for fluid behavior is called Bernoulli's principle. It is essentially just a reformulation of the law of conservation of mechanical energy for fluid mechanics.

The most common application of Bernoulli's principle is that pressure and speed are inversely related, assuming constant altitude. Thus, if the elevation of the fluid remains constant and the speed of a fluid particle increases as it travels along a streamline, the pressure will decrease. If the fluid slows down, the pressure will increase.

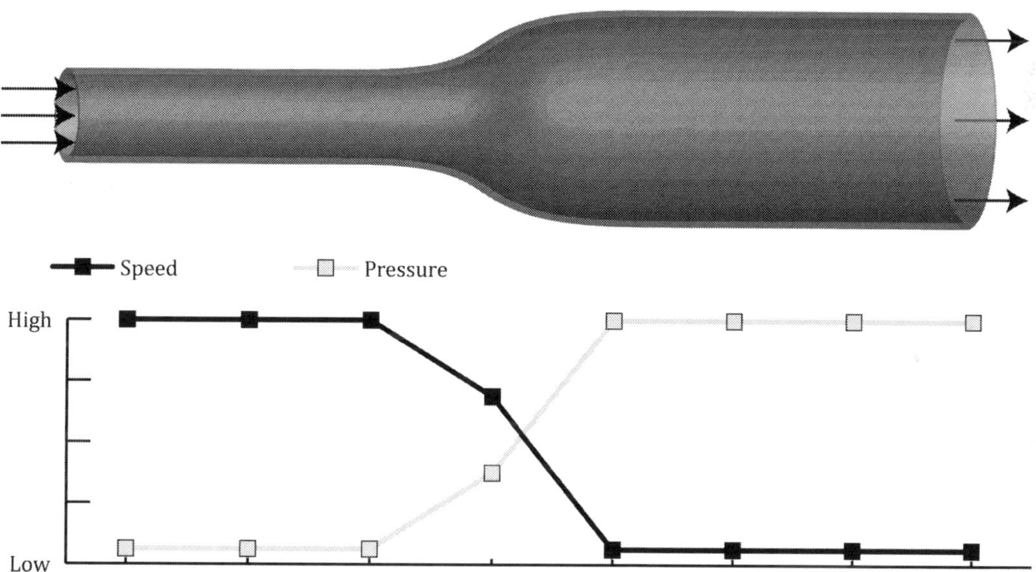

Heat Transfer

Heat Transfer

Heat is a type of energy. Heat transfers from the hot object to the cold object through the three forms of heat transfer: conduction, convection, and radiation.

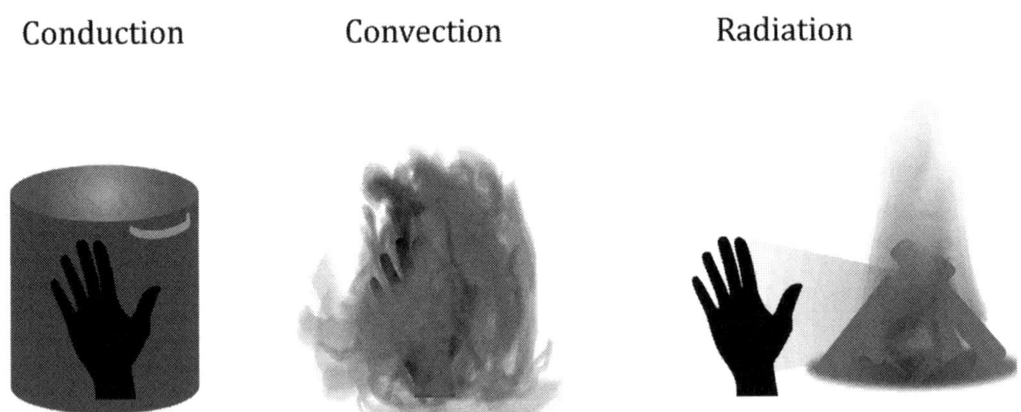

Conduction is the transfer of heat by physical contact. When you touch a hot pot, the pot transfers heat to your hand by conduction.

Convection is the transfer of heat by the movement of fluids. When you put your hand in steam, the steam transfers heat to your hand by convection.

Radiation is the transfer of heat by electromagnetic waves. When you put your hand near a campfire, the fire heats your hand by radiation.

Phase Changes

Materials exist in four phases or states: solid, liquid, gas, and plasma. However, as most tests will not cover plasma, we will focus on solids, liquids, and gases. The solid state is the densest in almost all cases (water is the most notable exception), followed by liquid, and then gas.

The impetus for phase change (changing from one phase to another) is heat. When a solid is heated, it will change into a liquid. The same process of heating will change a liquid into a gas.

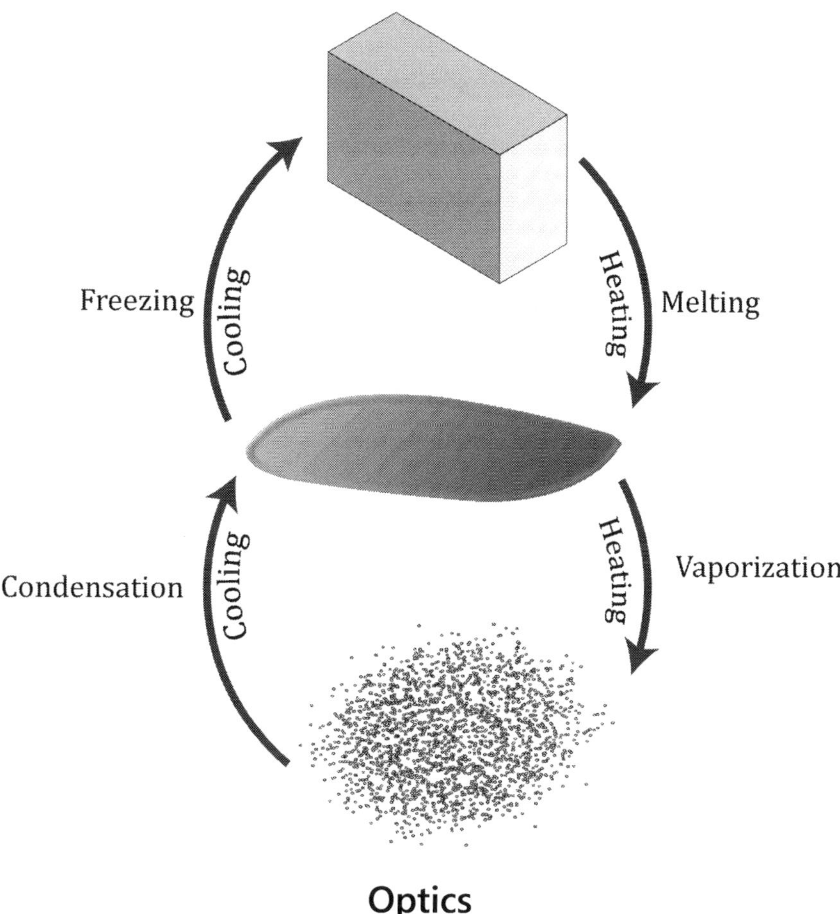

Optics

Optics

Lenses change the way light travels. Lenses are able to achieve this by the way in which light travels at different speeds in different mediums. The essentials to optics with lenses deal with concave and convex lenses. Concave lenses make objects appear smaller, while convex lenses make objects appear larger.

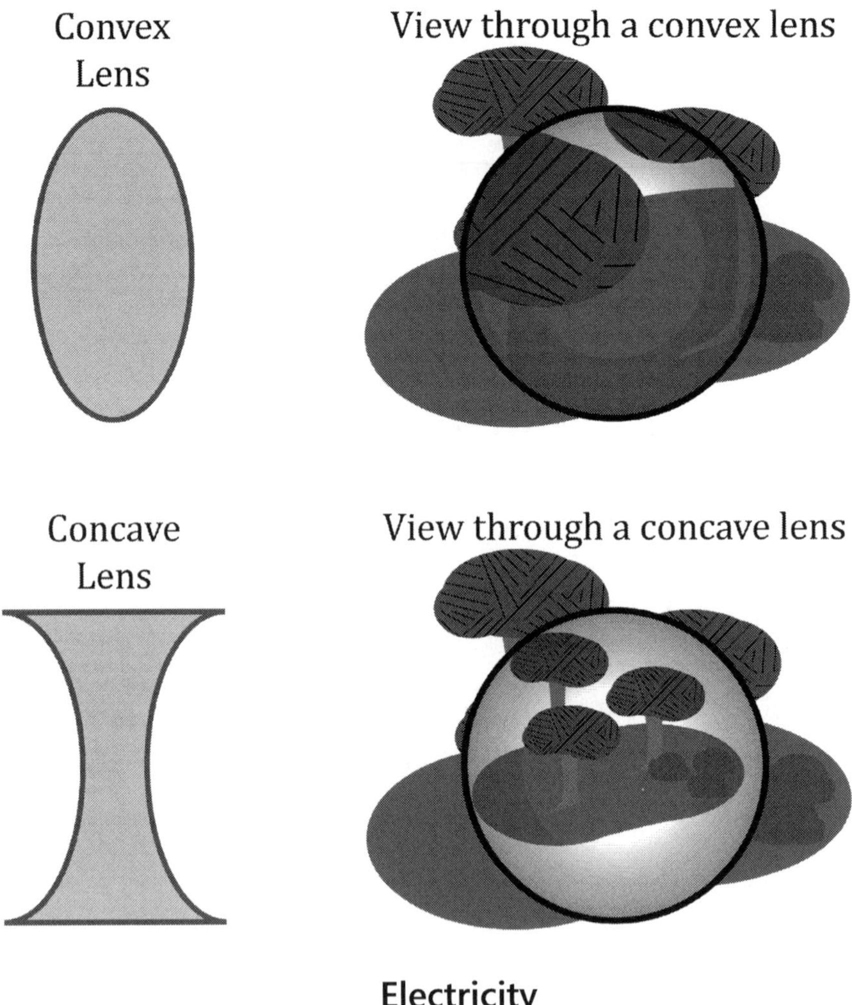

Electricity

Electric Charge

Much like gravity, electricity is an everyday observable phenomenon which is very complex, but may be understood as a set of behaviors. As the gravitational force exists between objects with mass, the electric force exists between objects with electrical charge. In all atoms, the protons have a positive charge, while the electrons have a negative charge. An imbalance of electrons and protons in an object results in a net charge. Unlike gravity, which only pulls, electrical forces can push objects apart as well as pulling them together.

Similar electric charges repel each other. Opposite charges attract each other.

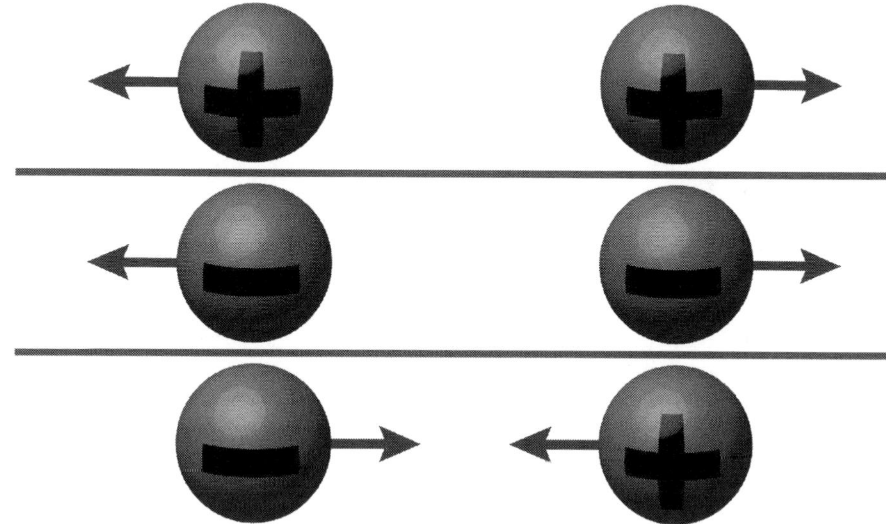

Current

Electrons (and electrical charge with it) move through conductive materials by switching quickly from one atom to another. This electrical flow can manipulate energy like mechanical systems.

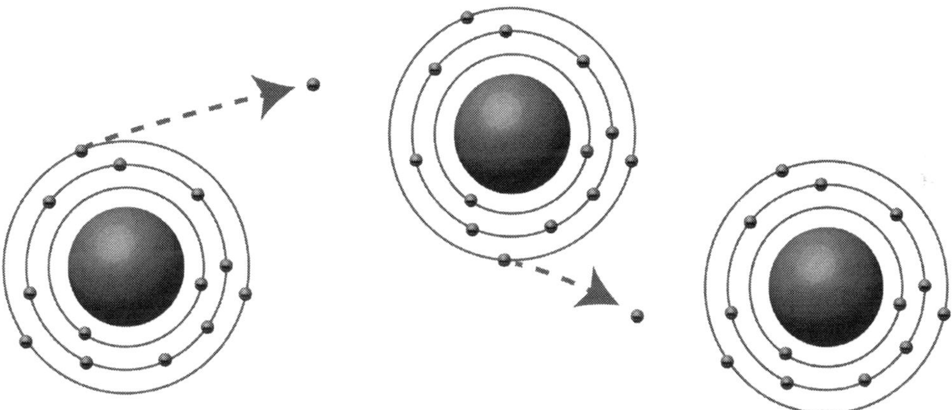

The term for the rate at which the charge flows through a conductive material is current. Because each electron carries a specific charge, current can be thought of as the number of electrons passing a point in a length of time. Current is measured in Amperes (A), each unit of which is approximately 6.24×10^{18} electrons per second.

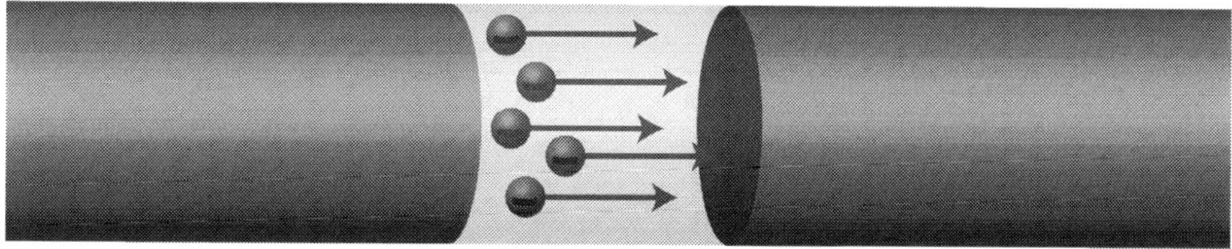

Electric current carries energy much like moving balls carry energy.

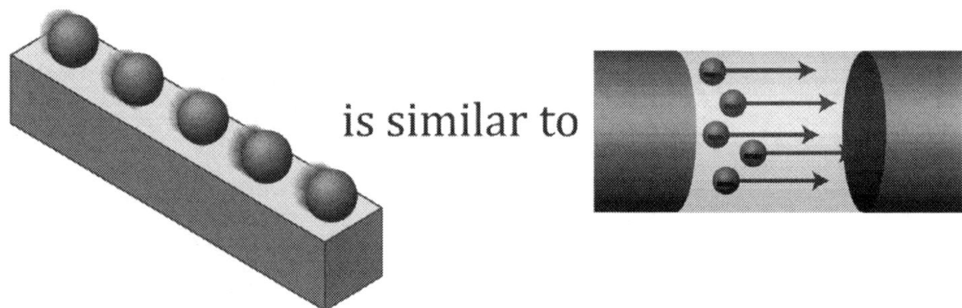

Voltage

Voltage is the potential for electric work. Voltage is the push behind electrical work. Voltage is similar to gravitational potential energy.

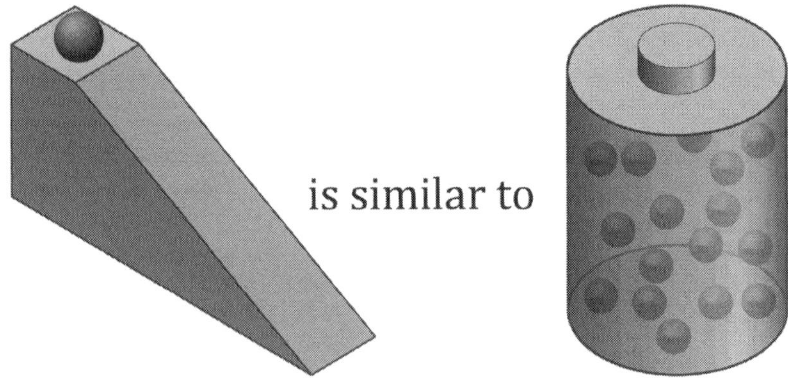

Anything used to generate a voltage, such as a battery or a generator, is called a voltage source. Voltage is conveniently measured in Volts (V).

Resistance

Resistance is the amount of pressure to slow electrical current. Electrical resistance is much like friction, resisting flow and dissipating energy.

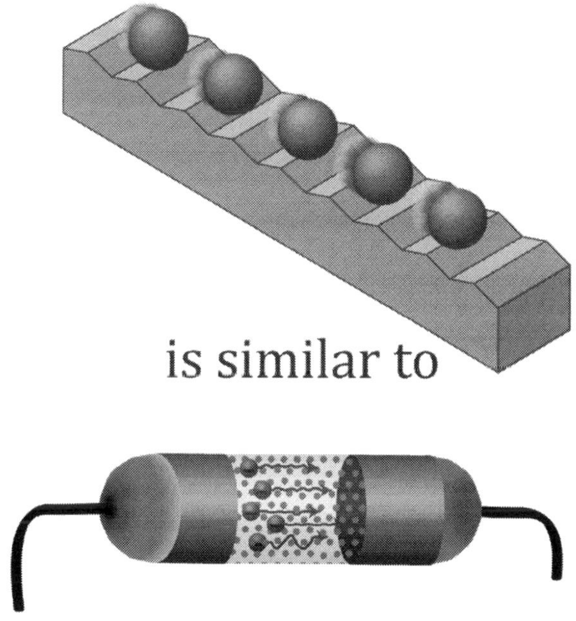

Different objects have different resistances. A resistor is an electrical component designed to have a specific resistance, measured in Ohms (Ω).

Basic Circuits

A circuit is a closed loop through which current can flow. A simple circuit contains a voltage source and a resistor. The current flows from the positive side of the voltage source through the resistor to the negative side of the voltage source.

If we plot the voltage of a simple circuit, the similarities to gravitational potential energy appear.

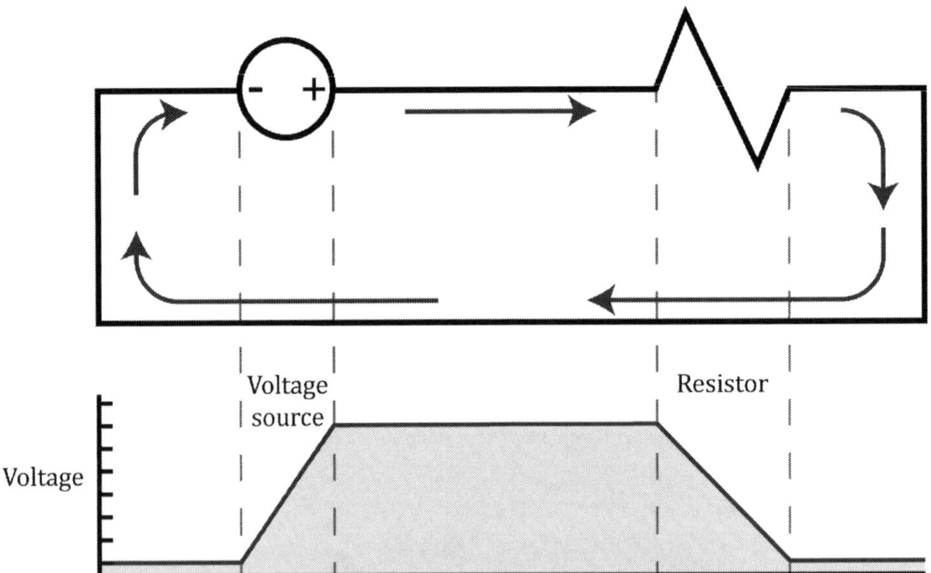

If we consider the circuit to be a track, the electrons would be balls, the voltage source would be a powered lift, and the resistor would be a sticky section of the track. The lift raises the balls, increasing their potential energy. This potential energy is expended as the balls roll down the sticky section of the track.

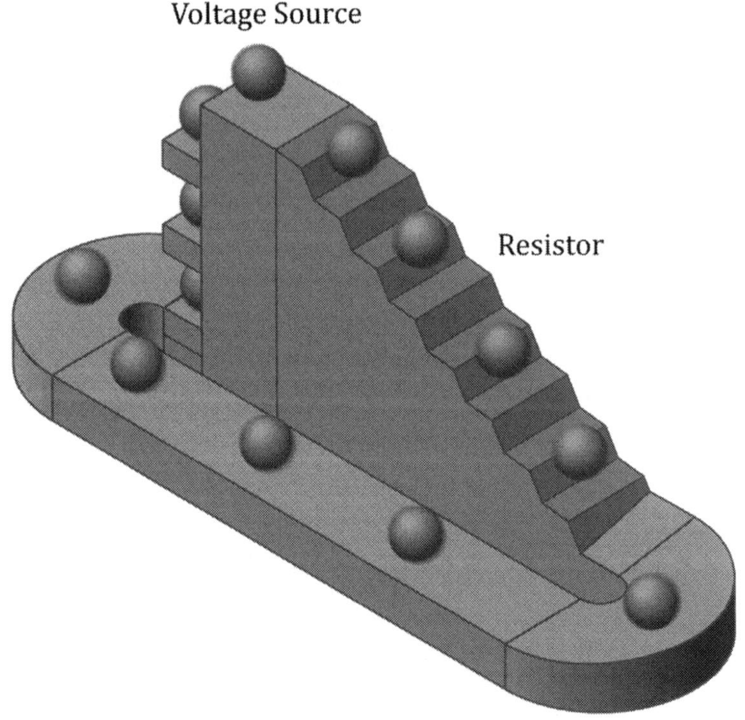

Ohm's Law

A principle called Ohm's Law explains the relationship between the voltage, current, and resistance. The voltage drop over a resistance is equal to the amount of current times the resistance:

$$\textbf{Voltage (V)} = \textbf{current (I)} \times \textbf{resistance (R)}$$

We can gain a better understanding of this equation by looking at a reference simple circuit and then changing one variable at a time to examine the results.

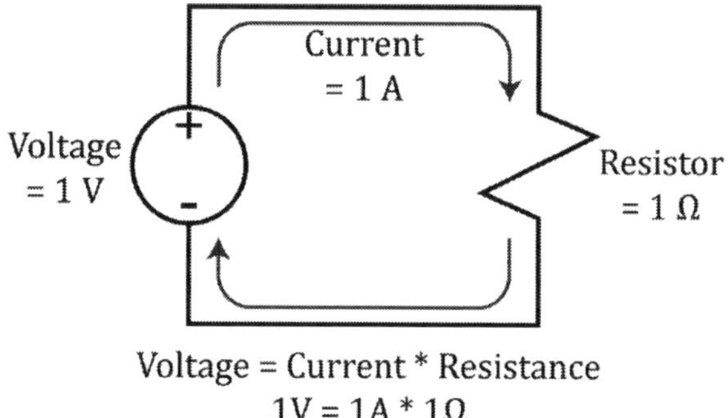

Voltage = Current * Resistance
1V = 1A * 1Ω

Increased Resistance

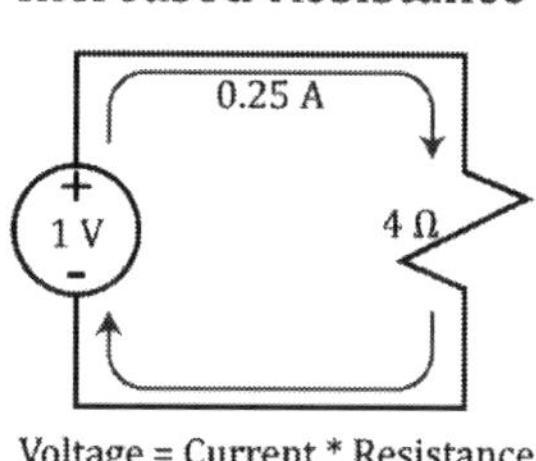

Voltage = Current * Resistance
1V = 0.25A * 4Ω

Increased Current

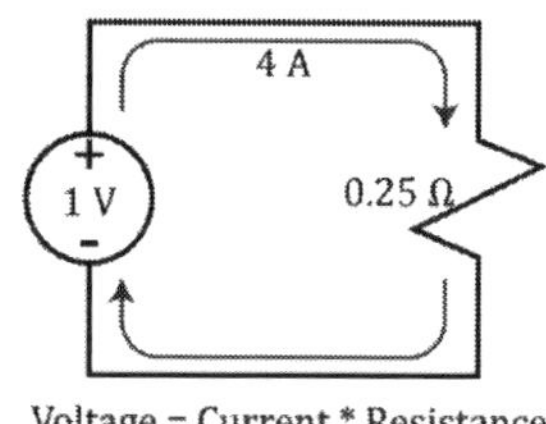

Voltage = Current * Resistance
1V = 4A * 0.25Ω

Increased Voltage

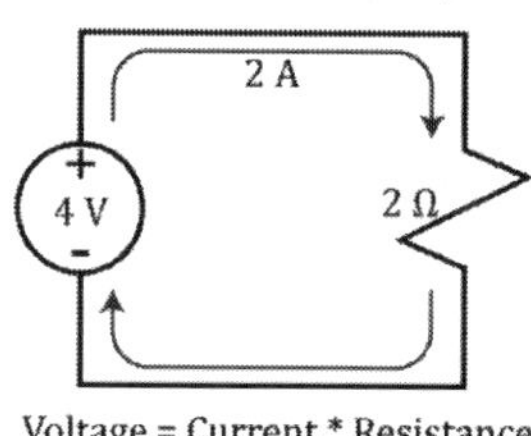

Voltage = Current * Resistance
4V = 2A * 2Ω

Series Circuits

A series circuit is a circuit with two or more resistors on the same path. The same current runs through both resistors. However, the total voltage drop splits between the resistors. The resistors in series can be added together to make an equivalent basic circuit.

$$\mathbf{R_{equiv} = R_1 + R_2}$$

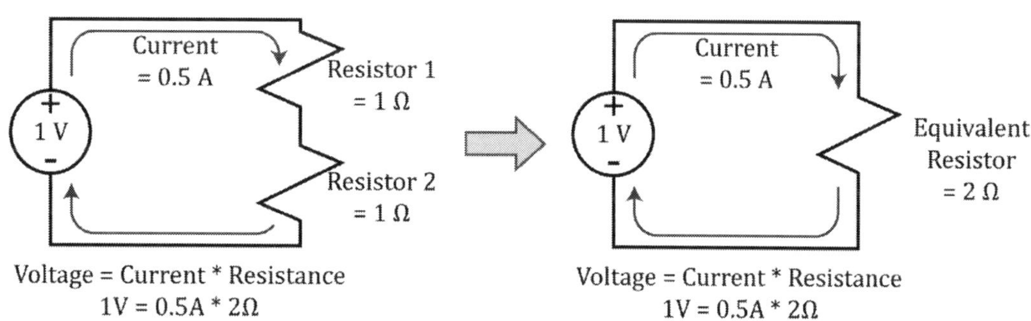

Voltage = Current * Resistance
1V = 0.5A * 2Ω

Voltage = Current * Resistance
1V = 0.5A * 2Ω

Parallel Circuits

A parallel circuit is a circuit with two or more resistors on different, parallel paths. Unlike the series circuit, the current splits between the different paths in a parallel circuit. Resistors in parallel can be reduced to an equivalent circuit, but not by simply adding the resistances. The inverse of the equivalent resistance of parallel resistors is equal to the sum of the inverses of the resistance of each leg of the parallel circuit. In equation form that means:

$$\frac{1}{R_{equiv}} = \frac{1}{R_1} + \frac{1}{R_2}$$

Or when solved for equivalent resistance:

$$\mathbf{R_{equiv}} = \frac{\mathbf{1}}{\frac{\mathbf{1}}{\mathbf{R_1}} + \frac{\mathbf{1}}{\mathbf{R_2}}}$$

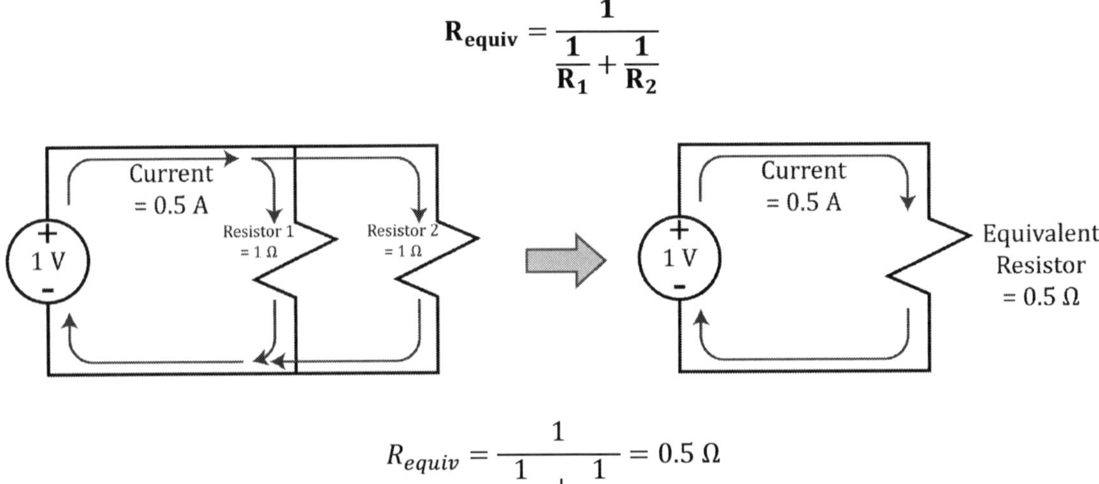

$$R_{equiv} = \frac{1}{\frac{1}{1\,\Omega} + \frac{1}{1\,\Omega}} = 0.5\,\Omega$$

Electrical Power

Electrical power, or the energy output over time, is equal to the current resulting from a voltage source times the voltage of that source:

$$\textbf{Power(P)} = \textbf{current (I)} \times \textbf{voltage (V)}$$

Thanks to Ohm's Law, we can write this relation in two other ways:

$$P = I^2R$$

$$P = \frac{V^2}{R}$$

For instance, if a circuit is composed of a 9 Volt battery and a 3 Ohm resistor, the power output of the battery will be:

$$Power = \frac{V^2}{R} = \frac{9^2}{3} = 27\ Watts$$

AC vs. DC

Up until this point, current has been assumed to flow in one direction. One directional flow is called Direct Current (DC). However, there is another type of electric current: Alternating Current (AC).

Many circuits use AC power sources, in which the current flips back and forth rapidly between directions.

Capacitors

Capacitors are electrical components which store voltage. Capacitors are made from two conductive surfaces separated from each other by a space and/or insulation. Capacitors resist changes to voltage. Capacitors don't stop AC circuits (although they do affect the current flow), but they do stop DC circuits, acting as open circuits.

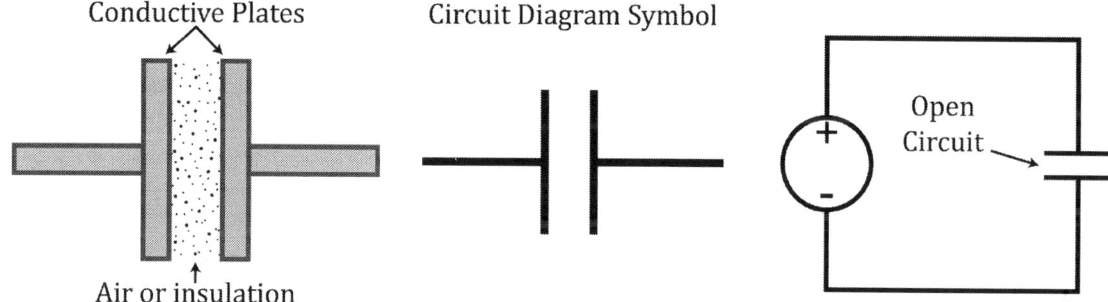

Inductors

Inductors are electrical components which effectively store current. Inductors use the relationship between electricity and magnetism to resist changes in current by running the current through coils of wire. Inductors don't stop DC circuits, but they do resist AC circuits as AC circuits utilize changing currents.

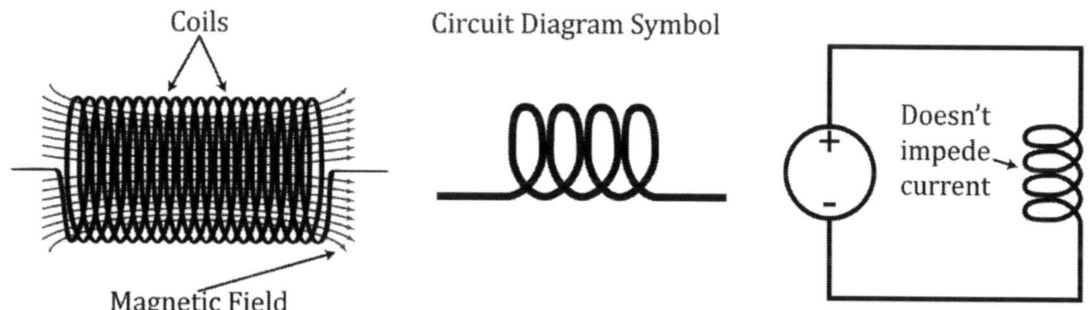

Diodes

Diodes are electrical components which limit the flow of electricity to one direction. If current flows through a diode in the intended direction, the diode will allow the flow. However, a diode will stop current if it runs the wrong way.

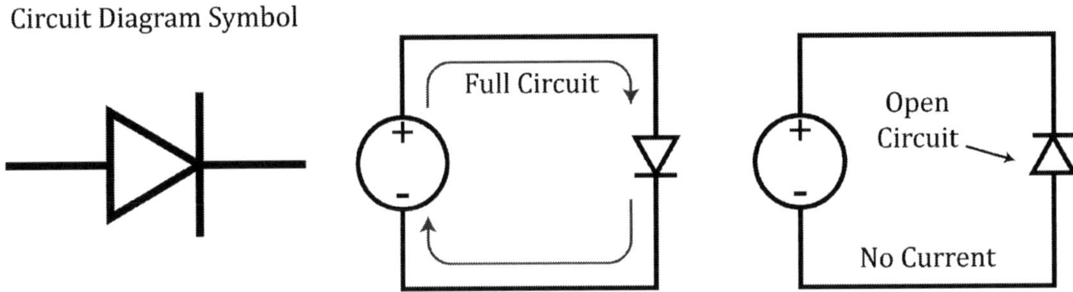

Magnetism

Magnetism

Magnetism is an attraction between opposite poles of magnetic materials and a repulsion between similar poles of magnetic materials. Magnetism can be natural or induced with the use of electric currents. Magnets almost always exist with two polar sides: north and south. A magnetic force exists between two poles on objects. Different poles attract each other. Like poles repel each other.

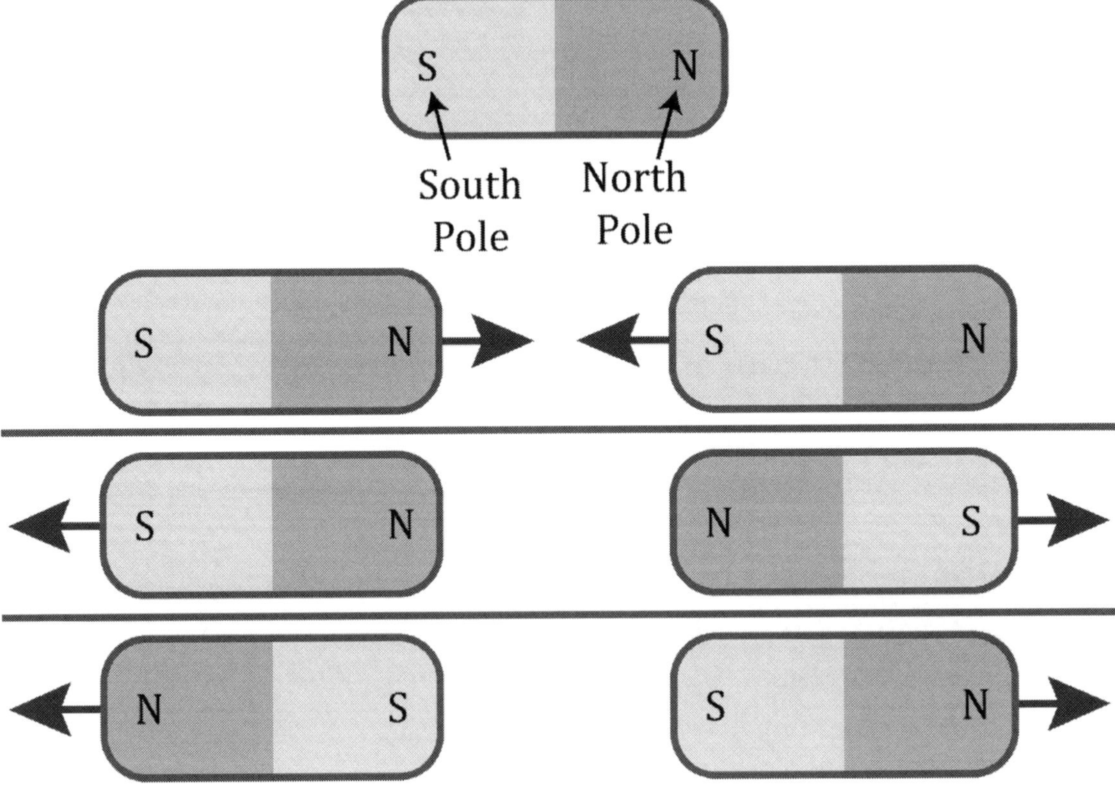

Final Notes

This concludes our review of the content of the SIFT subtests. Hopefully, a lot of this material was familiar to you, but if not, be sure to reread any sections you had difficulty with until you have a solid grasp of the important concepts. As you read, try to imagine the types of questions that will be asked on the test, and take frequent breaks to let the ideas sink in.

The SIFT tests a wide variety of knowledge and skills, so getting prepared for it is necessarily a difficult task, but so is training to be a pilot. If you can work hard enough to ace the SIFT, that's enough to convince the Army you can make it through flight training.

Good luck and good studying!

Simple Drawings Test

Instructions: Select the answer letter of the image that is different from the other four images shown. There are 100 questions in this section and the allotted time is 2 minutes.

1. (A) (B) (C) (D) (E)

2. (A) (B) (C) (D) (E)

3. (A) (B) (C) (D) (E)

4. (A) (B) (C) (D) (E)

5. (A) (B) (C) (D) (E)

6. (A) (B) (C) (D) (E)

7. (A) (B) (C) (D) (E)

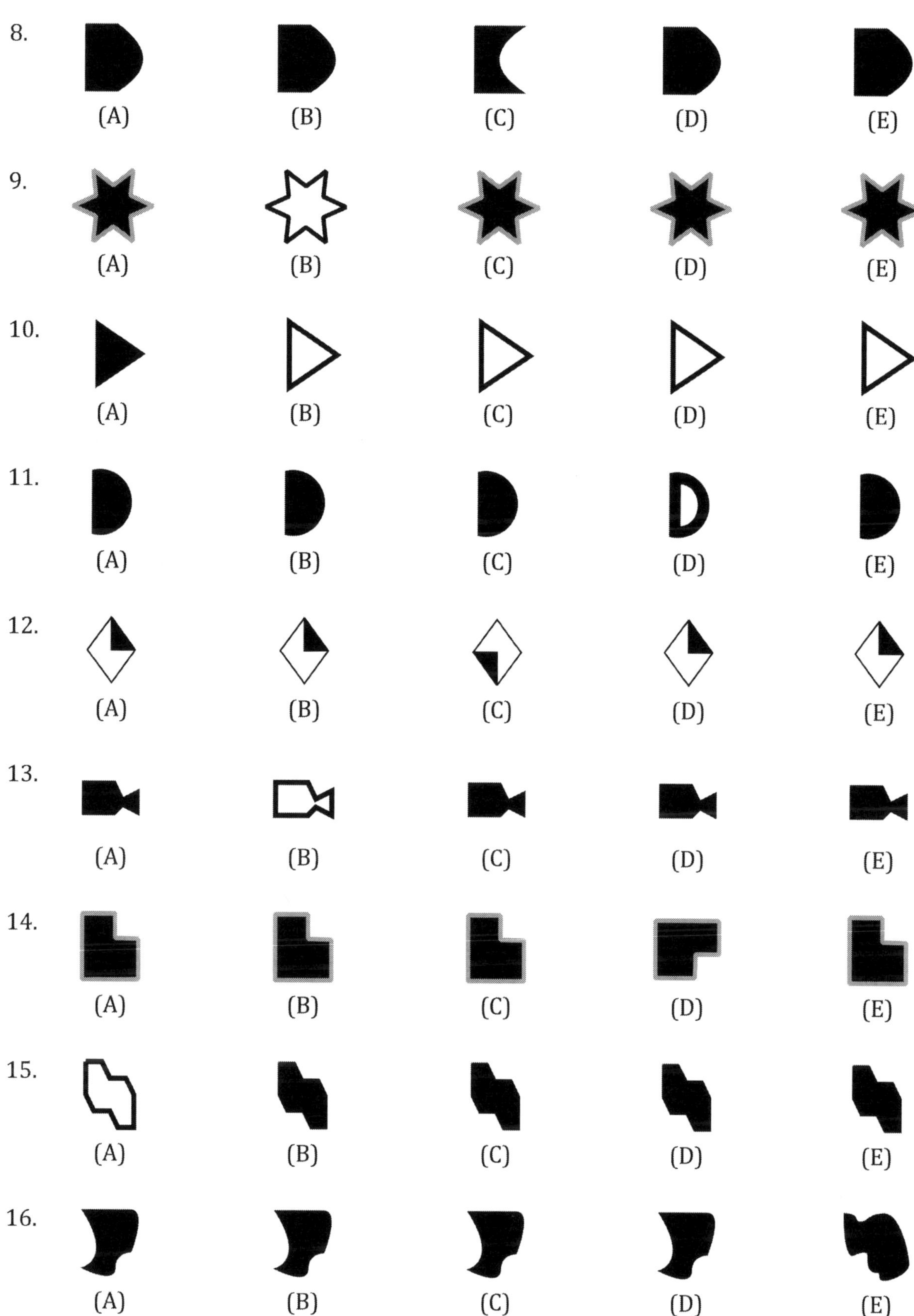
8.
(A)
(B)
(C)
(D)
(E)
9.
(A)
(B)
(C)
(D)
(E)
10.
(A)
(B)
(C)
(D)
(E)
11.
(A)
(B)
(C)
(D)
(E)
12.
(A)
(B)
(C)
(D)
(E)
13.
(A)
(B)
(C)
(D)
(E)
14.
(A)
(B)
(C)
(D)
(E)
15.
(A)
(B)
(C)
(D)
(E)
16.
(A)
(B)
(C)
(D)
(E)

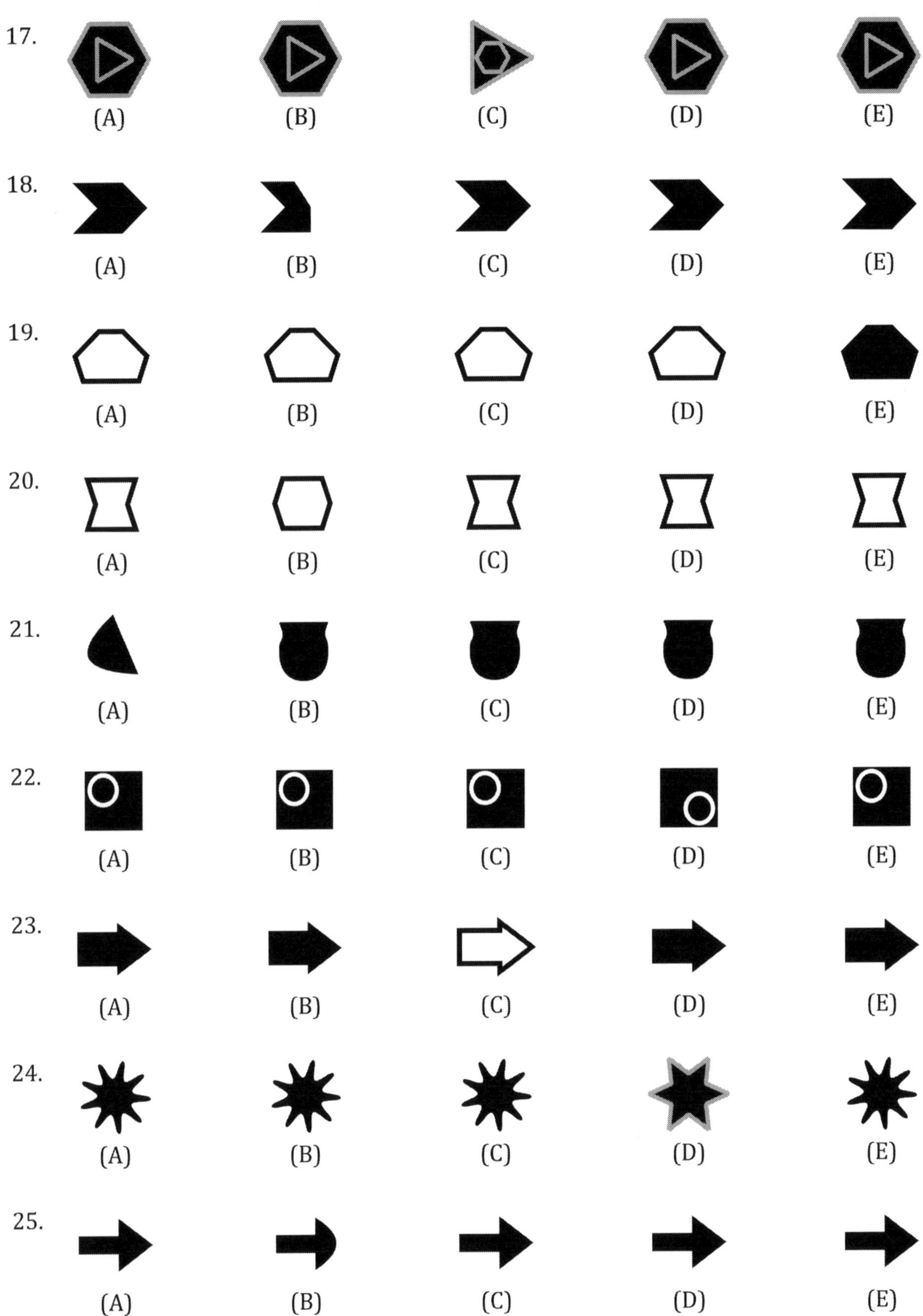
17.
(A)
(B)
(C)
(D)
(E)
18.
(A)
(B)
(C)
(D)
(E)
19.
(A)
(B)
(C)
(D)
(E)
20.
(A)
(B)
(C)
(D)
(E)
21.
(A)
(B)
(C)
(D)
(E)
22.
(A)
(B)
(C)
(D)
(E)
23.
(A)
(B)
(C)
(D)
(E)
24.
(A)
(B)
(C)
(D)
(E)
25.
(A)
(B)
(C)
(D)
(E)

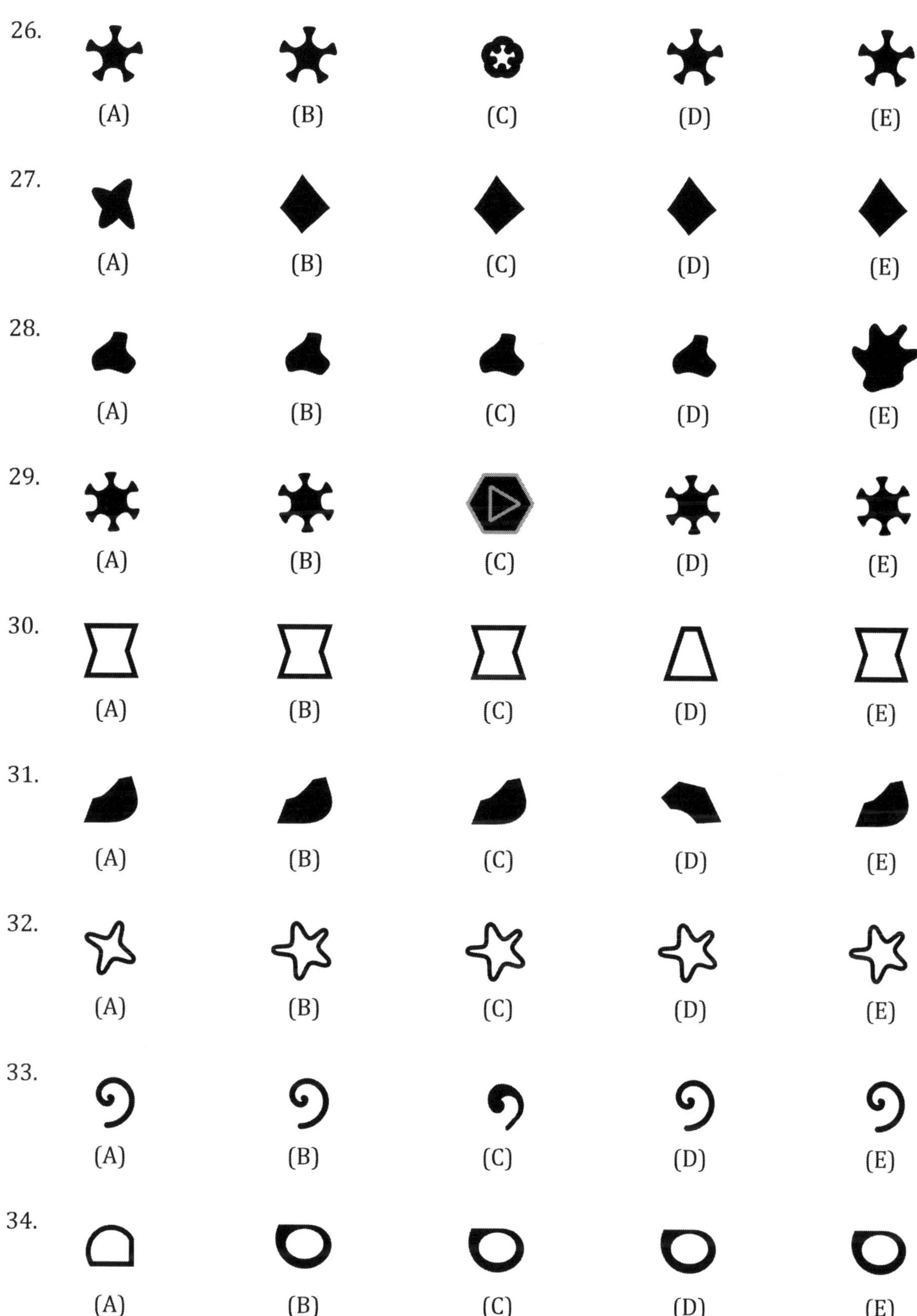
26.
(A) (B) (C) (D) (E)
27.
(A) (B) (C) (D) (E)
28.
(A) (B) (C) (D) (E)
29.
(A) (B) (C) (D) (E)
30.
(A) (B) (C) (D) (E)
31.
(A) (B) (C) (D) (E)
32.
(A) (B) (C) (D) (E)
33.
(A) (B) (C) (D) (E)
34.
(A) (B) (C) (D) (E)

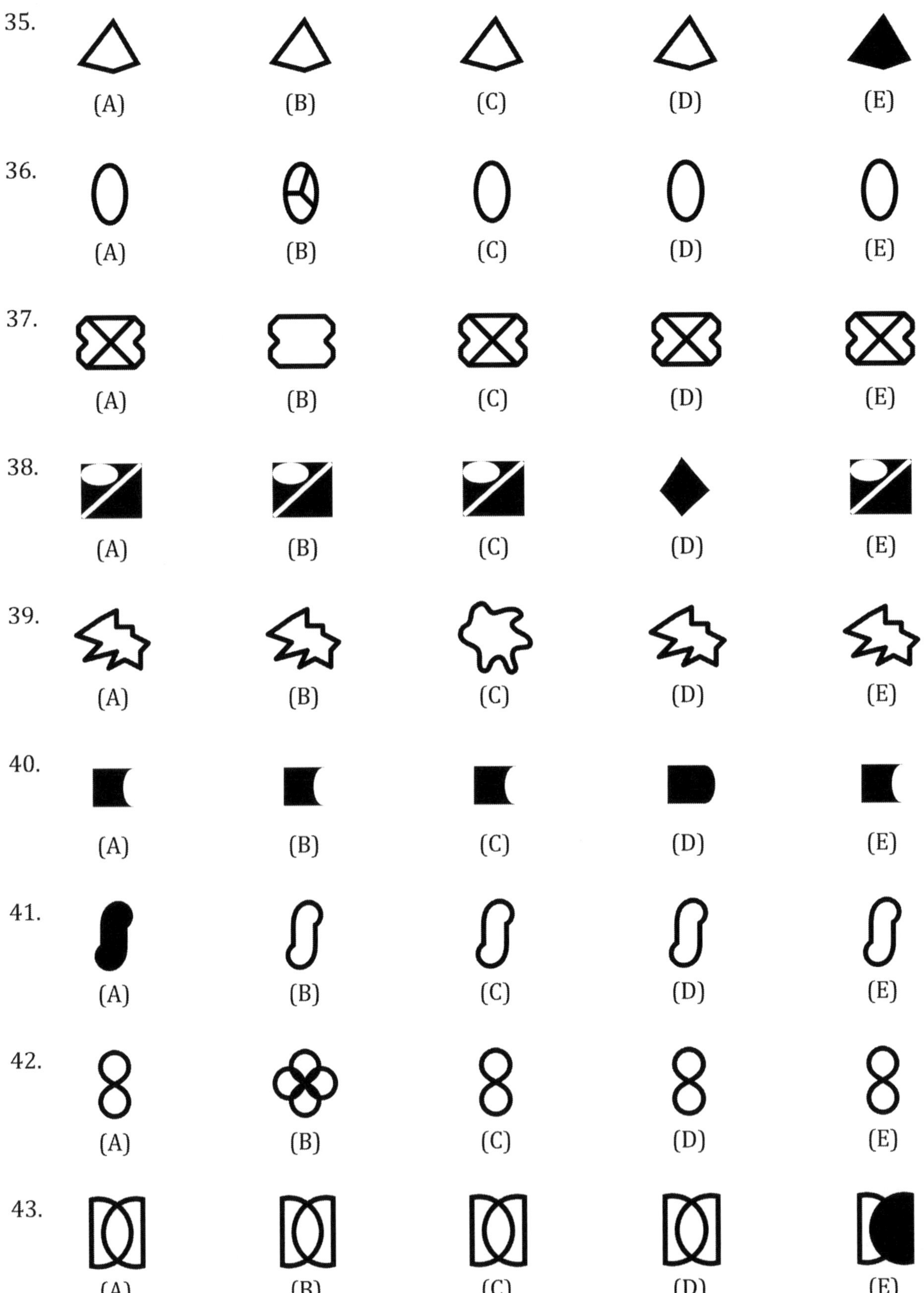
35.
(A) (B) (C) (D) (E)
36.
(A) (B) (C) (D) (E)
37.
(A) (B) (C) (D) (E)
38.
(A) (B) (C) (D) (E)
39.
(A) (B) (C) (D) (E)
40.
(A) (B) (C) (D) (E)
41.
(A) (B) (C) (D) (E)
42.
(A) (B) (C) (D) (E)
43.
(A) (B) (C) (D) (E)

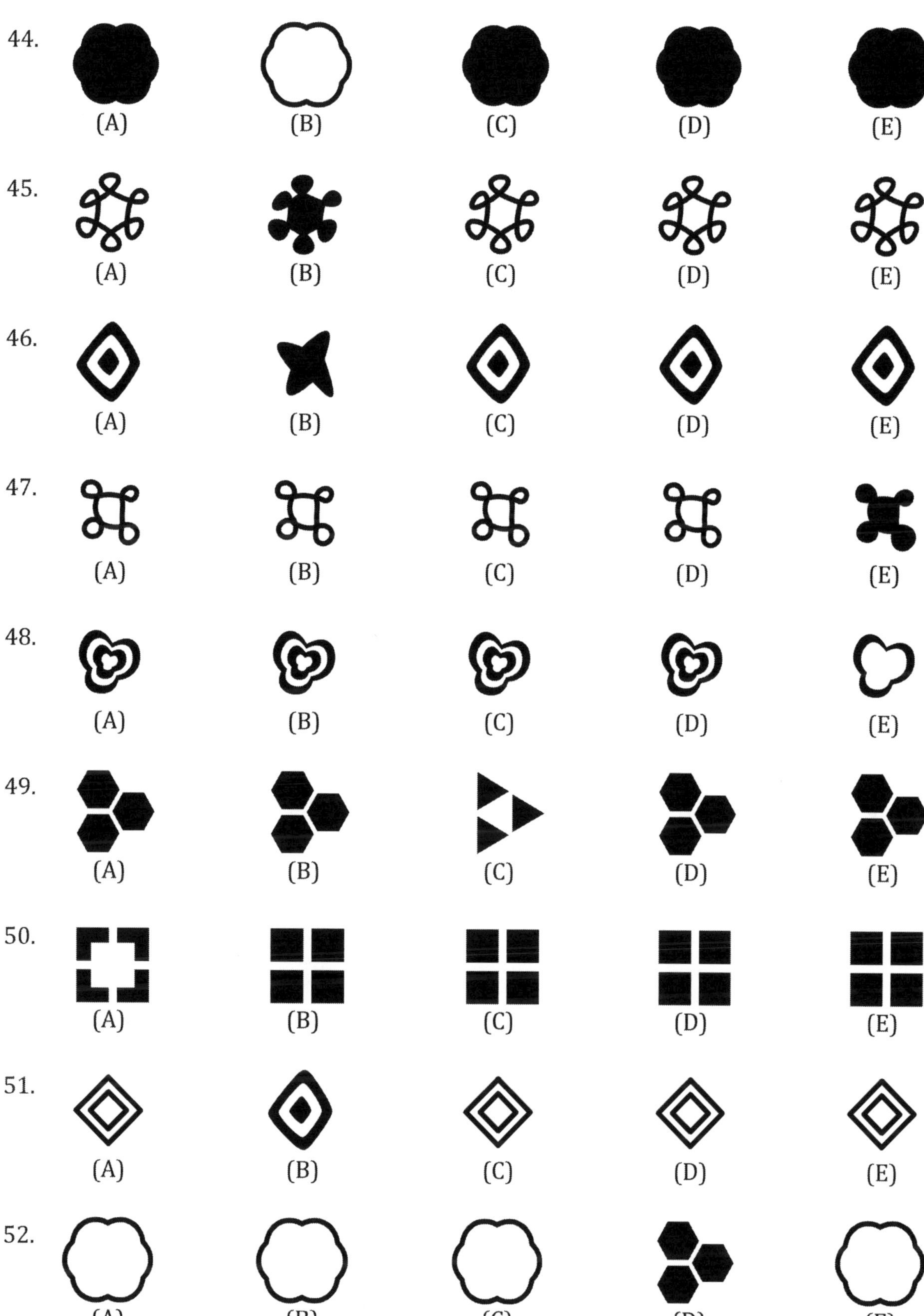
44.
(A)
(B)
(C)
(D)
(E)
45.
(A)
(B)
(C)
(D)
(E)
46.
(A)
(B)
(C)
(D)
(E)
47.
(A)
(B)
(C)
(D)
(E)
48.
(A)
(B)
(C)
(D)
(E)
49.
(A)
(B)
(C)
(D)
(E)
50.
(A)
(B)
(C)
(D)
(E)
51.
(A)
(B)
(C)
(D)
(E)
52.
(A)
(B)
(C)
(D)
(E)

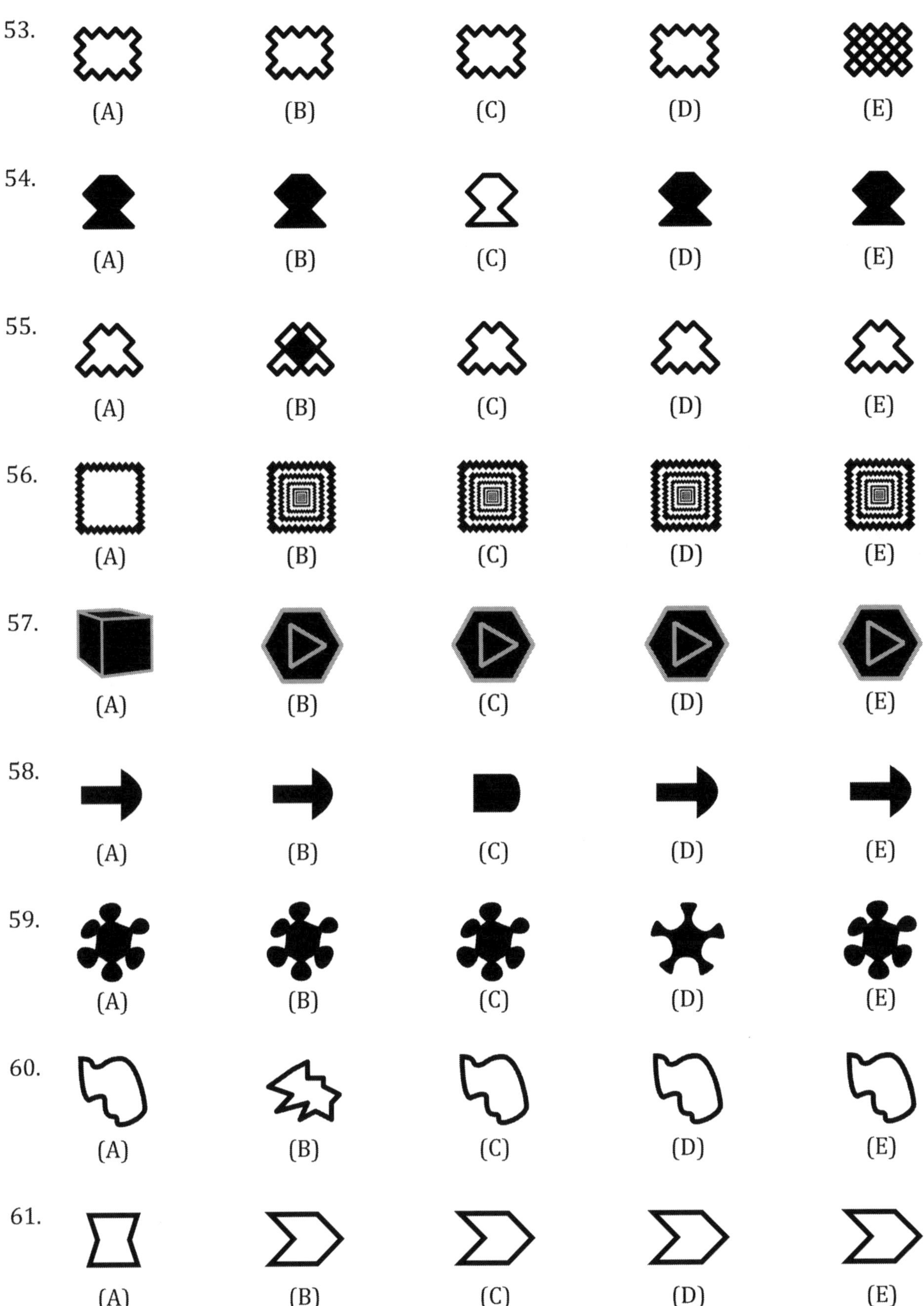
53.
(A)
(B)
(C)
(D)
(E)
54.
(A)
(B)
(C)
(D)
(E)
55.
(A)
(B)
(C)
(D)
(E)
56.
(A)
(B)
(C)
(D)
(E)
57.
(A)
(B)
(C)
(D)
(E)
58.
(A)
(B)
(C)
(D)
(E)
59.
(A)
(B)
(C)
(D)
(E)
60.
(A)
(B)
(C)
(D)
(E)
61.
(A)
(B)
(C)
(D)
(E)

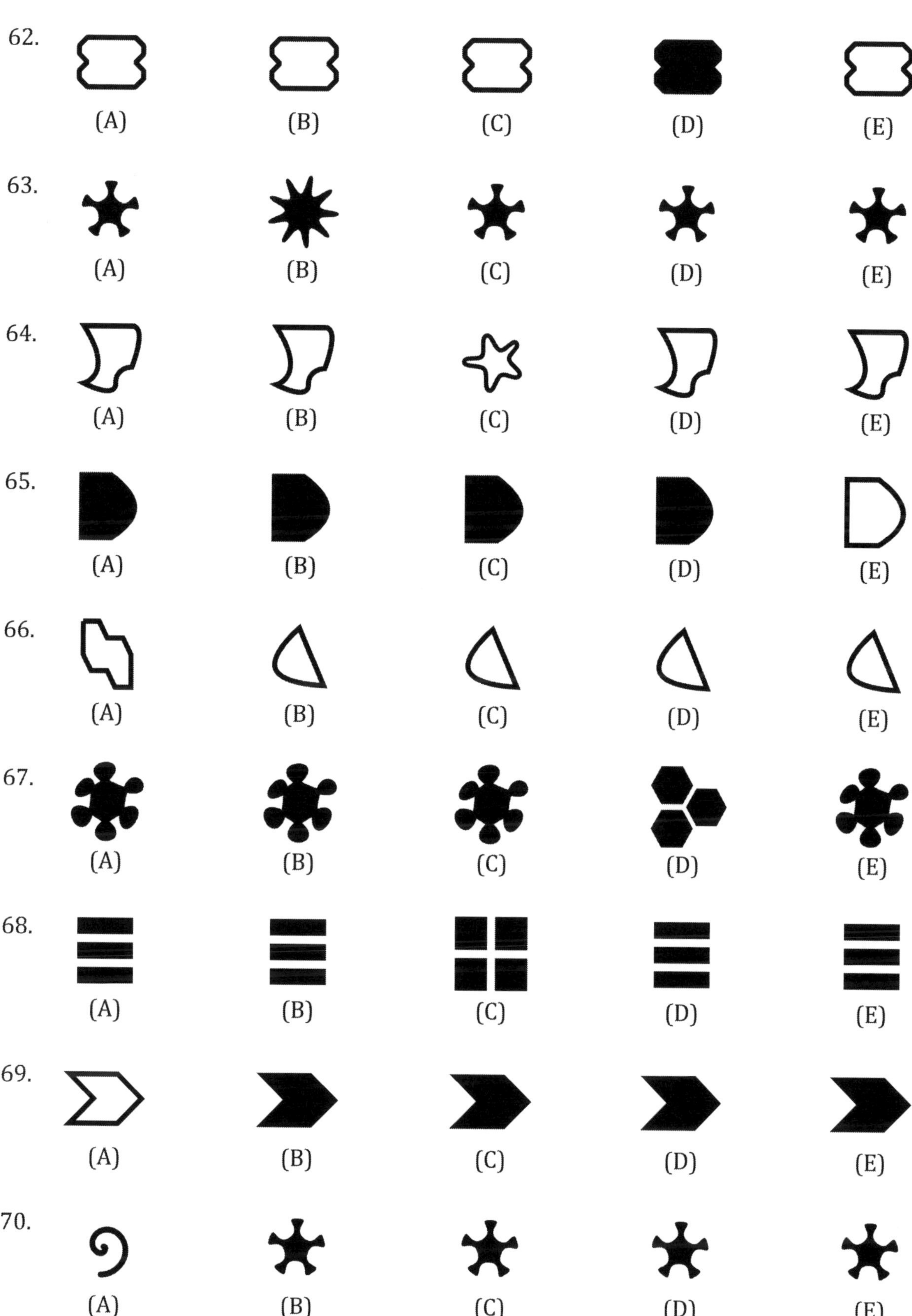
62. (A) (B) (C) (D) (E)
63. (A) (B) (C) (D) (E)
64. (A) (B) (C) (D) (E)
65. (A) (B) (C) (D) (E)
66. (A) (B) (C) (D) (E)
67. (A) (B) (C) (D) (E)
68. (A) (B) (C) (D) (E)
69. (A) (B) (C) (D) (E)
70. (A) (B) (C) (D) (E)

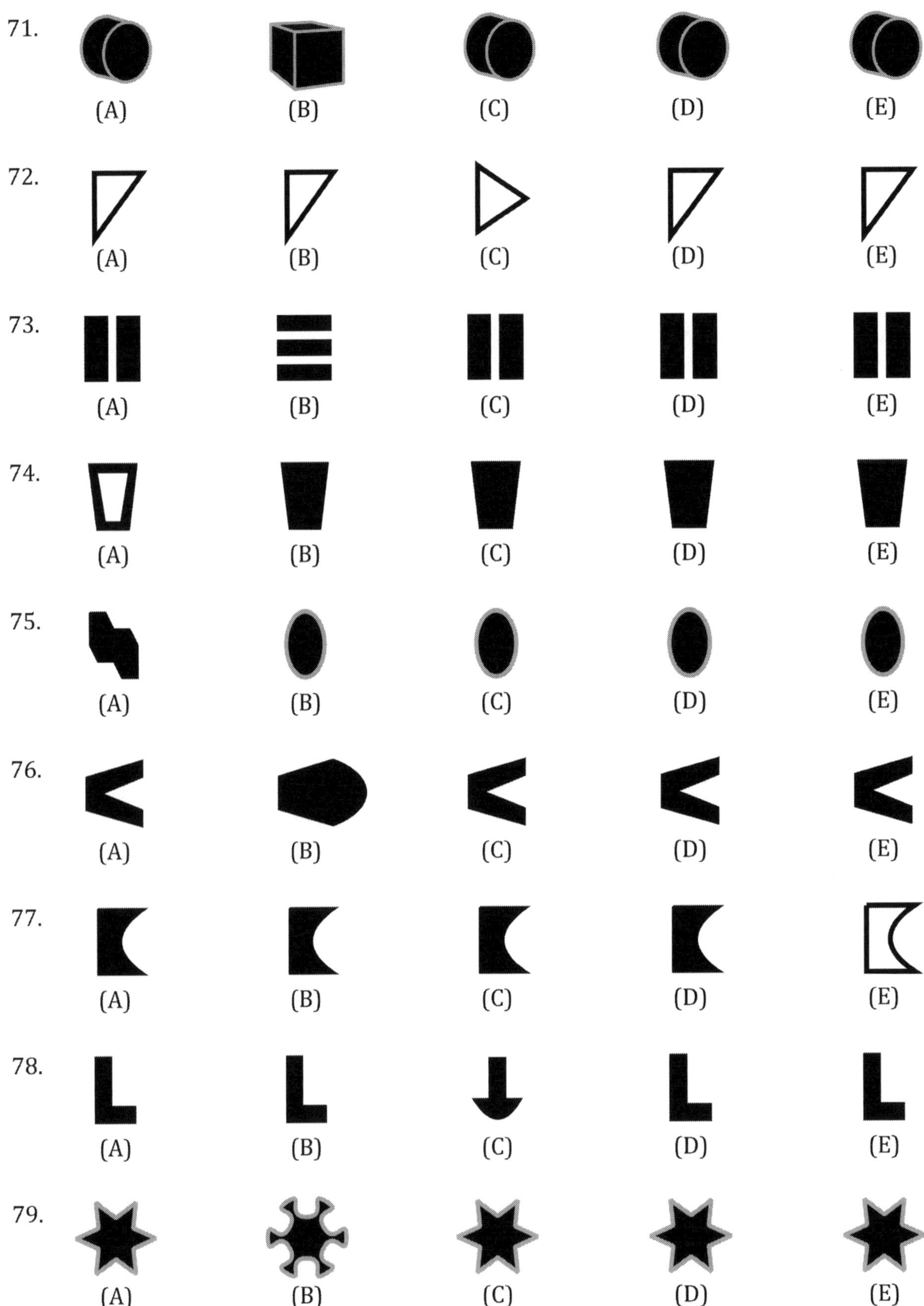
71.
(A)
(B)
(C)
(D)
(E)
72.
(A)
(B)
(C)
(D)
(E)
73.
(A)
(B)
(C)
(D)
(E)
74.
(A)
(B)
(C)
(D)
(E)
75.
(A)
(B)
(C)
(D)
(E)
76.
(A)
(B)
(C)
(D)
(E)
77.
(A)
(B)
(C)
(D)
(E)
78.
(A)
(B)
(C)
(D)
(E)
79.
(A)
(B)
(C)
(D)
(E)

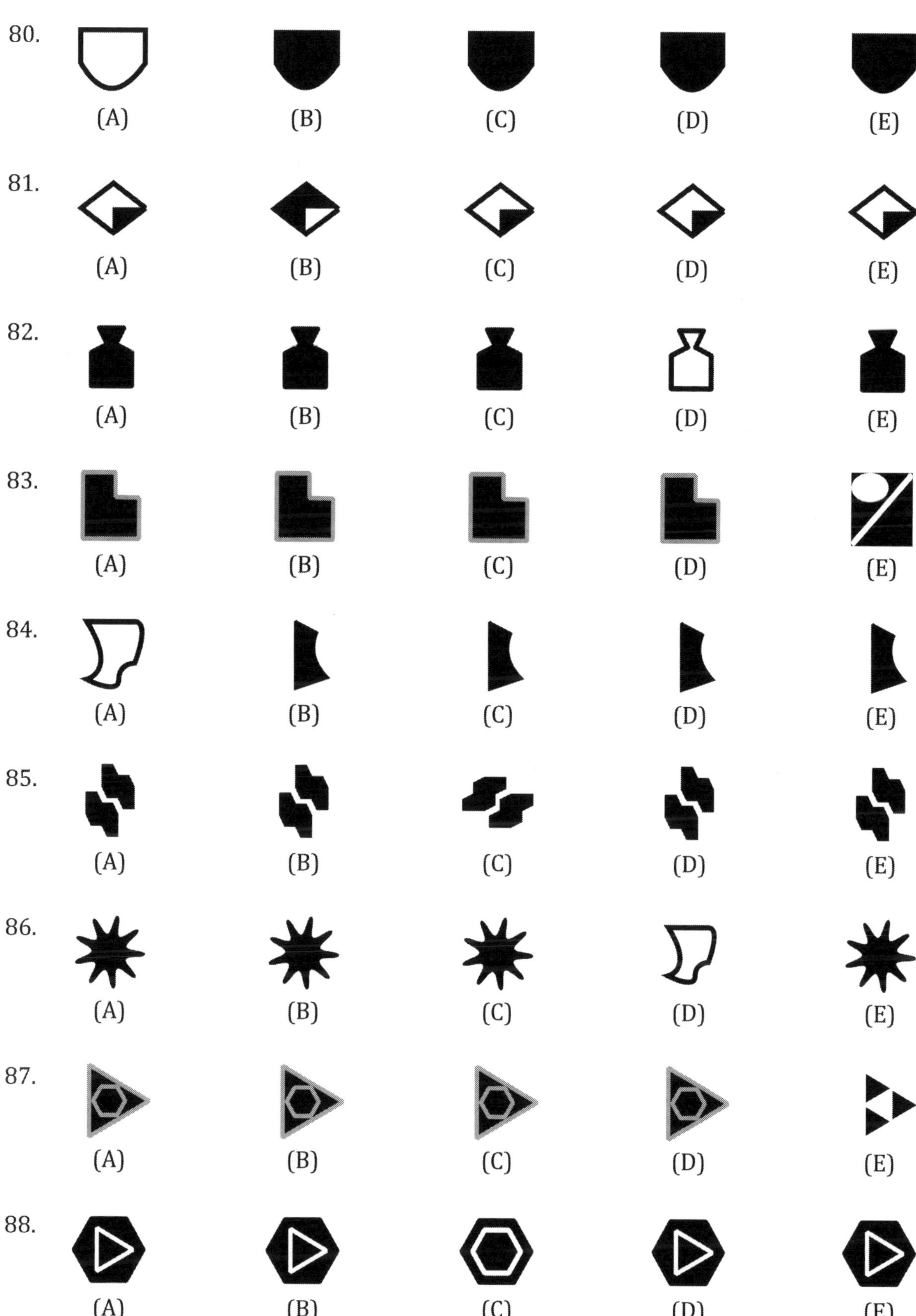
80.
(A)
(B)
(C)
(D)
(E)
81.
(A)
(B)
(C)
(D)
(E)
82.
(A)
(B)
(C)
(D)
(E)
83.
(A)
(B)
(C)
(D)
(E)
84.
(A)
(B)
(C)
(D)
(E)
85.
(A)
(B)
(C)
(D)
(E)
86.
(A)
(B)
(C)
(D)
(E)
87.
(A)
(B)
(C)
(D)
(E)
88.
(A)
(B)
(C)
(D)
(E)

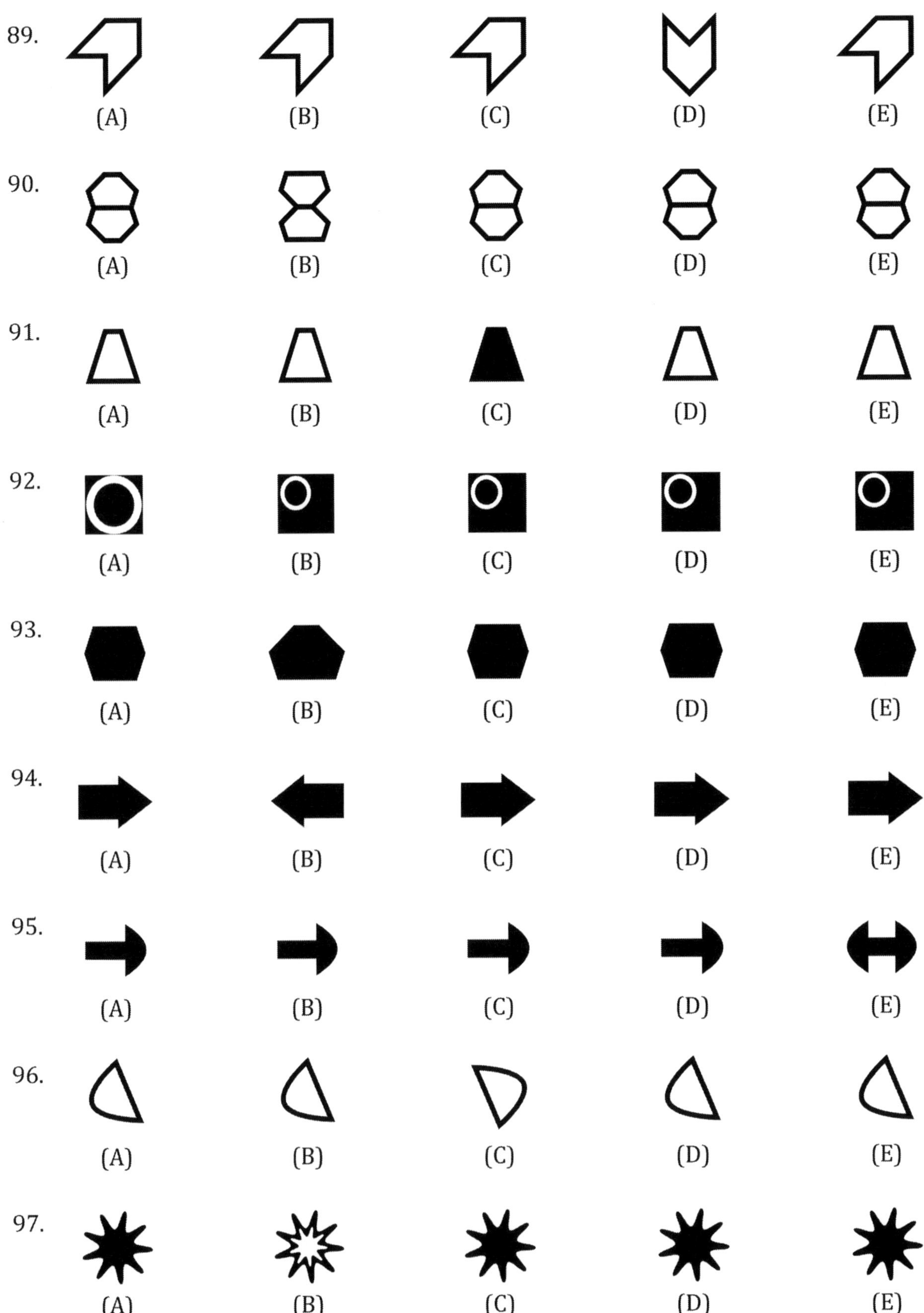
89.
(A)
(B)
(C)
(D)
(E)
90.
(A)
(B)
(C)
(D)
(E)
91.
(A)
(B)
(C)
(D)
(E)
92.
(A)
(B)
(C)
(D)
(E)
93.
(A)
(B)
(C)
(D)
(E)
94.
(A)
(B)
(C)
(D)
(E)
95.
(A)
(B)
(C)
(D)
(E)
96.
(A)
(B)
(C)
(D)
(E)
97.
(A)
(B)
(C)
(D)
(E)

98. (A) (B) (C) (D) (E)

99. (A) (B) (C) (D) (E)

100. (A) (B) (C) (D) (E)

Hidden Figures Test

Instructions: For each question, select the answer letter of the figure at the top of the page that appears within the image shown. The figure that appears within the image will have the same size and orientation as the figure shown at the top of the page.

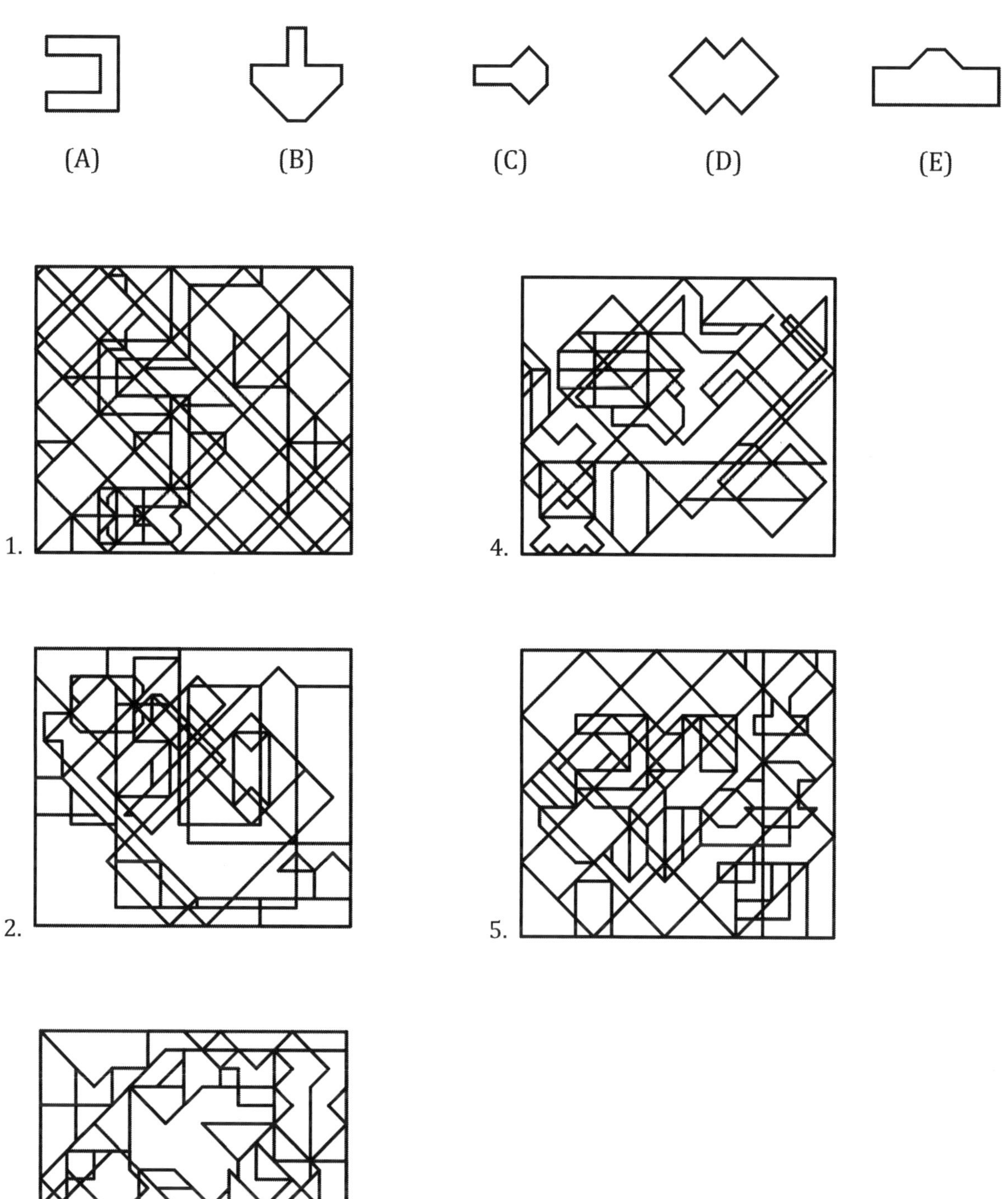
(A)
(B)
(C)
(D)
(E)
1.
2.
3.
4.
5.

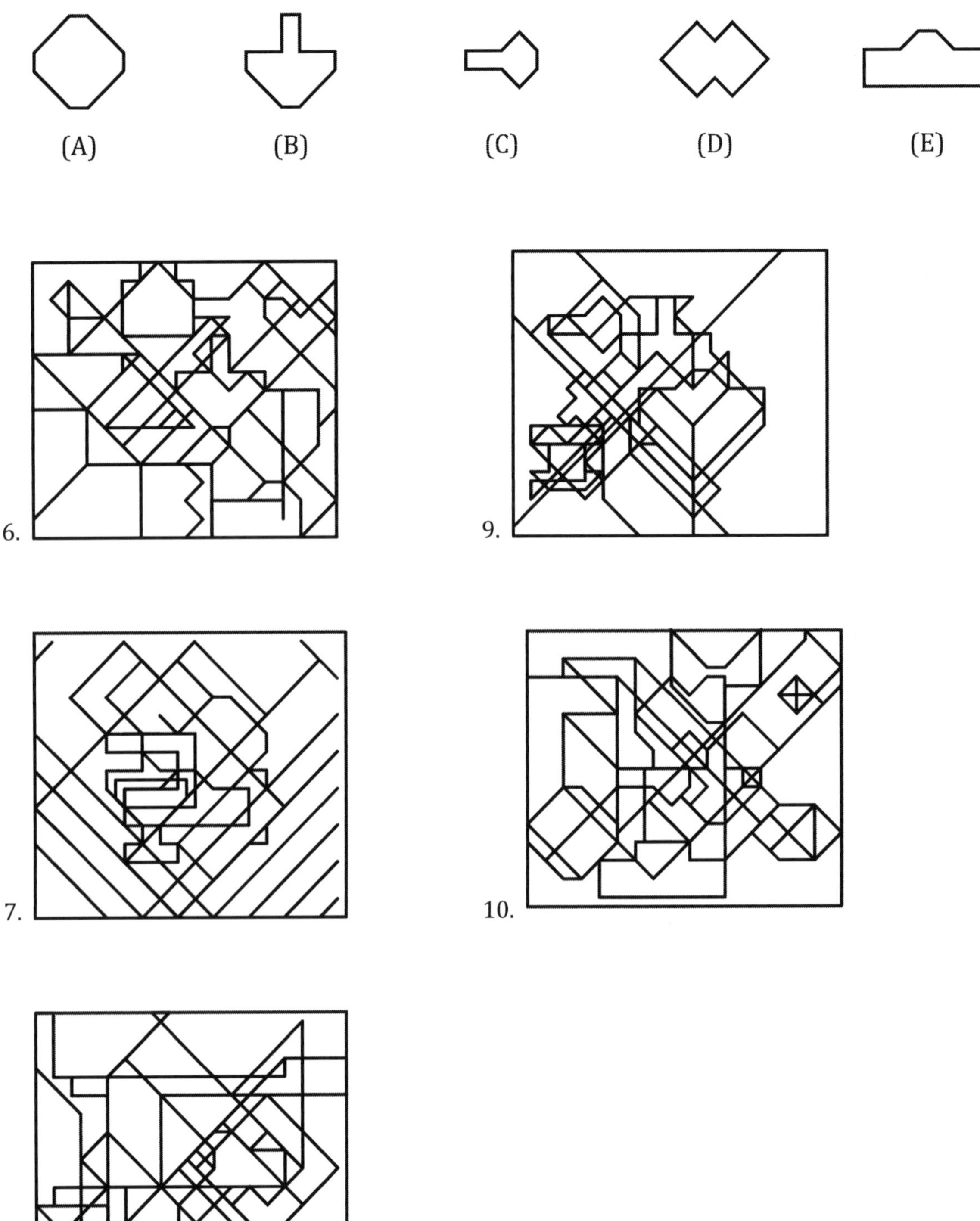
(A)
(B)
(C)
(D)
(E)
6.
9.
7.
10.
8.

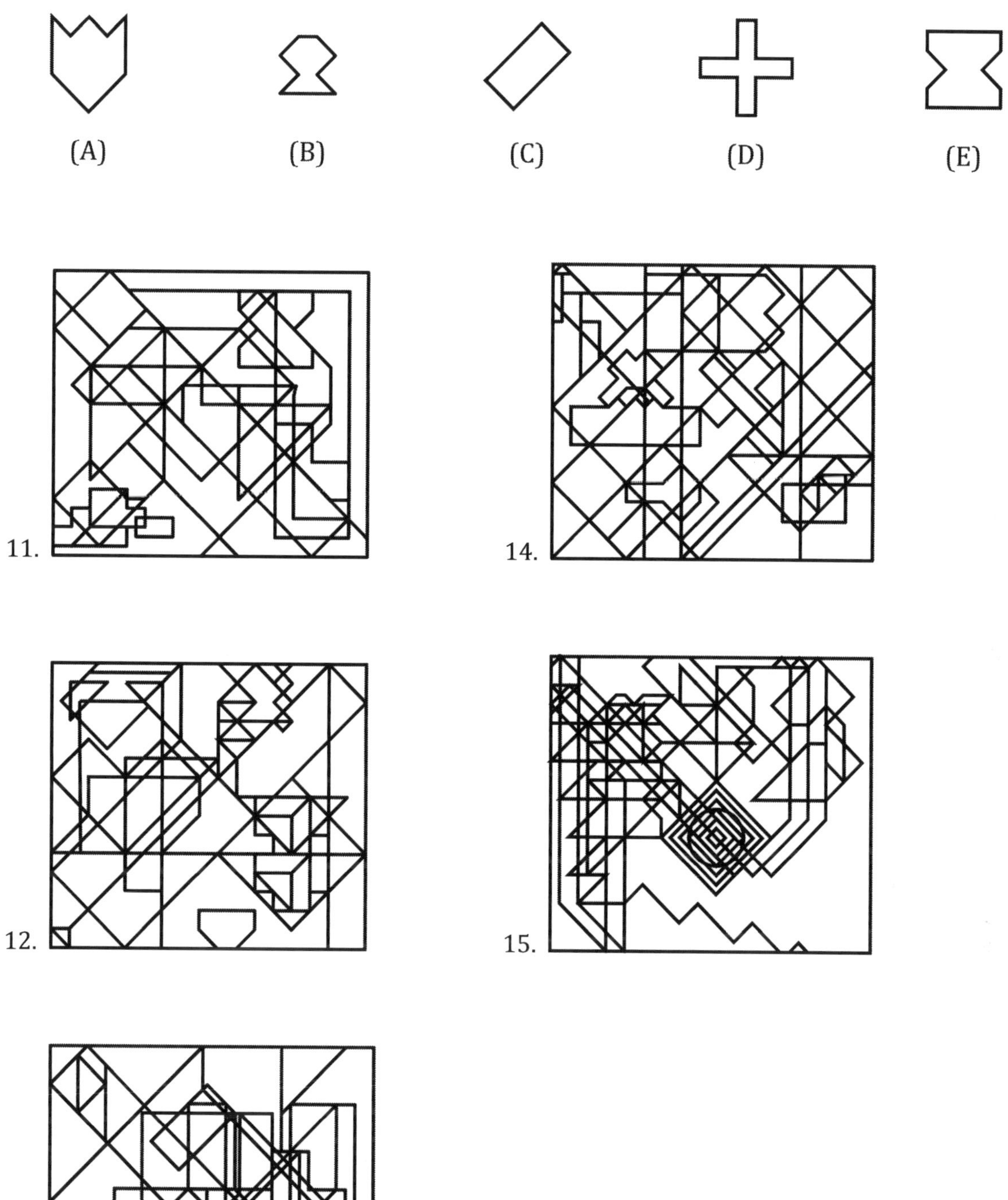
(A)
(B)
(C)
(D)
(E)
11.
14.
12.
15.
13.

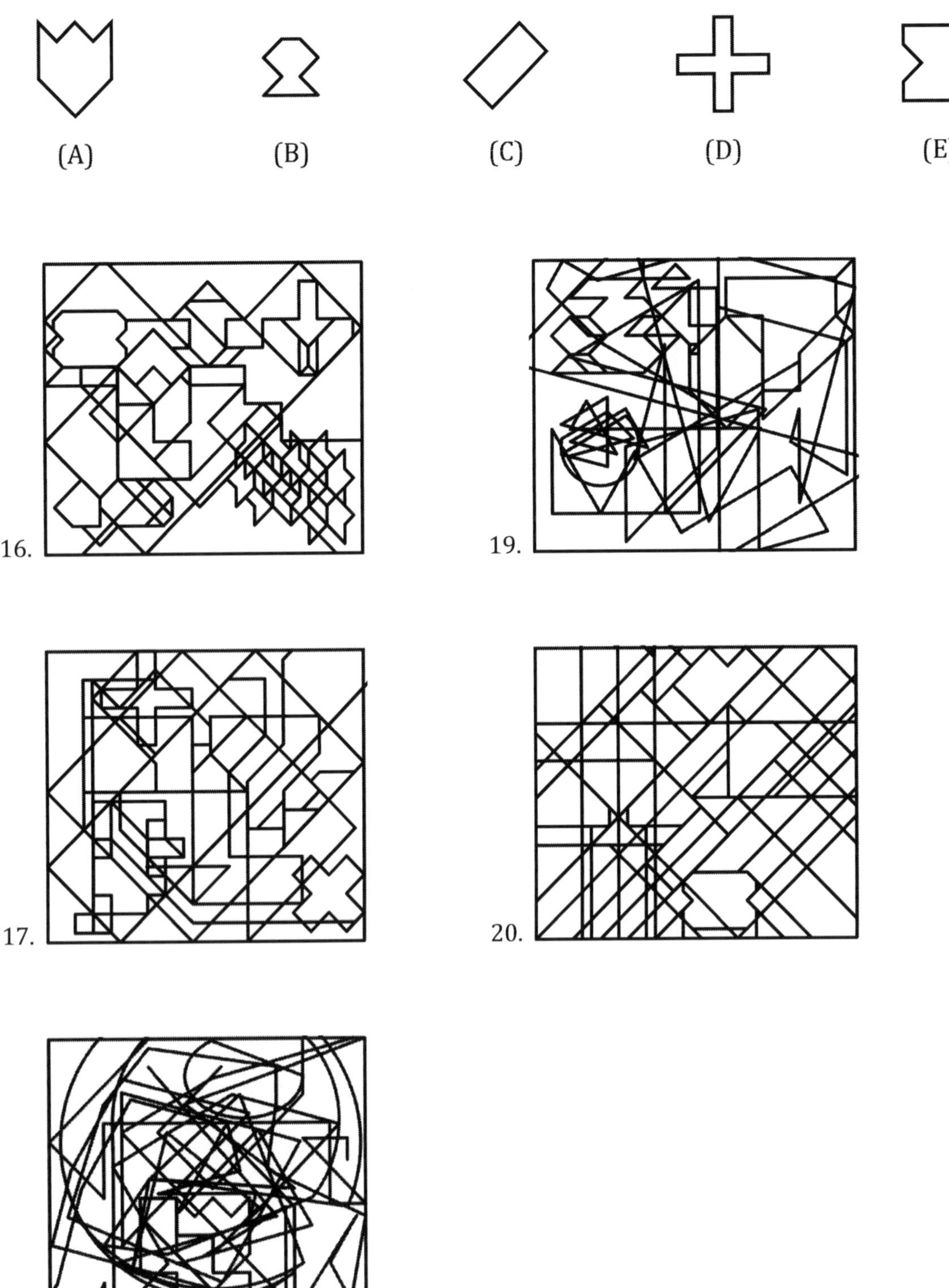
(A)
(B)
(C)
(D)
(E)
16.
19.
17.
20.
18.

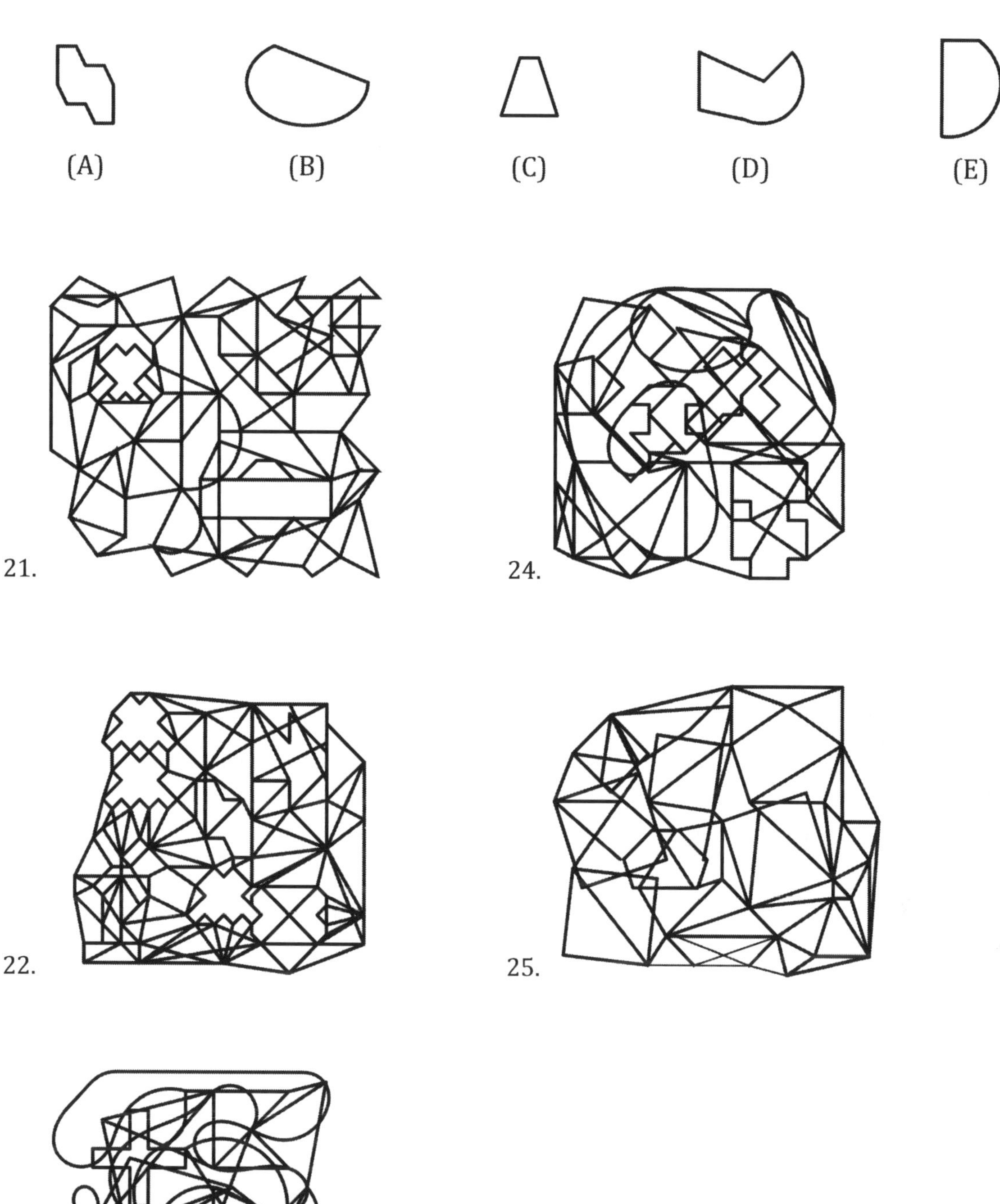
(A)
(B)
(C)
(D)
(E)
21.
24.
22.
25.
23.

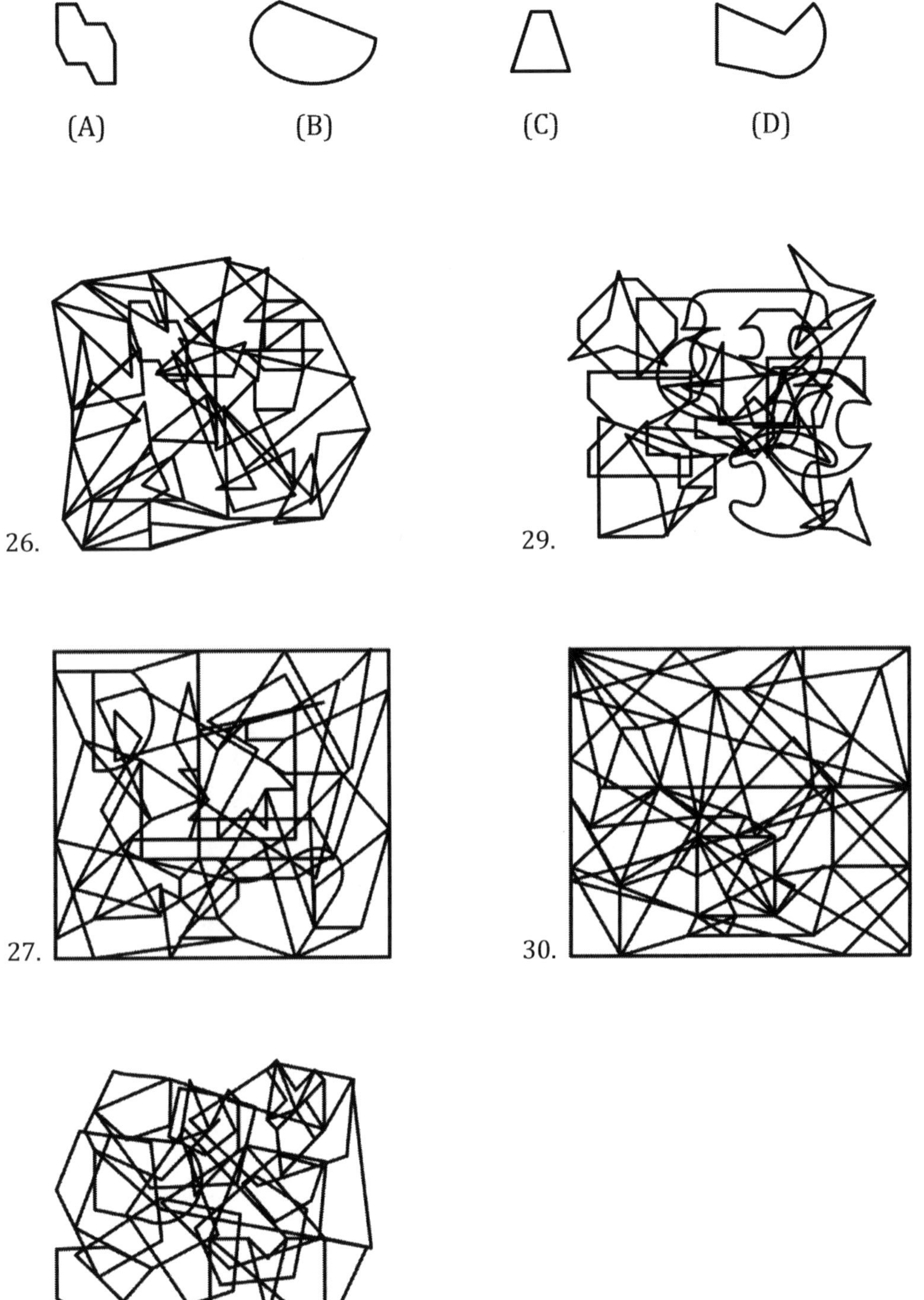
(A)
(B)
(C)
(D)
(E)
26.
29.
27.
30.
28.

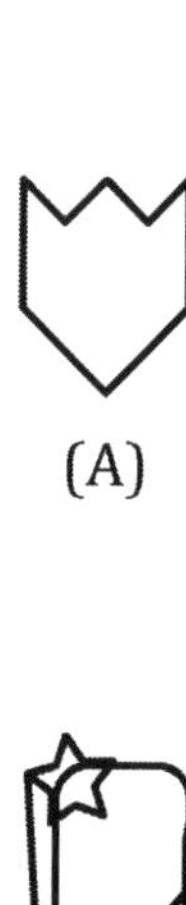
(A)

(B)

(C)

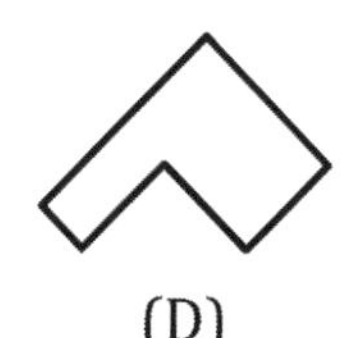
(D)

(E)

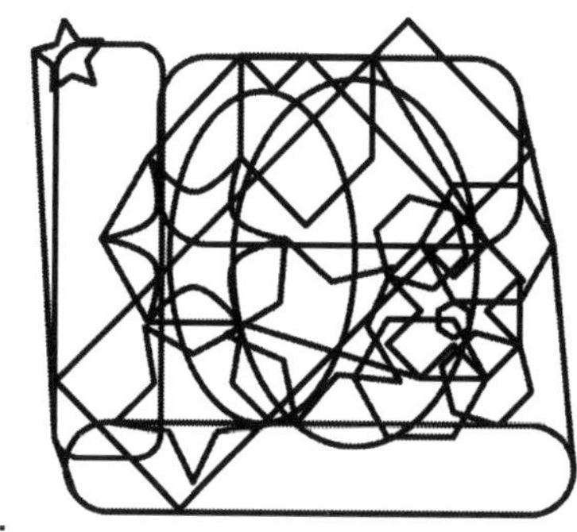
31.

34.

32.

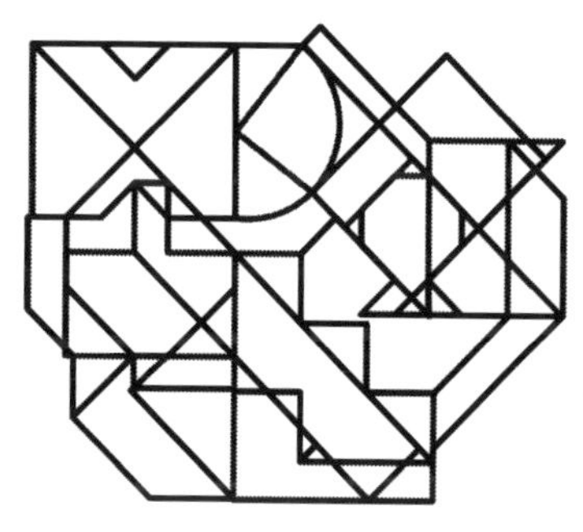
35.

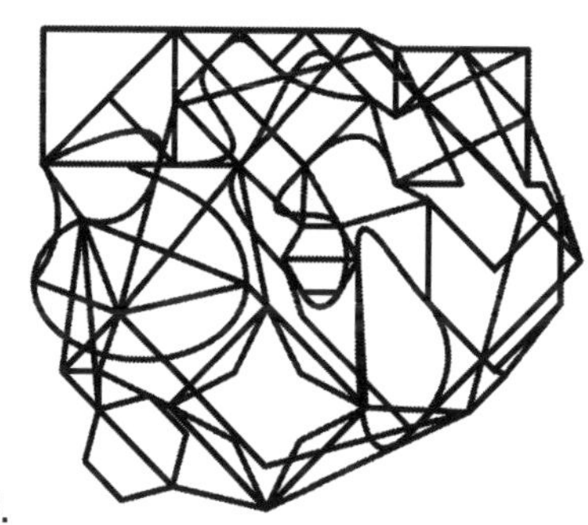
33.

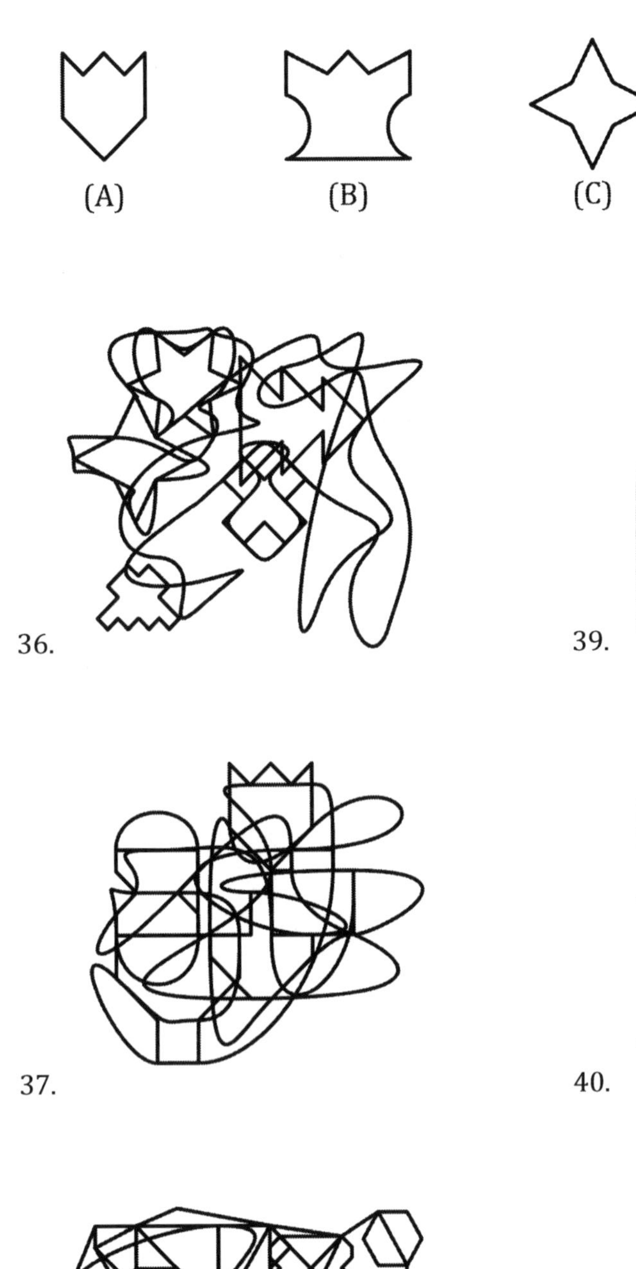

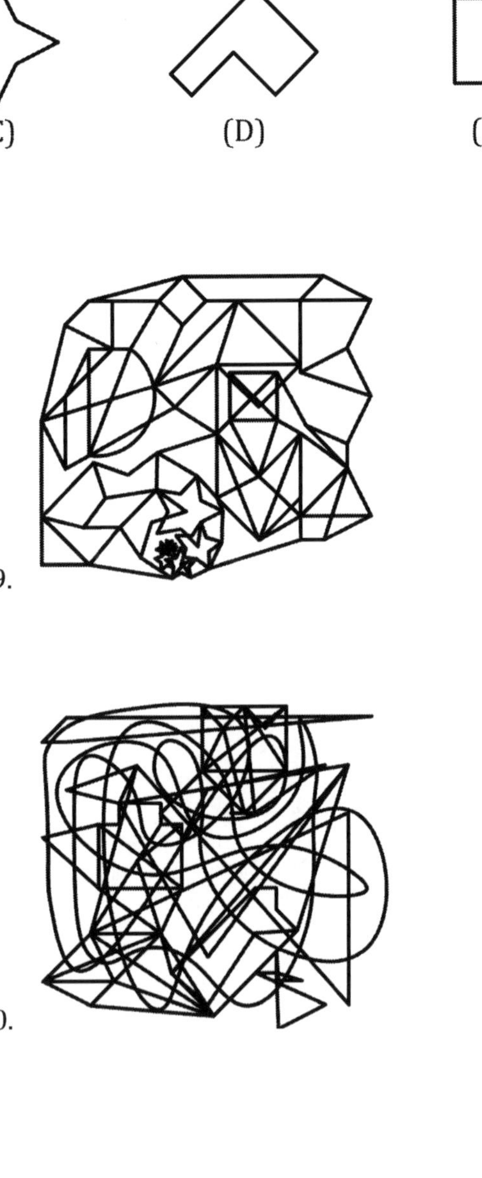

(A) (B) (C) (D) (E)

36.

39.

37.

40.

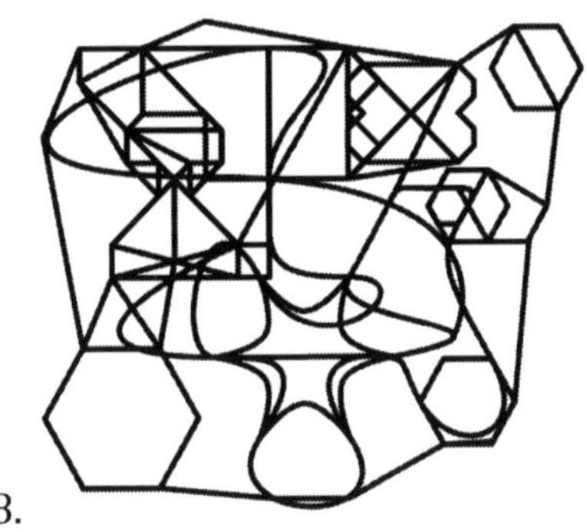

38.

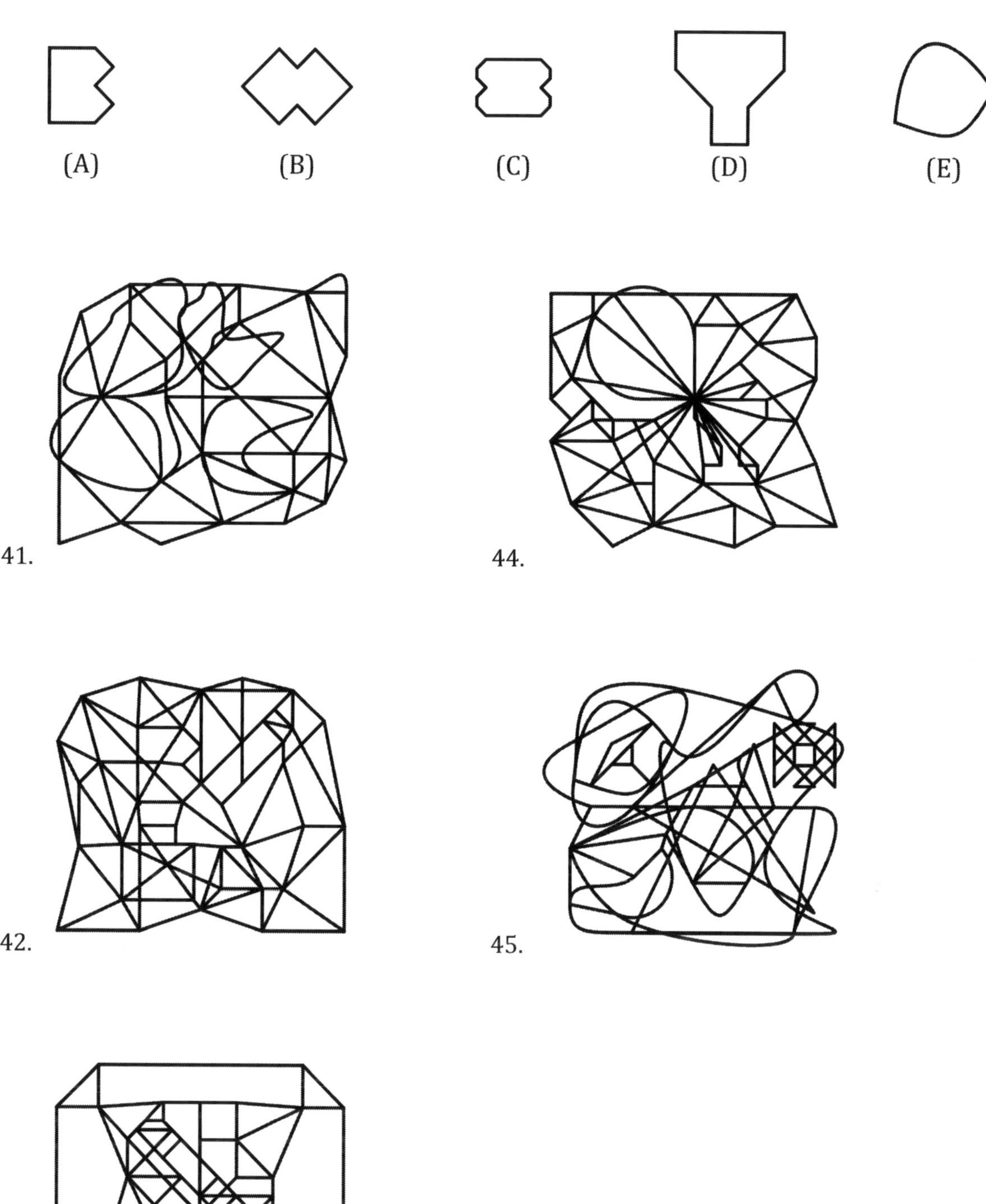
(A)
(B)
(C)
(D)
(E)
41.
44.
42.
45.
43.

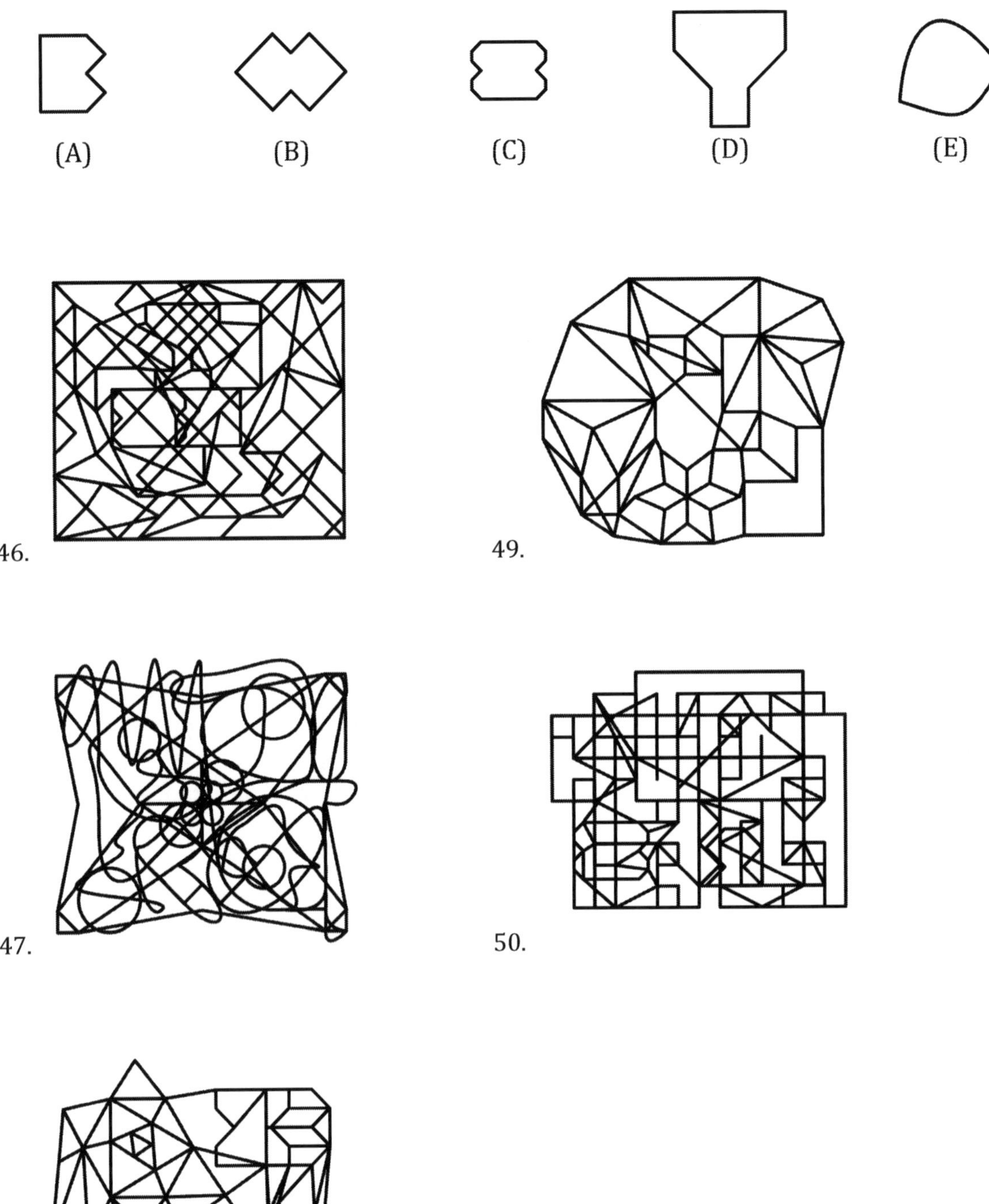
(A)
(B)
(C)
(D)
(E)
46.
49.
47.
50.
48.

Army Aviation Information Test

1. Which of these is one of the three types of drag that constitute total drag?
   a. Inversion
   b. Paradox
   c. Subduction
   d. Accelerated
   e. Parasite

2. Which of the following is common to all turbine helicopters, but is only on some piston powered helicopters?
   a. Governor
   b. Thrust control
   c. Heading control
   d. Antitorque rotor
   e. Intermeshing rotor

3. Where is the horizontal reference datum located?
   a. Three feet forward of the helicopter's nose
   b. The tip of the helicopter's nose
   c. The rotor mast
   d. One foot forward of the rotor mast
   e. It varies by helicopter

4. The ________ position relative to the horizon determines the helicopter's travel and attitude
   a. Main rotor
   b. Cyclic
   c. Nose
   d. Tail rotor
   e. Collective

5. When training for a rapid deceleration, in most helicopters the entry speed should be approximately:
   a. 30 knots
   b. 35 knots
   c. 40 knots
   d. 45 knots
   e. 50 knots

6. Which of the following has been the Army's primary training helicopter since 1993?
   a. Eurocopter UH-72
   b. Bell TH-67
   c. Bell OH-58
   d. Boeing AH-64
   e. Sikorsky UH-60

7. Which of the following occurs when the tail rotor becomes more aerodynamically efficient during the transition from hover to forward flight?

a. Downwash
b. In Ground Effect
c. Out of Ground Effect
d. Translational thrust
e. Coning

8. The solidity ratio is the:

a. Ratio of thrust to drag
b. Ratio of lift to thrust
c. Ratio of the total rotor blade area to the total rotor disk area
d. Ratio of the total rotor disk area to the total rotor blade area squared
e. Ratio of the helicopter's total length to its total width

9. Which of the following is NOT one of the controls used by a helicopter pilot during flight?

a. Collective pitch
b. Torque pedals
c. Antitorque pedals
d. Cyclic pitch
e. Throttle

10. Each gallon of reciprocating engine oil weighs ____ lbs.

a. 6.5
b. 7.0
c. 7.5
d. 8.0
e. 8.5

11. To maintain airspeed in a 2G/60° turn, rotor thrust/engine power must increase by ___ percent.

a. 25
b. 50
c. 75
d. 100
e. 150

12. A high reconnaissance should be flown at an altitude of ___ to ___ feet above the surface.

a. 100 and 200
b. 150 and 250
c. 200 and 400
d. 300 and 500
e. 500 and 750

13. The twin-engine, tandem rotor helicopter that came to prominence in the Vietnam War and is still in current use is the:

a. UH-60 Black Hawk
b. OH-58 Kiowa
c. CH-47 Chinook
d. AH-64 Apache
e. UH-72 Lakota

14. _______________ changes angle of incidence differentially around the rotor system.

a. Lift coefficient
b. Collective feathering
c. Cyclic feathering
d. Increased velocity
e. Decrease velocity

15. Which of the following describes the relationship between internal fluid pressure and fluid velocity?

a. Venturi Flow Theory
b. Newton's Third Law of Motion
c. Bernoulli's Principle
d. Kensington's Rule of Lift
e. Reynolds' Theory

16. What power setting should be used during terminations to a hover?

a. 25% of maximum
b. 50% of maximum
c. 75% of maximum
d. 100% of maximum
e. The correct power setting varies by make and model.

17. During the approach to a pinnacle, the apparent rate of closure:

a. Should not be a critical factor
b. Should be steadily increasing
c. Should be about the pace of a brisk walk
d. Should be about the pace of a fast run
e. Should vary by make and model of the aircraft

18. Which of these Army helicopters is the lightest (i.e., has the lowest empty weight)?

a. UH-60 Black Hawk
b. Bell TH-67
c. OH-58A Kiowa
d. AH-64 Apache
e. UH-72 Lakota

19. During hovering flight, a single main rotor helicopter tends to move in the direction of tail rotor thrust. This sideward movement is called ________ ________.

a. Sideward tendency
b. Translating tendency
c. Lateral tendency
d. Translating bias
e. Lateral bias

20. Which of the following changes the helicopter's angle of attack?

a. Collective pitch
b. Torque pedals
c. Antitorque pedals
d. Cyclic pitch
e. Throttle

21. Which of these has the same meaning as *load factor*?

a. Weight
b. Effective weight
c. Basic empty weight
d. Cargo
e. Maximum gross weight

22. Which of the following is <u>false</u> regarding most helicopters?

a. During left turns, torque increases.
b. During right turns, torque decreases.
c. During application of aft cyclic, torque decreases and rotor speed increases.
d. During application of forward cyclic, torque increases and rotor speed decreases.
e. None of these are false.

23. When climbing to a ridgeline, the approach flightpath should be:

a. Parallel to the ridgeline and into the wind
b. Parallel to the ridgeline and with the wind
c. Diagonal to the ridgeline and with the wind
d. Perpendicular to the ridgeline and into the wind
e. Perpendicular to the ridgeline and with the wind

24. Which of these helicopters is the US Army's primary light utility helicopter?

a. UH-60 Black Hawk
b. OH-58 Kiowa
c. CH-47 Chinook
d. AH-64 Apache
e. UH-72 Lakota

25. The law of conservation of angular momentum is another name for the:

a. Coriolis Effect
b. Law of Hovering
c. Friedrich Momentum Principle
d. Principle of Autonomy
e. Angle of Attack Theorem

26. Which of the following is located on the left of the pilot's seat?

a. Collective pitch
b. Torque pedals
c. Antitorque pedals
d. Cyclic pitch
e. Throttle

27. A forward CG is not obvious when:

a. Hovering in a crosswind
b. Taking off in a crosswind
c. Hovering in a strong tailwind
d. Hovering in a strong headwind
e. A forward CG is always obvious.

28. Which of the following is a required action while entering a climb while maintaining air speed?

a. Increase right antitorque pedal pressure
b. Apply forward cyclic
c. Increase the collective
d. Lower the collective
e. Apply aft cyclic

29. An approach angle of approximately __ to __ degrees is considered a steep approach.

a. 3 and 5
b. 6 and 8
c. 10 and 12
d. 13 and 15
e. 16 and 18

30. Which of the following is an attack helicopter that features four hardpoints mounted on stub-wing pylons, and usually carries a combination of AGM-114 Hellfire missiles and Hydra 70 rocket pods?

a. UH-60 Black Hawk
b. OH-58 Kiowa
c. CH-47 Chinook
d. AH-64 Apache
e. UH-72 Lakota

31. Which of these conditions can make it hazardous to operate the helicopter at or near its maximum gross weight?

a. High altitude
b. Low temperature
c. Low humidity
d. B and C
e. A, B, and C

32. In a standard airplane traffic pattern, which of the five legs is known as the crosswind leg?

a. 1st
b. 2nd
c. 3rd
d. 4th
e. 5th

33. For slope landings, a slope of __ degrees is considered maximum for normal operation of most helicopters.

a. 2
b. 5
c. 8
d. 10
e. 12

34. Which of these Army helicopters has the highest maximum speed?

a. UH-60 Black Hawk
b. OH-58 Kiowa
c. CH-47 Chinook
d. AH-64 Apache
e. AH-6 Little Bird

35. While transitioning to forward flight at about __ to __ knots, the helicopter goes through effective translational lift (ETL).

a. 5 and 10
b. 10 and 20
c. 16 and 24
d. 6 and 12
e. 5 and 15

36. Which of the following controls the direction in which the nose of the helicopter points?

a. Collective pitch
b. Torque pedals
c. Antitorque pedals
d. Cyclic pitch
e. Throttle

37. Each gallon of JP-4 jet fuel weighs ____ lbs.

a. 5.0
b. 5.5
c. 6.0
d. 6.5
e. 7.0

38. A hover taxi is used when operating below __ feet above ground level (AGL).

a. 15
b. 20
c. 25
d. 30
e. 35

39. During a steep approach, the helicopter should be kept in trim just prior to loss of effective translational lift (approximately 25 knots). Below ____ feet AGL, the antitorque pedals should be adjusted to align the helicopter with the intended touchdown point.

a. 75
b. 100
c. 125
d. 150
e. 200

40. The primary use of OH-58 Kiowa helicopters is:

a. Armed reconnaissance in support of ground troops
b. Electronic warfare and special operations
c. Troop movement, battlefield resupply, and artillery placement
d. Tactical transport and special operations
e. Attack and multi-role combat

Spatial Apperception Test

Instructions: The view shown on each question is a view from the cockpit of an aircraft in flight. Select the answer letter that best represents the orientation of the aircraft as seen from the ground.

1.

a. b. c. d. e.

2.

a. b. c. d. e.

3.

a. b. c. d. e.

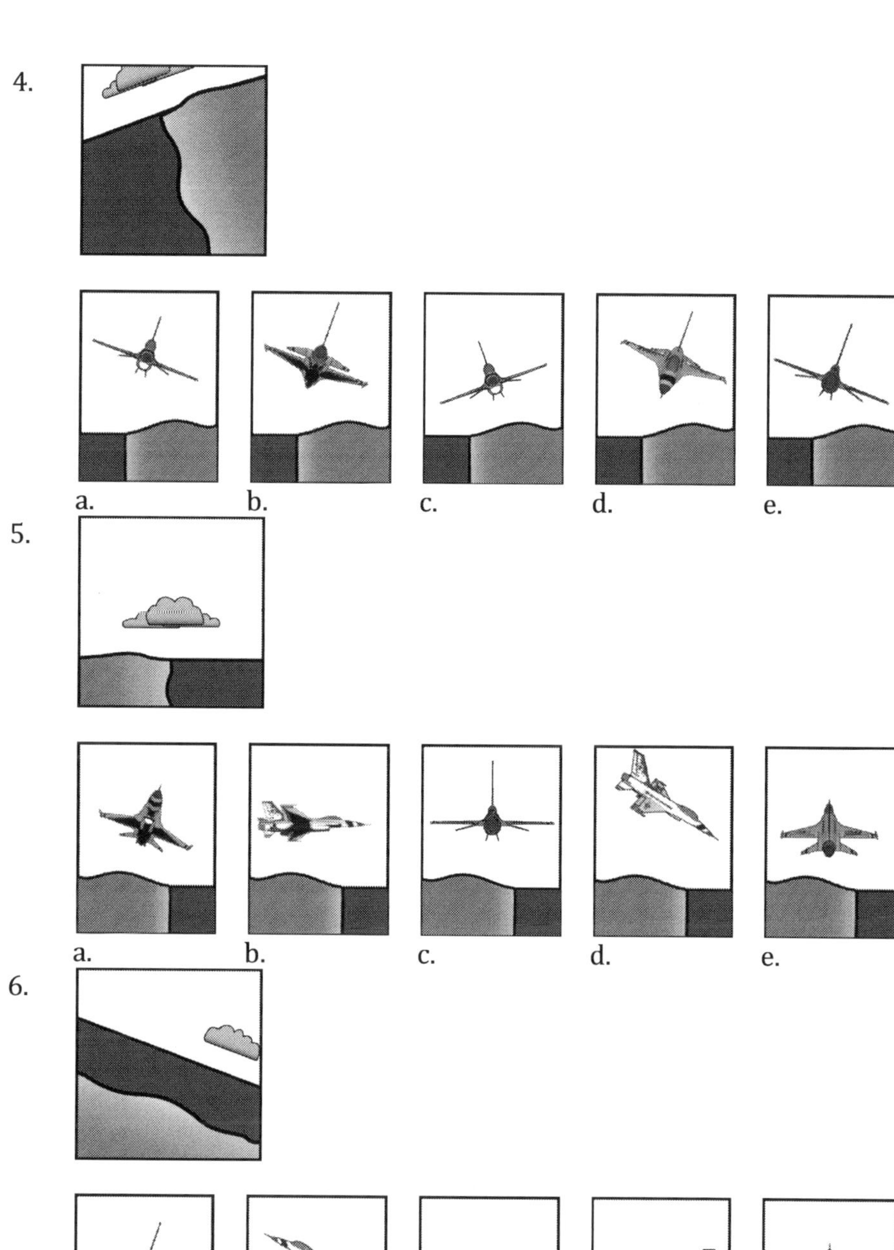

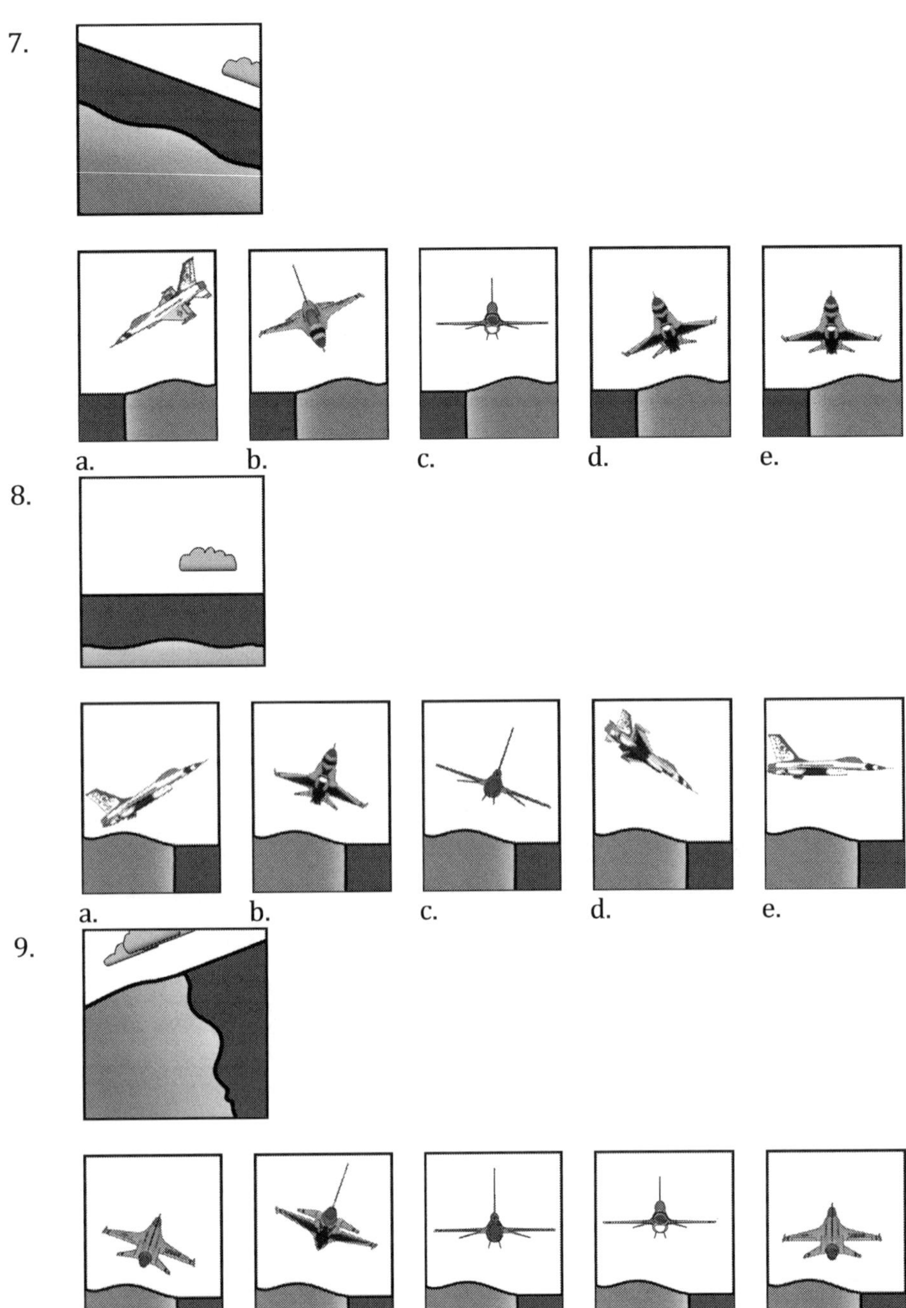
7.
a.
b.
c.
d.
e.
8.
a.
b.
c.
d.
e.
9.
a.
b.
c.
d.
e.

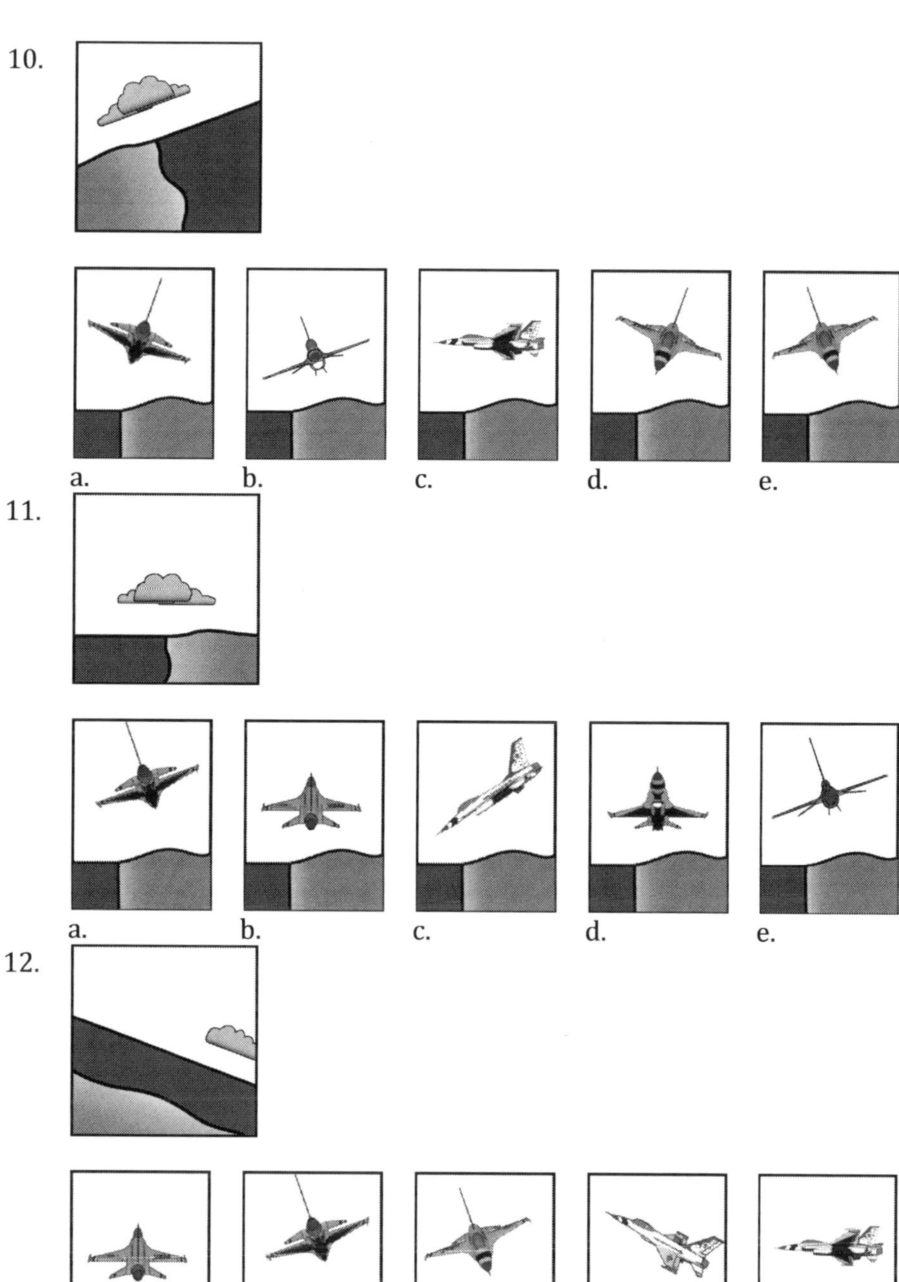
10.
a.
b.
c.
d.
e.
11.
a.
b.
c.
d.
e.
12.
a.
b.
c.
d.
e.

13.

14.

15.

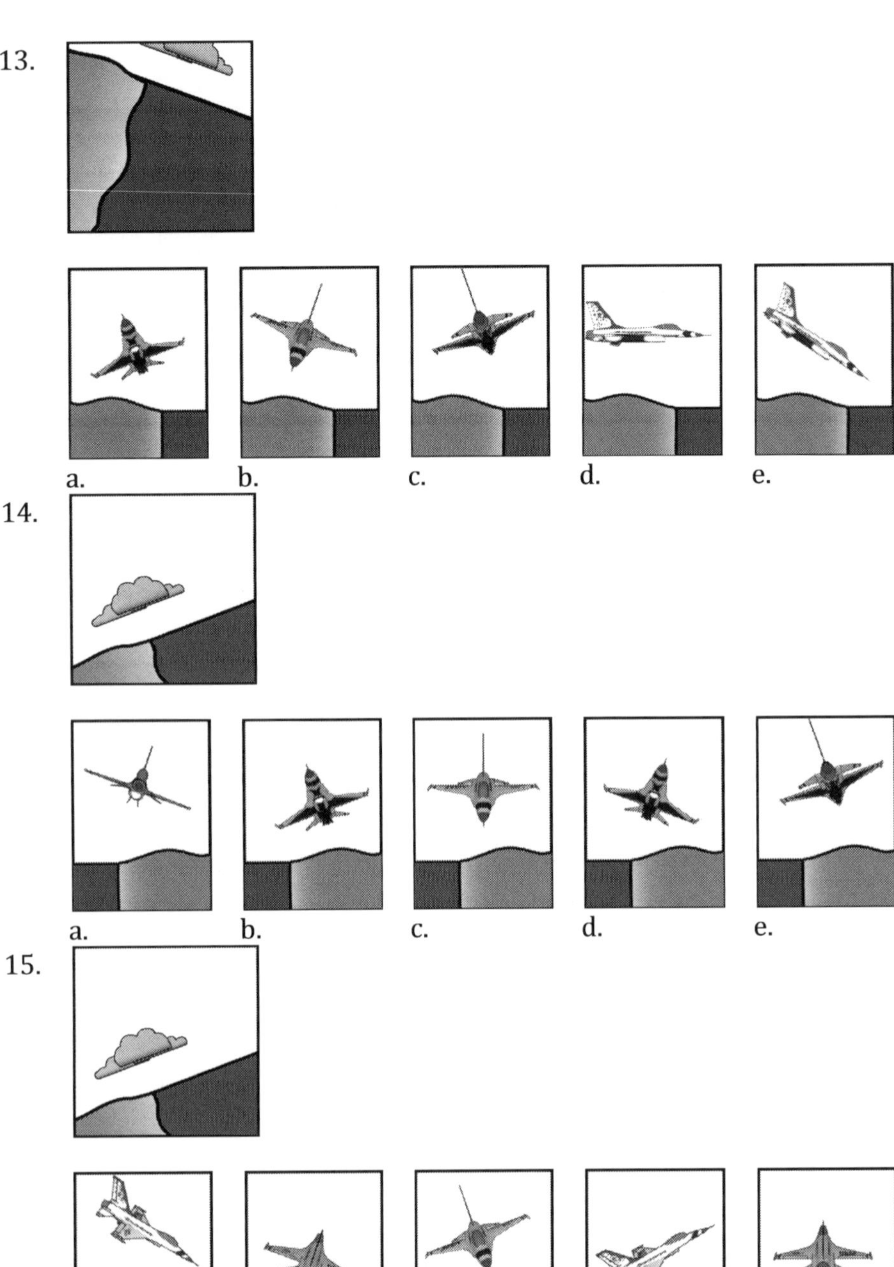

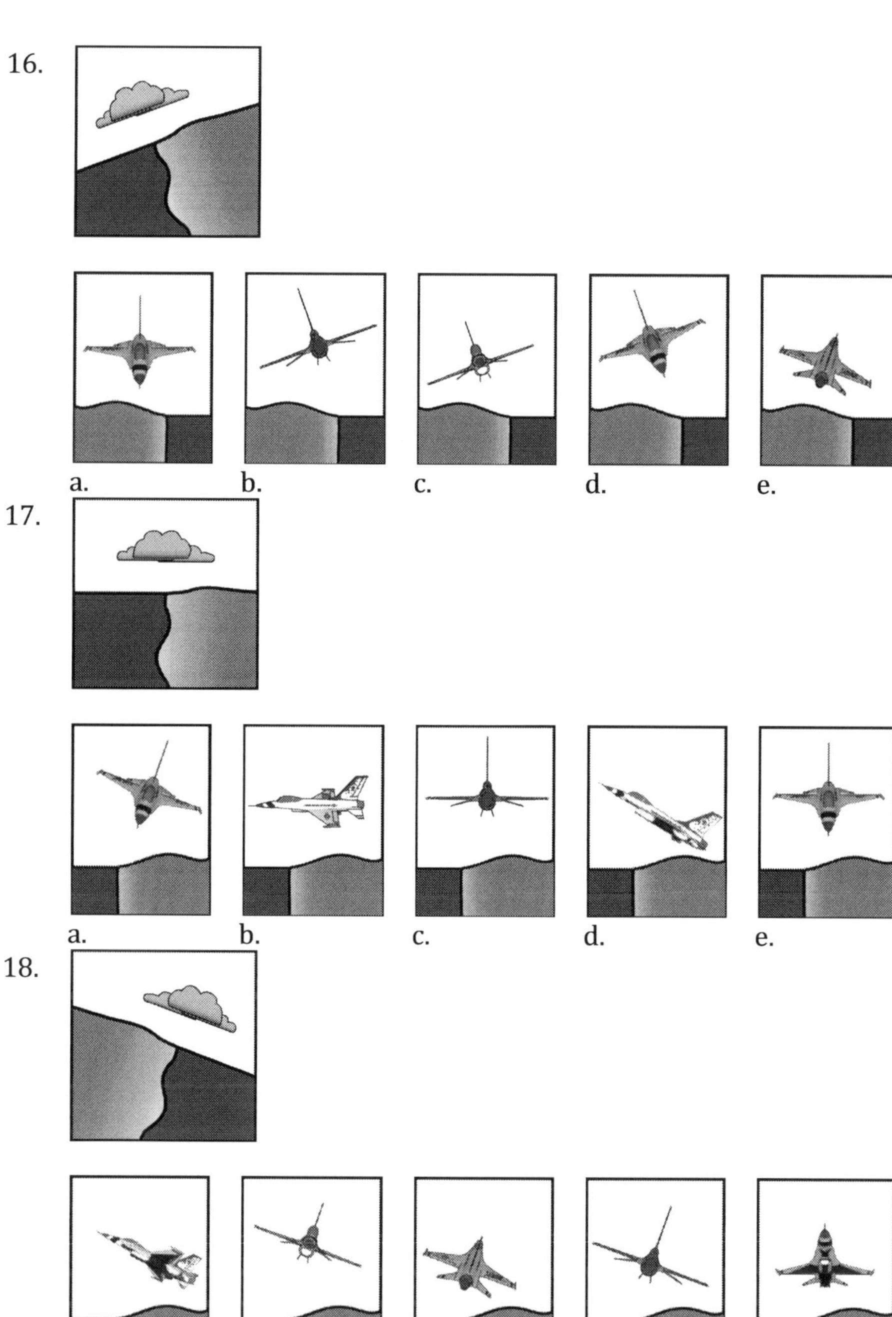
16.
a.
b.
c.
d.
e.
17.
a.
b.
c.
d.
e.
18.
a.
b.
c.
d.
e.

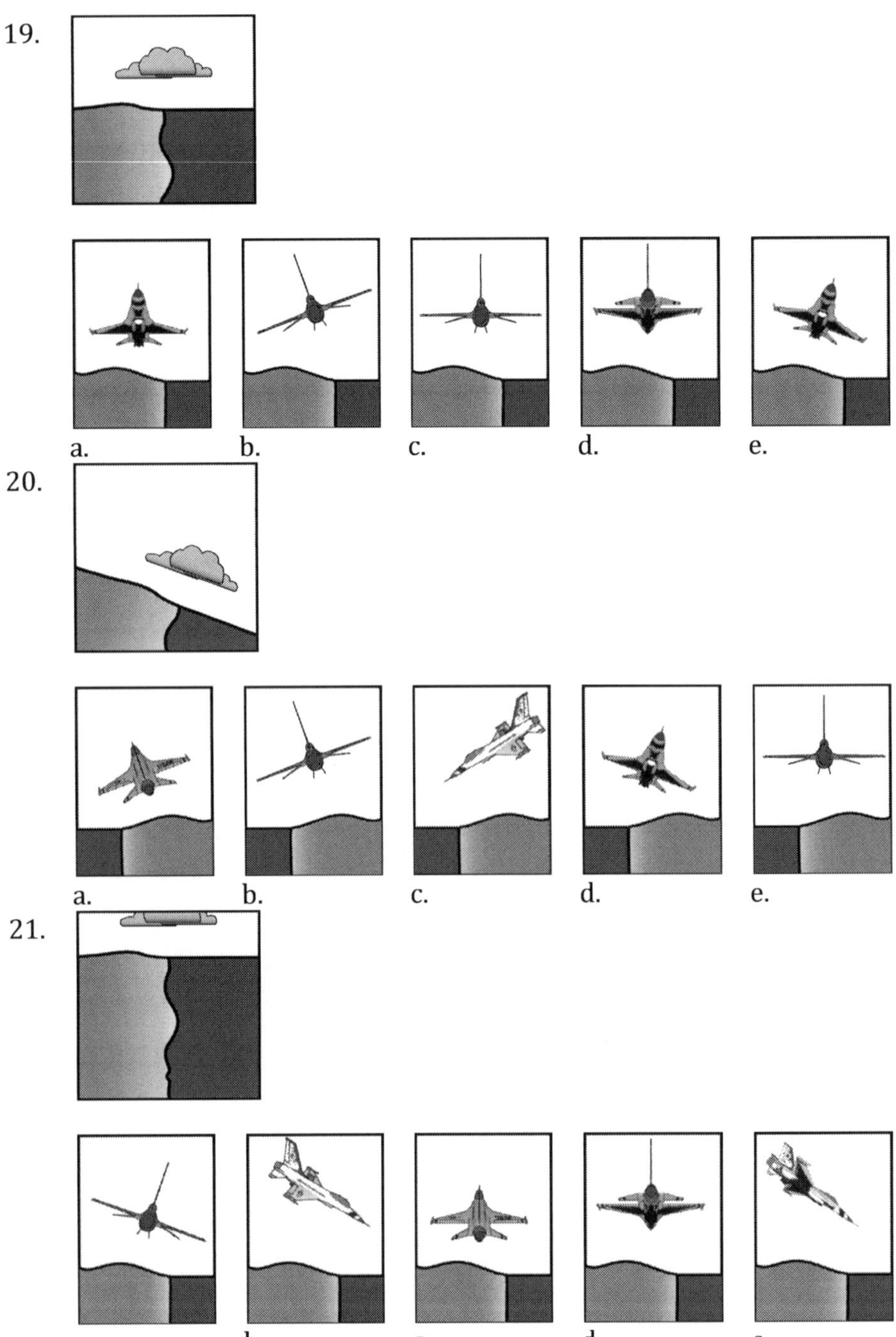
19.
a.
b.
c.
d.
e.
20.
a.
b.
c.
d.
e.
21.
a.
b.
c.
d.
e.

22.

23.

24.

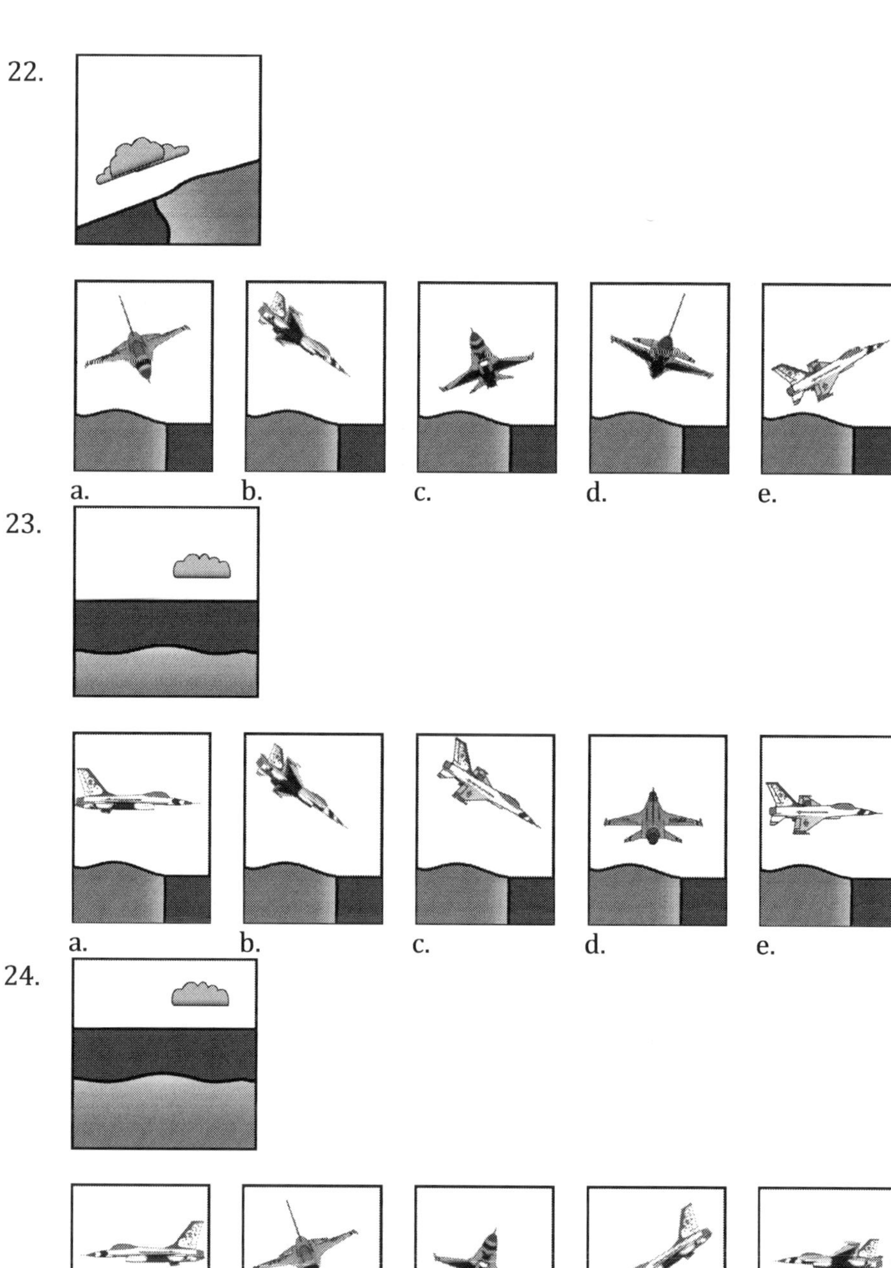

25. 

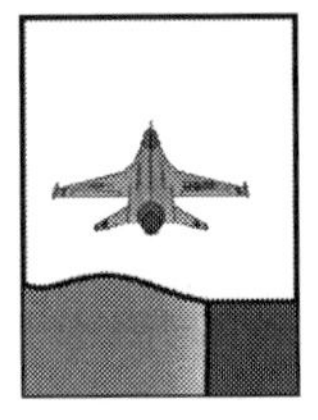
a.

b.

c.

d.

e.

Reading Comprehension Test

1. Although helicopters were developed and built during the first half-century of flight, some even reaching limited production; it was not until 1942 that a helicopter designed by Igor Sikorsky reached full-scale production, with 131 aircraft built. Even though most previous designs used more than one main rotor, it was the single main rotor with an antitorque tail rotor configuration design that would come to be recognized worldwide as the helicopter. In 1951, at the urging of his contacts at the Department of the Navy, Charles H. Kaman modified his K-225 helicopter with a new kind of engine, the turbo-shaft engine. This adaptation of the turbine engine provided a large amount of horsepower to the helicopter with a lower weight penalty than piston engines, heavy engine blocks, and auxiliary components. On December 11, 1951, the K-225 became the first turbine-powered helicopter in the world. Two years later, on March 26, 1954, a modified Navy HTK-1, another Kaman helicopter, became the first twin-turbine helicopter to fly. However, it was the Sud Aviation Alouette II that would become the first helicopter to be produced with a turbine engine. Reliable helicopters capable of stable hover flight were developed decades after fixed-wing aircraft. This is largely due to higher engine power density requirements than fixed-wing aircraft. Improvements in fuels and engines during the first half of the 20th century were a critical factor in helicopter development. The availability of lightweight turbo-shaft engines in the second half of the 20th century led to the development of larger, faster, and higher-performance helicopters. The turbine engine has the following advantages over a reciprocating engine: less vibration, increased aircraft performance, reliability, and ease of operation. While smaller and less expensive helicopters still use piston engines, turboshaft engines are the preferred powerplant for helicopters today.

Which of these is most responsible for a huge increase in the number of helicopters in use?

a. The military demand for helicopters in World War I
b. The military demand for helicopters in World War II
c. The development of an antitorque tail rotor configuration design
d. The development of turbine engine powered helicopters
e. The development of piston engine helicopters

2. The helicopter rotor system is the rotating part of a helicopter that generates lift. A rotor system may be mounted horizontally, as main rotors are, providing lift vertically; it may be mounted vertically, such as a tail rotor, to provide lift horizontally as thrust to counteract torque effect. In the case of tilt rotors, the rotor is mounted on a nacelle that rotates at the edge of the wing to transition the rotor from a horizontal mounted position, providing lift horizontally as thrust, to a vertical mounted position providing lift exactly as a helicopter. Tandem rotor (sometimes referred to as dual rotor) helicopters have two large horizontal rotor assemblies; a twin rotor system, instead of one main assembly and a smaller tail rotor. Single rotor helicopters need a tail rotor to neutralize the twisting momentum produced by the single large rotor. Tandem rotor helicopters, however, use counter-rotating rotors, with each canceling out the other's torque. Counter-rotating rotor blades won't collide with and destroy each other if they flex into the other rotor's pathway. This configuration also has the advantage of being able to hold more weight with shorter blades, since there are two sets. Also, all of the power from the engines can be used for lift, whereas a single rotor helicopter uses power to counter the torque. Because of this, tandem helicopters are among some of the most powerful and fastest.

Which of these is not discussed in the passage?

a. A horizontal rotor
b. A vertical rotor
c. Twin horizontal rotors
d. Twin tilt rotors
e. Tandem rotor helicopters

3. Displacing the cyclic forward causes the nose to pitch down initially, with a resultant increase in airspeed and loss of altitude. Aft cyclic causes the nose to pitch up initially, slowing the helicopter and causing it to climb; however, as the helicopter reaches a state of equilibrium, the horizontal stabilizer levels the helicopter airframe to minimize drag, unlike an airplane. Therefore, the helicopter has very little pitch deflection up or down when the helicopter is stable in a flight mode. The variation from absolutely level depends on the particular helicopter and the horizontal stabilizer function. Increasing collective (power) while maintaining a constant airspeed induces a climb while decreasing collective causes a descent. Coordinating these two inputs, down collective plus aft cyclic or up collective plus forward cyclic, results in airspeed changes while maintaining a constant altitude. The pedals serve the same function in both a helicopter and a fixed-wing aircraft, to maintain balanced flight. This is done by applying a pedal input in whichever direction is necessary to center the ball in the turn and bank indicator.

According to this article, what is one of the main factors when it comes to variation from absolute level?

a. The horizontal stabilizer
b. The direction of the wind
c. The speed of the wind
d. How much experience the pilot has
e. Whether the weight of passengers and cargo is properly balanced

4. Making good choices sounds easy enough. However, there are a multitude of factors that come into play when these choices, and subsequent decisions, are made in the aeronautical world. Many tools are available for pilots to become more self-aware and assess the options available, along with the impact of their decision. Yet, with all the available resources, accident rates are not being reduced. Poor decisions continue to be made, frequently resulting in lives being lost and/or aircraft damaged or destroyed. The Risk Management Handbook discusses aeronautical decision-making (ADM) and single-pilot resource management (SRM) in detail and should be thoroughly read and understood. While progress is continually being made in the advancement of pilot training methods, aircraft equipment and systems, and services for pilots, accidents still occur. Historically, the term "pilot error" has been used to describe the causes of these accidents. Pilot error means an action or decision made by the pilot was the cause of, or a contributing factor that led to, the accident. This definition also includes the pilot's failure to make a decision or take action. From a broader perspective, the phrase "human factors related" more aptly describes these accidents since it is usually not a single decision that leads to an accident, but a chain of events triggered by a number of factors. The poor judgment chain, sometimes referred to as the "error chain," is a term used to describe this concept of contributing factors in a human factors related accident. Breaking one link in the chain is often the only event necessary to change the outcome of the sequence of events.

Which of the following statements would the author be most likely to agree with?

- a. The problem of aircraft accidents has never been worse.
- b. Realistically, the number of aircraft accidents is probably about as low as it's ever going to be.
- c. There is still much room for improvement when it comes to reducing aircraft accidents.
- d. The FAA is too lax, and often gives licenses to pilots who are not fully qualified.
- e. Great strides have been made in recent years in reducing the number of aircraft accidents.

5. The roots of aviation are firmly based on curiosity. Where would we be today had it not been for the dreams of Leonardo da Vinci, the Wright Brothers, and Igor Sikorsky? They all were infatuated with flight, a curiosity that led to the origins of aviation. The tale of aviation is full of firsts: first flight, first helicopter, first trans-Atlantic flight, and so on. But, along the way there were many setbacks, fatalities, and lessons learned. Today, we continue to learn and investigate the limits of aviation. We've been to the moon, and soon beyond. Our curiosity will continue to drive us to search for the next challenge. However, curiosity can also have catastrophic consequences. Despite over 100 years of aviation practice, we still see accidents that are caused by impaired judgment formed from curious behavior. Pilots commonly seek to determine the limits of their ability as well as the limits of the aircraft. Unfortunately, too often this leads to mishaps with deadly results. Inquisitive behavior must be harnessed and displayed within personal and material limits. Deadly curiosity may not seem as obvious to some as it is to others. Simple thoughts such as, "Is visibility really as bad as what the ATIS is reporting?" or "Does the 20-minute fuel light really indicate only 20 minutes worth of fuel?" can lead to poor decisions and disastrous outcomes. Some aviators blatantly violate rules and aircraft limitations without thinking through the consequences. "What indications and change in flight characteristics will I see if I fly this helicopter above its maximum gross weight?" or "I've heard this helicopter can do aerobatic flight. Why is it prohibited?" are examples of extremely harmful curiosity. Even more astounding is their ignoring the fact that the damage potentially done to the aircraft will probably manifest later in the aircraft's life, affecting other crews. Spontaneous excursions in aviation can be deadly. Curiosity is natural, and promotes learning. Airmen should abide by established procedures until proper and complete hazard assessment and risk management can be completed.

Which of these statements most closely matches the theme of this passage?

a. Fortune favors the bold.
b. A stitch in time saves nine.
c. Curiosity killed the cat.
d. Fools rush in where angels fear to tread.
e. An ounce of prevention is worth a pound of cure.

6. As found in the Pilot's Handbook of Aeronautical Knowledge, the FAA has designed a personal minimums checklist. To help pilots with self-assessment, which in turn helps mitigate risk, the acronym PAVE divides the risks of flight into four categories. For each category, think of the applicability specific to helicopter operations:

- Pilot (pilot in command)
    - Physical, emotional readiness.
    - Flight experience, recency, currency, total time in type.
- Aircraft
    - Is the helicopter capable of performing the task?
    - Can it carry the necessary fuel?
    - Does it provide adequate power margins for the task to be accomplished?
    - Can it carry the weight and remain within CG?
    - Will there be external loads?
- Environment
    - Helicopters are susceptible to the impact of changing weather conditions.
    - How will the change in moderating temperatures and DA affect performance?
    - Will controllability be jeopardized by winds, terrain, and turbulence?
- External pressures
    - Do not let the notion to accomplish "the mission" override good judgment and safety.
    - Many jobs include time lines. How often do we hear "time is money" or "time is wasting"?
    - Don't sacrifice safety for an implied or actual need to meet the deadline!
    - Do not allow yourself to feel pressured by coworkers, family events, or friends.

Incorporated into preflight planning, the PAVE checklist provides the pilot with a simple way to remember each category to examine for risk prior to each flight. Once the pilot identifies the risks of a flight, he or she needs to decide whether the risk or combination of risks can be managed safely and successfully. Remember, the PIC is responsible for deciding about canceling the flight. If the pilot decides to continue with the flight, he or she should develop strategies to mitigate the risks. One way to control risk is by setting personal minimums for items in each risk category. Remember, these are limits unique to an individual pilot's current level of experience and proficiency. They should be reevaluated periodically based upon experience and proficiency.

Which category of PAVE does the pilot have the least control over?

a. Pilot
b. Aircraft
c. EnVironment
d. External Pressures
e. The pilot has equal control over all four PAVE categories.

7. Many of the concepts utilized in crew resource management (CRM) have been successfully applied to single-pilot operations which led to the development of single-pilot resource management (SRM). Defined as the art and science of managing all the resources (both on board the aircraft and from outside resources) available to a single pilot (prior to and during flight), SRM ensures the successful outcome of the flight. This includes risk management, situational awareness, and controlled flight into terrain (CFIT) awareness. SRM training helps the pilot maintain situational awareness by managing automation, associated control, and navigation tasks. This enables the pilot to accurately assess hazards, manage resulting risk potential, and make good decisions. To make informed decisions during flight operations, a pilot must be aware of the resources found both inside and outside the cockpit. Since useful tools and sources of information may not always be readily apparent, learning to recognize these resources is an essential part of SRM training. Resources must not only be identified, but a pilot must also develop the skills to evaluate whether he or she has the time to use a particular resource and the impact its use has upon the safety of flight.

What is the author's purpose in writing this passage?

a. To describe single-pilot resource management
b. To compare single-pilot resource management to crew resource management
c. To persuade readers to use single-pilot resource management
d. To answer objections to single-pilot resource management
e. To raise questions about single-pilot resource management

8. Checklists are essential cockpit resources used to verify the aircraft instruments and systems are checked, set, and operating properly. They also ensure proper procedures are performed if there is a system malfunction or inflight emergency. Pilots at all levels of experience refer to checklists. The more advanced the aircraft is, the more crucial checklists are.

Many accidents could and should be avoided by simply using the resources, internal and external, that are available. Internal resources are found in the cockpit during flight. Since some of the most valuable internal resources are ingenuity, knowledge, and skill, a pilot can expand cockpit resources immensely by improving these capabilities. This can be accomplished by frequently reviewing flight information publications, such as 14 CFR and the AIM, as well as by pursuing additional training. No other internal resource is more important than the pilot's ability to control the situation, thereby controlling the aircraft. Helicopter pilots quickly learn that it is not possible to hover, single pilot, and pick up the checklist, a chart, or publication without endangering themselves, the aircraft, or those nearby. Checklists are essential cockpit resources used to verify the aircraft instruments and systems are checked, set, and operating properly. They also ensure proper procedures are performed if there is a system malfunction or inflight emergency. Pilots at all levels of experience refer to checklists. The more advanced the aircraft is, the more crucial checklists are.

The author of this passage would most strongly agree with which of these statements?

a. As technology brings us more and more advanced aircraft, checklists become less important.
b. Checklists should be referred to frequently during operation of the aircraft.
c. Autopilot technology has significantly reduced the importance of pilots' skill level.
d. Checklists are used primarily by pilots who do not yet have enough experience to operate by instinct.
e. Improving a pilot's knowledge and skills is an effective way to promoting safe operation.

9. When an operator requests a Minimum Equipment List (MEL) and a Letter of Authorization (LOA) is issued by the FAA, then the use of the MEL becomes mandatory for that helicopter. All maintenance deferrals must be accomplished in accordance with the terms and conditions of the MEL and the operator-generated procedures document. Exercise extreme caution when hovering near buildings or other aircraft. The use of an MEL for rotorcraft operated under part 91 also allows for the deferral of inoperative items or equipment. The primary guidance becomes the FAA-approved MEL issued to that specific operator and N-numbered helicopter. The FAA has developed master minimum equipment lists (MMELs) for rotorcraft in current use. Upon written request by a rotorcraft operator, the local FAA Flight Standards District Office (FSDO) may issue the appropriate make and model MMEL, along with an LOA, and the preamble. The operator then develops operations and maintenance (O&M) procedures from the MMEL. This MMEL with O&M procedures now becomes the operator's MEL. The MEL, LOA, preamble, and procedures document developed by the operator must be on board the helicopter when it is operated. The FAA considers an approved MEL to be a supplemental type certificate (STC) issued to an aircraft by serial number and registration number. It therefore becomes the authority to operate that aircraft in a condition other than originally type certificated. With an approved MEL, if the position lights were discovered inoperative prior to a daytime flight, the pilot would make an entry in the maintenance record or discrepancy record provided for that purpose. The item is then either repaired or deferred in accordance with the MEL. Upon confirming that daytime flight with inoperative position lights is acceptable in accordance with the provisions of the MEL, the pilot would leave the position lights switch OFF, open the circuit breaker (or whatever action is called for in the procedures document), and placard the position light switch as INOPERATIVE.

What resource would a pilot use to determine if an inoperative part or system rendered daytime flight unacceptable?

a. LOA
b. O&M
c. FSDO
d. MEL
e. Any of the above

10. Since few helicopters carry cabin attendants, the pilot must conduct the pretakeoff and prelanding briefings, usually before takeoff due to noise and cockpit layout. The type of operation dictates what sort of briefing is necessary. All briefings should include the following:

1. The use and operation of seatbelts for takeoff, en route, and landing.
2. For over water flights, the location and use of flotation gear and other survival equipment that might be on board. Also include how and when to abandon the helicopter should ditching become necessary.
3. For flights over rough or isolated terrain, all occupants should be told where maps and survival gear are located.
4. Passengers should be informed as to what actions and precautions to take in the event of an emergency, such as the body position for best spinal protection against a high vertical impact landing (erect with back firmly against the seat back); and when and how to exit after landing. Ensure that passengers are aware of the location of the fire extinguisher, survival equipment and, if equipped, how to use and locate the Emergency Position Indicator Radio Beacon (EPIRB).
5. Smoking should not be permitted within 50 feet of an aircraft on the ground. Smoking could be permitted upwind from any possible fuel fumes, at the discretion of the pilot, except under the following conditions:
    a. During all ground operations.
    b. During takeoff or landing.
    c. When carrying flammable or hazardous materials.

When passengers are approaching or leaving a helicopter that is sitting on a slope with the rotors turning, they should approach and depart downhill. This affords the greatest distance between the rotor blades and the ground. If this involves walking around the helicopter, they should always go around the front—never the rear.

After listening to a briefing that follows these guidelines, which of the following issues might a passenger be unsure about?

a. Which direction to head when exiting the aircraft
b. Where to light a cigarette during a refueling stop
c. Where to find terrain maps of the flight area
d. How long to wait before exiting the aircraft
e. Where to collect items stowed for the flight

11. Many helicopter operators have been lured into a "quick turnaround" ground operation to avoid delays at airport terminals and to minimize stop/start cycles of the engine. As part of this quick turn-around, the pilot might leave the cockpit with the engine and rotors turning. Such an operation can be extremely hazardous if a gust of wind disturbs the rotor disk, or the collective flight control moves causing lift to be generated by the rotor system. Either occurrence may cause the helicopter to roll or pitch, resulting in a rotor blade striking the tail boom or the ground. Good operating procedures dictate that, generally, pilots remain at the flight controls whenever the engine is running and the rotors are turning. If operations require the pilot to leave the cockpit to refuel, the throttle should be rolled back to flight idle and all controls firmly frictioned to prevent uncommanded control movements. The pilot should be well trained on setting controls and exiting the cockpit without disturbing the flight or power controls.

When the flight is terminated, park the helicopter where it does not interfere with other aircraft and is not a hazard to people during shutdown. For many helicopters, it is advantageous to land with the wind coming from the right over the tail boom (counterrotating blades). This tends to lift the blades over the tail boom, but lowers the blades in front of the helicopter. This action decreases the likelihood of a main rotor strike to the tail boom due to gusty winds. Rotor downwash can cause damage to other aircraft in close proximity, and spectators may not realize the danger or see the rotors turning. Passengers should remain in the helicopter with their seats belts secured until the rotors have stopped turning. During the shutdown and postflight inspection, follow the manufacturer's checklist. Any discrepancies should be noted and, if necessary, reported to maintenance personnel.

What is the main reason leaving the cockpit with the engines running and rotors going during turnarounds should be avoided?

a. It violates FAA regulations.
b. It adds wear and tear to the engine and rotors.
c. It is unsafe.
d. It wastes fuel.
e. It looks unprofessional.

12. Today, helicopters are quite reliable. However, emergencies do occur, whether as a result of mechanical failure or pilot error, and should be anticipated. Regardless of the cause, the recovery needs to be quick and precise. By having a thorough knowledge of the helicopter and its systems, a pilot is able to handle the situation more readily. Helicopter emergencies and the proper recovery procedures should be discussed and, when possible, practiced in flight. In addition, by knowing the conditions that can lead to an emergency, many potential accidents can be avoided. Emergencies should always be anticipated. Knowledge of the helicopter, possible malfunctions and failures, and methods of recovery can help the pilot avoid accidents and be a safer pilot. Helicopter pilots should always expect the worst hazards and possible aerodynamic effects and plan for a safe exit path or procedure to compensate for the hazard.

Which of the following best sums up this passage?

a. Helicopters are extremely reliable these days.
b. Planning ahead is the best way to prepare for emergencies.
c. Many helicopter emergencies are due to faulty equipment.
d. In helicopter emergencies, there is little margin for error.
e. Helicopter emergencies can arise at any time and for a variety of reasons.

13. Medium-frequency vibrations (1,000–2,000 cycles per minute) range between the low frequencies of the main rotor (100–500 cycles per minute) and the high frequencies (2,100 cycles per minute or higher) of the engine and tail rotor. Depending on the helicopter, medium-frequency vibration sources may be engine and transmission cooling fans, and accessories such as air conditioner compressors, or driveline components. Medium-frequency vibrations are felt through the entire airframe, and prolonged exposure to the vibrations will result in greater pilot fatigue. Most tail rotor vibrations fall into the high-frequency range (2,100 cycles per minute or higher) and can be felt through the tail rotor pedals as long as there are no hydraulic actuators to dampen out the vibration. This vibration is felt by the pilot through his or her feet, which are usually "put to sleep" by the vibration. The tail rotor operates at approximately a 6:1 ratio with the main rotor, meaning for every one rotation of the main rotor the tail rotor rotates 6 times. A main rotor operating rpm of 350 means the tail rotor rpm would be 2,100 rpm. Any imbalance in the tail rotor system is very harmful as it can cause cracks to develop and rivets to work loose. Piston engines usually produce a normal amount of high-frequency vibration, which is aggravated by engine malfunctions, such as spark plug fouling, incorrect magneto timing, carburetor icing and/or incorrect fuel/air mixture. Vibrations in turbine engines are often difficult to detect as these engines operate at a very high rpm. Turbine engine vibration can be at 30,000 rpm internally, but common gearbox speeds are in the 1,000 to 3,000 rpm range for the output shaft. The vibrations in turbine engines may be short lived as the engine disintegrates rapidly when damaged due to high rpm and the forces present.

Which frequencies can result in the pilot experiencing numbness in the pilot's leg?

a. Low frequency vibrations
b. Medium frequency vibrations
c. High frequency vibrations
d. Both low and medium frequency vibrations
e. Both medium and high frequency vibrations

14. Under certain conditions of high weight, high temperature, or high density altitude, a pilot may get into a low rotor rpm situation. Although the pilot is using maximum throttle, the rotor rpm is low and the lifting power of the main rotor blades is greatly diminished. In this situation, the main rotor blades have an AOA that has created so much drag that engine power is not sufficient to maintain or attain normal operating rpm. When rotor rpm begins to decrease, it is essential to recover and maintain it. As soon as a low rotor rpm condition is detected, apply additional throttle if it is available. If there is no throttle available, lower the collective. The amount the collective can be lowered depends on altitude. Rotor rpm is life! If the engine rpm is too low, it cannot produce its rated power for the conditions because power generation is defined at a qualified rpm value. An rpm that is too low equals low power. Main rotor rpm must be maintained. When operating at altitude, the collective may need to be lowered only once to regain rotor speed. If power is available, throttle can be added and the collective raised. Once helicopter rotor blades cone excessively due to low rotor rpm, return the helicopter to the surface to allow the main rotor rpm to recover. Maintain precise landing gear alignment with the direction of travel in case a landing is necessary. Low inertia rotor systems can become unrecoverable in 2 seconds or less if the rpm is not regained immediately. Since the tail rotor is geared to the main rotor, low main rotor rpm may prevent the tail rotor from producing enough thrust to maintain directional control. If pedal control is lost and the altitude is low enough that a landing can be accomplished before the turning rate increases dangerously, slowly decrease collective pitch, maintain a level attitude with cyclic control, and land.

According to this passage, what is the primary determining factor when it comes to how much the collective can be lowered?

a. Wind speed and direction
b. The altitude of the helicopter
c. The attitude of the helicopter
d. The angle of attack of the main rotor blades
e. The amount of throttle available

15. Control of the helicopter is the result of accurately interpreting the flight instruments and translating these readings into correct control responses. Helicopter control involves adjustment to pitch, bank, power, and trim in order to achieve a desired flightpath. Pitch attitude control is control of the movement of the helicopter about its lateral axis. After interpreting the helicopter's pitch attitude by reference to the pitch instruments (attitude indicator, altimeter, airspeed indicator, and VSI), cyclic control adjustments are made to affect the desired pitch attitude. A pilot transitioning from airplanes to helicopters must understand that the attitude indicator is mounted in the airframe beneath the main rotor system and does not directly indicate what the main rotor system is doing to the flightpath. Therefore, the helicopter can take off and climb with the nose below the horizon. The helicopter can slow down and land with the nose above the horizon. In contrast, the airplane must be pointed generally in the direction of travel (up or down) since the attitude indicator is firmly attached to the airframe that is firmly attached to the wings. The helicopter tends to fly through the air at some stabilized attitude, an effect developed by the horizontal stabilizer and designed to minimize drag in forward flight. As a helicopter begins to take off, acceleration begins. As the airflow increases over the horizontal stabilizer, it produces a downward force to bring the nose into a stabilized attitude to streamline the airframe into the relative wind. Therefore, the helicopter's attitude indicator is about level when at a stable airspeed and altitude. A nose-low attitude indicates acceleration, not necessarily a descent, and a nose-high attitude indicates a decelerating attitude, not necessarily a climb. These effects make the helicopter pilot interpretation of the instruments even more important because the pilot must integrate the results of the entire instrument scan to achieve complete situational awareness of the helicopter's to flightpath.

Which of the following is the best definition of *attitude*?

a. The relation of the helicopter to the horizon
b. The distance between the helicopter and the surface of the earth
c. The angle of the helicopter
d. The ratio of the helicopter's speed to its altitude
e. The angle of the main rotor blades

16. Common Errors of Attitude Instrument Flying

Fixation

Fixation, or staring at one instrument, is a common error observed in pilots first learning to utilize instruments. The pilot may initially fixate on an instrument and make adjustments with reference to that instrument alone.

Omission

Another common error associated with attitude instrument flying is omission of an instrument from the cross-check. Pilots tend to omit the stand-by instruments, as well as the magnetic compass from their scans. The position of the instrument is often the reason for the omission. One of the most commonly omitted instruments from the scan is the slip/skid indicator.

Emphasis

In initial training, placing emphasis on a single instrument is very common and can become a habit if not corrected. When the importance of a single instrument is elevated above another, the pilot begins to rely solely on that instrument for guidance. When rolling out of a 180° turn, the attitude indicator, heading indicator, slip/skid indicator, and altimeter need to be referenced. If a pilot omits the slip/skid indicator, coordination is sacrificed.

Inadvertent Entry into IMC

Prior to any flight, day or night, an inadvertent IMC plan should be carefully planned and, if possible, rehearsed. Many aircraft mishaps can be blamed on the pilot's inability to recover an aircraft after inadvertently entering IMC. The desire to stay outside visually is very strong and can only be overcome through training. IMC-trained helicopter pilots should climb to a safe altitude free of obstacles and obtain an instrument clearance from ATC. However, for the nonrated pilot and, more importantly, a non-IFR equipped helicopter, remaining VMC is critical. Pilots who are not trained in IMC have a tendency to try and chase favorable weather by flying just above the tree tops or following roads. The thought process is that as long as they can see what is below them, then they can fly to their intended destination. Experience shows us that continuing VFR flight in IMC is often fatal. Pilots get too fixated on what they see below them and fail to see what is ahead of them, such as power lines, towers, and taller trees. By the time the pilot sees the obstacle, it is too close to avoid collision. Helicopter pilots should always remain aware of flight visibility by comparing how much can be seen ahead. As soon as the pilot notices a marked decrease in visibility, that pilot must reevaluate the flight plan and landing options. A suitable landing area can always be used to sit out bad weather and let conditions improve.

Which of these errors is the most dangerous during attitude instrument flying?

a. Fixation
b. Omission
c. Emphasis
d. Inadvertent Entry into IMC
e. All of these errors can be equally dangerous.

17. A semirigid rotor system is usually composed of two blades that are rigidly mounted to the main rotor hub. The main rotor hub is free to tilt with respect to the main rotor shaft on what is known as a teetering hinge. This allows the blades to flap together as a unit. As one blade flaps up, the other flaps down. Since there is no vertical drag hinge, lead/lag forces are absorbed and mitigated by blade ending. The semirigid rotor is also capable of feathering, which means that the pitch angle of the blade changes. This is made possible by the feathering hinge. [Figure 4-2] The underslung rotor system mitigates the lead/lag forces by mounting the blades slightly lower than the usual plane of rotation, so the lead and lag forces are minimized. As the blades cone upward, the center of pressures of the blades are almost in the same plane as the hub. Whatever stresses are remaining bend the blades for compliance. If the semirigid rotor system is an underslung rotor, the center of gravity (CG) is below where it is attached to the mast. This underslung mounting is designed to align the blade's center of mass with a common flapping hinge so that both blades' centers of mass vary equally in distance from the center of rotation during flapping. The rotational speed of the system tends to change, but this is restrained by the inertia of the engine and flexibility of the drive system. Only a moderate amount of stiffening at the blade root is necessary to handle this restriction. Simply put, underslinging effectively eliminates geometric imbalance. Helicopters with semirigid rotors are vulnerable to a condition known as mast bumping which can cause the rotor flap stops to shear the mast. The mechanical design of the semirigid rotor system dictates downward flapping of the blades must have some physical limit. Mast bumping is the result of excessive rotor flapping. Each rotor system design has a maximum flapping angle. If flapping exceeds the design value, the static stop will contact the mast. It is the violent contact between the static stop and the mast during flight that causes mast damage or separation. This contact must be avoided at all costs. Mast bumping is directly related to how much the blade system flaps. In straight and level flight, blade flapping is minimal, perhaps 2° under usual flight conditions. Flapping angles increase slightly with high forward speeds, at low rotor rpm, at high-density altitudes, at high gross weights, and when encountering turbulence. Maneuvering the aircraft in a sideslip or during low-speed flight at extreme CG positions can induce larger flapping angles.

Feathering means:

a. Mounting the blades slightly lower than the usual plane of rotation
b. Both blades flapping together as a unit
c. The slight increase of flapping angles at high forward speeds
d. Changing the pitch angle of the blade
e. Excessive rotor flapping

18. Rigid rotor systems tend to behave like fully articulated systems through aerodynamics, but lack flapping or lead/ lag hinges. Instead, the blades accommodate these motions by bending. They cannot flap or lead/lag but they can be feathered. As advancements in helicopter aerodynamics and materials continue to improve, rigid rotor systems may become more common because the system is fundamentally easier to design and offers the best properties of both semirigid and fully articulated systems. The rigid rotor system is very responsive and is usually not susceptible to mast bumping like the semirigid or articulated systems because the rotor hubs are mounted solid to the main rotor mast. This allows the rotor and fuselage to move together as one entity and eliminates much of the oscillation usually present in the other rotor systems. Other advantages of the rigid rotor include a reduction in the weight and drag of the rotor hub and a larger flapping arm, which significantly reduces control inputs. Without the complex hinges, the rotor system becomes much more reliable and easier to maintain than the other rotor configurations. A disadvantage of this system is the quality of ride in turbulent or gusty air. Because there are no hinges to help absorb the larger loads, vibrations are felt in the cabin much more than with other rotor head designs. There are several variations of the basic three rotor head designs. The bearingless rotor system is closely related to the articulated rotor system, but has no bearings or hinges. This design relies on the structure of blades and hub to absorb stresses. The main difference between the rigid rotor system and the bearingless system is that the bearingless system has no feathering bearing—the material inside the cuff is twisted by the action of the pitch change arm. Nearly all bearingless rotor hubs are made of fiber-composite materials.

The author of this passage would probably agree most strongly with which statement about rigid rotor systems?

a. They are less popular than they used to be.
b. They result in fewer vibrations than semirigid and fully articulated systems.
c. Overall, they're superior to semirigid and fully articulated systems.
d. Overall, they're inferior to semirigid and fully articulated systems.
e. They are not as safe as semirigid and fully articulated systems.

19. While RFMs may appear similar for the same make and model of aircraft, each flight manual is unique since it contains specific information about a particular aircraft, such as the equipment installed, and weight and balance information. Therefore, manufacturers are required to include the serial number and registration on the title page to identify the aircraft to which the flight manual belongs. If a flight manual does not indicate a specific aircraft registration and serial number, it is limited to general study purposes only.

The general information section provides the basic descriptive information on the rotorcraft and the powerplant. In some manuals there is a three-view drawing of the rotorcraft that provides the dimensions of various components, including the overall length and width, and the diameter of the rotor systems. This is a good place for pilots to quickly familiarize themselves with the aircraft. Pilots need to be aware of the dimensions of the helicopter since they often must decide the suitability of an operations area for themselves, as well as hanger space, landing pad, and ground handling needs. Pilots can find definitions, abbreviations, explanations of symbology, and some of the terminology used in the manual at the end of this section. At the option of the manufacturer, metric and other conversion tables may also be included.

The operating limitations section contains only those limitations required by regulation or that are necessary for the safe operation of the rotorcraft, powerplant, systems, and equipment. It includes operating limitations, instrument markings, color coding, and basic placards. Some of the areas included are: airspeed, altitude, rotor, and powerplant limitations, including fuel and oil requirements; weight and loading distribution; and flight limitations. Concise checklists describing the recommended procedures and airspeeds for coping with various types of emergencies or critical situations can be found in this section. Some of the emergencies covered include: engine failure in a hover and at altitude, tail rotor failures, fires, and systems failures. The procedures for restarting an engine and for ditching in the water might also be included. Manufacturers may first show the emergencies checklists in an abbreviated form with the order of items reflecting the sequence of action. This is followed by amplified checklists providing additional information to clarify the procedure. To be prepared for an abnormal or emergency situation, learn the first steps of each checklist, if not all the steps. If time permits, refer to the checklist to make sure all items have been covered. For more information on emergencies, refer to Chapter 11, Helicopter Emergencies. Manufacturers are encouraged to include an optional area titled Abnormal Procedures, which describes recommended procedures for handling malfunctions that are not considered to be emergencies. This information would most likely be found in RFMs for larger helicopters.

According to this passage, which of the following information is not usually found in most RFMs?

a. How to deal with engine failure in a hover
b. The dimensions of the rotor systems
c. Operating limitations
d. How to deal with non-emergency malfunctions
e. How to deal with tail rotor failures

20. Prior to departing an unfamiliar location, make a detailed analysis of the area. There are several factors to consider during this evaluation. Besides determining the best departure path and identifying all hazards in the area, select a route that gets the helicopter from its present position to the takeoff point while avoiding all hazards, especially to the tail rotor and landing gear. Some things to consider while formulating a takeoff plan are the aircraft load, height of obstacles, the shape of the area, direction of the wind, and surface conditions. Surface conditions can consist of dust, sand and snow, as well as mud and rocks. Dust landings and snow landings can lead to a brownout or whiteout condition, which is the loss of the horizon reference. Disorientation may occur, leading to ground contact, often with fatal results. Taking off or landing on uneven terrain, mud, or rocks can cause the tail rotor to strike the surface or if the skids get caught can lead to dynamic rollover. If the helicopter is heavily loaded, determine if there is sufficient power to clear the obstacles. Sometimes it is better to pick a path over shorter obstacles than to take off directly into the wind. Also evaluate the shape of the area so that a path can be chosen that will provide you the most room to maneuver and abort the takeoff if necessary. Positioning the helicopter to the most downwind portion of the confined area gives the pilot the most distance to clear obstacles. Wind analysis also helps determine the route of takeoff. The prevailing wind can be altered by obstructions on the departure path and can significantly affect aircraft performance. There are several ways to check the wind direction before taking off. One technique is to watch the tops of the trees; another is to look for any smoke in the area. If there is a body of water in the area, look to see which way the water is rippling. If wind direction is still in question revert back to the last report that was received by either ATIS or airport tower.

The main theme of this passage is:

a. How to come up with a takeoff plan in an unfamiliar location
b. The biggest risks of taking off from an unfamiliar location
c. The importance of relying on past experience when taking off from an unfamiliar location
d. How critical wind analysis becomes when taking off from an unfamiliar location
e. Listing the different problems that can occur when taking off from an unfamiliar location

Math Skills Test

1. If $16x + 4 = 100$, what is the value of x?
   a. 6
   b. 7
   c. 8
   d. 9

2. Simplify the following expression:
   $(2x - 20)(5x + 10)$
   a. $10x^2 - 80x - 200$
   b. $70x - 200$
   c. $10x^2 - 80x + 200$
   d. $10x^2 - 120x - 200$

3. Which of the following are complementary angles?
   a. 71° and 19°
   b. 90° and 90°
   c. 90° and 45°
   d. 15° and 30°

4. Simply the following expression:
   $(2x^4)^3 + 2(y^5)^5$
   a. $8x^{64} + 2y^{3125}$
   b. $6x^7 + 2y^{10}$
   c. $6x^{12} + 2y^{25}$
   d. $8x^{12} + 2y^{25}$

5. If the measures of the three angles in a triangle are 2 : 6 : 10, what is the measure of the smallest angle?
   a. 20 degrees
   b. 40 degrees
   c. 60 degrees
   d. 80 degrees

6. If a circle has a diameter of 12cm, what is its area?
   a. $38cm^2$
   b. $113cm^2$
   c. $276cm^2$
   d. $452cm^2$

7. The length of a square is 15cm. What is its area?
   a. $30cm^2$
   b. $60cm^2$
   c. $150cm^2$
   d. $225cm^2$

8. A rectangular solid measures 12cm by 3cm by 9cm. What is its volume?

a. $36cm^3$
b. $108cm^3$
c. $324cm^3$
d. $407cm^3$

9. If $2x^2 = -4x^2 + 216$, what is the value of x?

a. 4
b. 5
c. 6
d. 7

10. The perimeter of a square is 24 m. What is its area?

a. $30m^2$
b. $36m^2$
c. $42m^2$
d. $24m^2$

11. If a rectangle has a length of 5cm and a width of 7cm, what is its area?

a. $24cm^2$
b. $35cm^2$
c. $42cm^2$
d. $56cm^2$

12. On a six-sided die, each side has a number between 1 and 6. What is the probability of throwing a 3 or a 4?

a. 1 in 6
b. 1 in 3
c. 1 in 2
d. 1 in 4

13. Solve for y in the following inequality:

$-2y \geq 24 + 6$

a. $y \leq 15$
b. $y \geq 15$
c. $y \leq -15$
d. $y \geq -15$

14. If $2x = 5x - 30$, what is the value of x?

a. 10
b. -10
c. 4.3
d. -4.3

15. Given the functions, $f(x) = 3x + 6$ and $g(x) = 2x - 8$, what is the solution of the equation, $f(x) = g(x)$?

a. $x = -12$
b. $x = -8$
c. $x = -14$
d. $x = -10$

16. Suppose the area of the square in the diagram to the right is 64 in^2. (The square is not shown actual size.) What is the area of the circle?

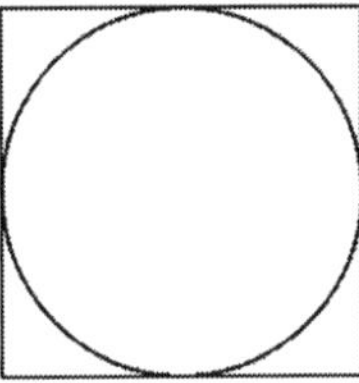

a. 16π in^2
b. 64π in^2
c. $\frac{64}{\pi}$ in^2
d. $(64 + \pi)$ in^2

17. Solve for x in the following inequality:

$4x + 23 > -3x - 6$

a. $x > -4.14$
b. $x < -4.14$
c. $x > 4.14$
d. $x < 4.14$

18. If $2x + 5x = 3x + x + 30$, what is the value of x?

a. 2.72
b. 4.29
c. 6
d. 10

19. $3x^2y + y/2 - 6x$

If x=4 and y=10, what is the value of the expression

a. 221
b. 461
c. 872
d. 1916

20. At a school carnival, three students spend an average of $10. Six other students spend an average of $4. What is the average amount of money spent by all nine students?

a. $5
b. $6
c. $7
d. $8

21. If w=7, calculate the value of the following expression:

$8w^2 - 12w + (4w - 5) + 6$

a. 279
b. 285
c. 337
d. 505

22. If x/3 + 7 = 35, what is the value of x?

a. 9.33
b. 14
c. 84
d. 126

23. In the following equation, solve for x by factoring:

$2x^2 - 7x = x^2 - 12$

a. x = -3, -4
b. x = 3, 4
c. x = 3, -4
d. x = -3, 4

24. If x is 25% of 250, what is the value of x?

a. 62.5
b. 100
c. 1000
d. 6250

25. Which of the following inequalities is correct?

a. $\frac{1}{3} < \frac{2}{7} < \frac{5}{12}$
b. $\frac{2}{7} < \frac{1}{3} < \frac{5}{12}$
c. $\frac{5}{12} < \frac{2}{7} < \frac{1}{3}$
d. $\frac{5}{12} < \frac{1}{3} < \frac{2}{7}$

26. If the volume of a cube is $8cm^3$, what is the length of the cube?

a. 1cm
b. 2cm
c. 3cm
d. 4cm

27. Simply the following expression:

$(2x^2 + 3)(2x - 1)$

a. $4x^3 - 2x^2 + 6x - 3$
b. $2x^2 + 6x - 3$
c. $4x^3 - 2x^2 + 6x + 3$
d. $4x^3 - 2x^2 - 6x - 3$

28. Simply the following expression

$(2x^4y^7m^2z) * (5x^2y^3m^8)$

a. $10x^6y^9m^{10}z$
b. $7x^6y^{10}m^{10}z$
c. $10x^5y^{10}m^{10}z$
d. $10x^6y^{10}m^{10}z$

29. A classroom contains 13 boys and 18 girls. If a student's name is chosen randomly, what is the probability it will be a girl's name?

a. 36%
b. 42%
c. 58 %
d. 72%

30. What is 10% of 40%?

a. 4%
b. 30%
c. 50%
d. 400%

Mechanical Comprehension Test

1. A cannon fires off a ship up towards a mountain range. Neglecting air resistance, where will the velocity of the projectile be greatest?

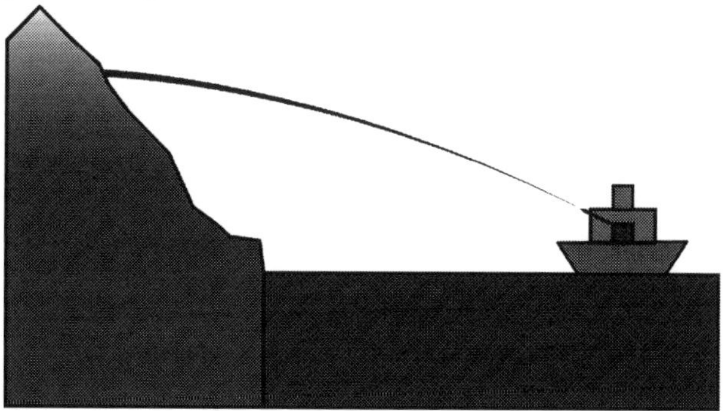

a. Exiting the muzzle
b. Halfway to the mountains
c. As it impacts the mountains

2. These pulleys are connected by belts. Which pulley travels the fastest?

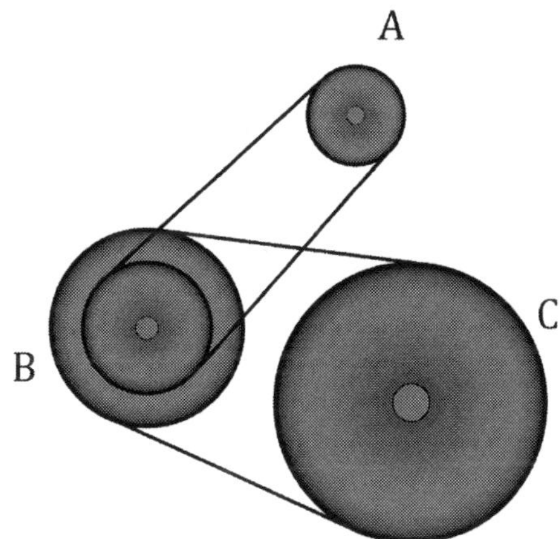

a. Pulley A
b. Pulley B
c. Pulley C

3. If Gear A is traveling at 10 rpm, how many times will Gear C rotate in 3 minutes?

a. 1.7 times
b. 3 times
c. 30 times

4. Where should the fulcrum be located to balance this beam?

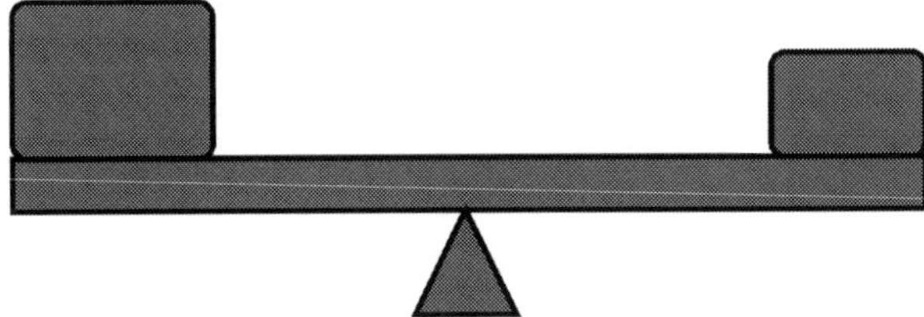

a. closer to the large mass
b. closer to the small mass
c. exactly between the two masses

5. Which orientation will require more force to pull?

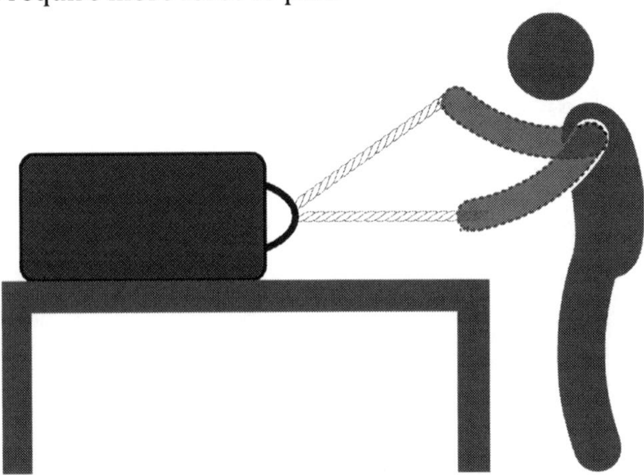

a. with the rope at an angle to the table
b. with the rope parallel to the table
c. both orientations are equal

6. The larger piston has four times as much horizontal area as the smaller piston. If the small piston is compressed 8 inches, how far will the larger piston move?

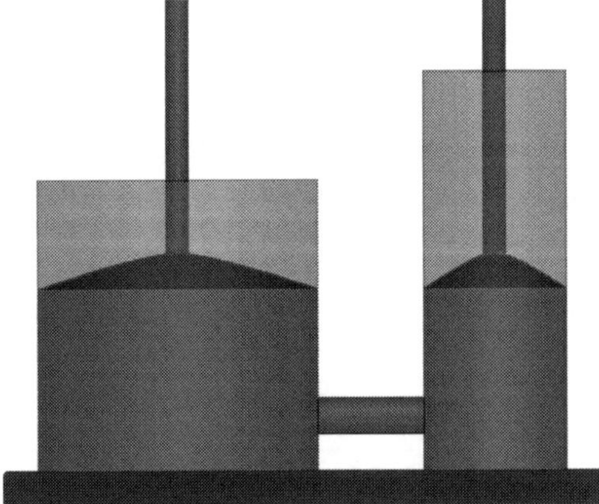

a. 8 inches
b. 2 inches
c. 32 inches

7. A wing in flight has a set of pressures causing the overall forces on the top and bottom of the wing. Where will the total force on the wing point?

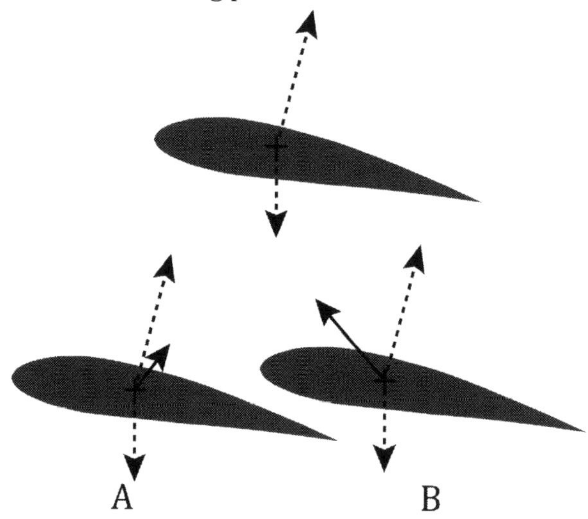

a. up and to the right
b. up and to the left
c. neither A or B

8. River water enters a section where the water spreads out into a wide, deep area. Is the water likely to speed up, slow down, or remain at a constant speed?

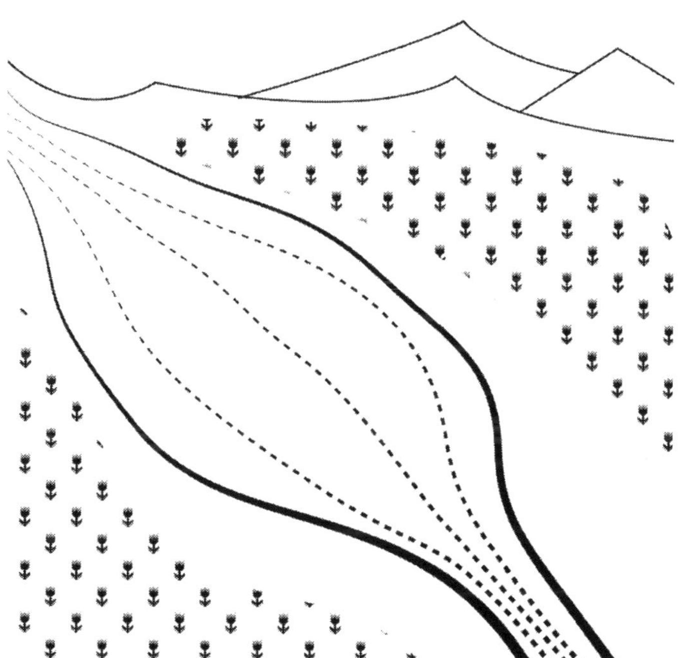

a. speed up
b. slow down
c. remain at a constant speed

9. A magnet is placed in the middle of two identical, anchored magnets. Which direction will the magnet go?

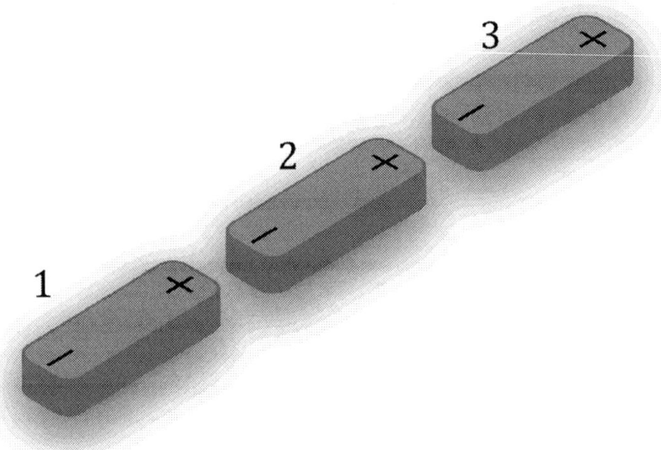

a. towards magnet 1
b. towards magnet 2
c. the magnet won't move

10. A solid substance melts at -21°C. If the object is known to change phase at 81°C, will the object be a solid, liquid, or gas at 90°C?

a. solid
b. liquid
c. gas

11. If the resistors in the circuits are identical, which circuit will have the greatest overall resistance?

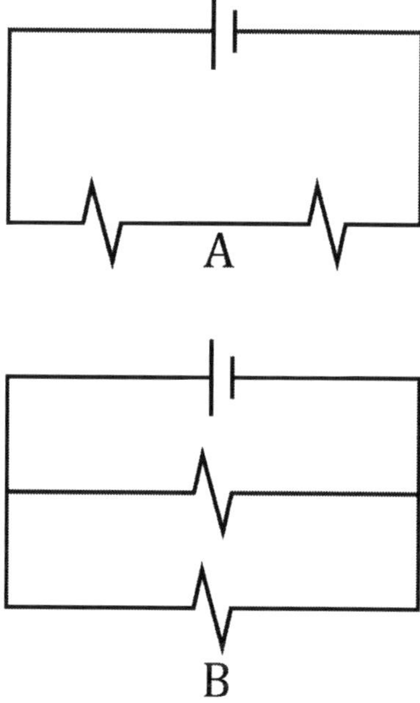

a. circuit A
b. circuit B
c. circuit A and B have the same overall resistance

12. A pendulum swings back and forth once per second. The pendulum is shortened by removing half of the string. The new frequency is 1.4 Hz (Hz=1/sec). How often will the pendulum swing back and forth in a minute?

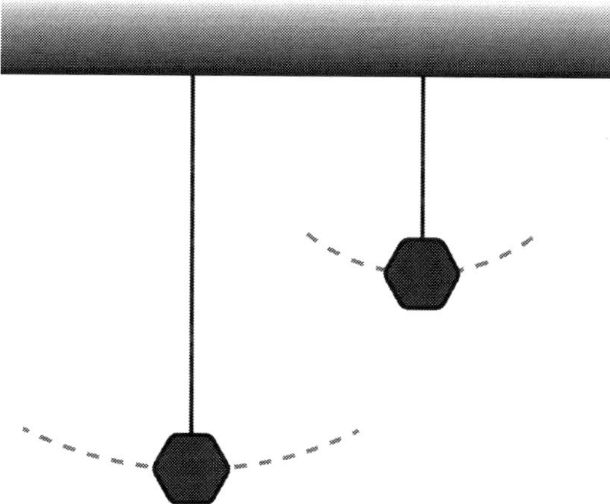

a. 84
b. 92
c. 72

13. Two identical pistons are connected by a pipe. What is the mechanical advantage of the piston system?

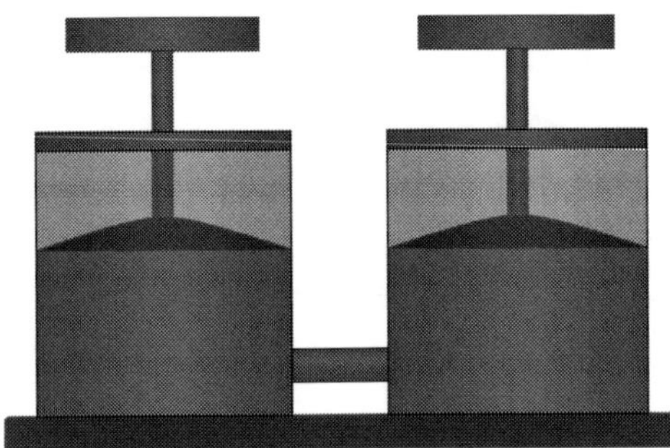

a. 0.5
b. 1
c. 2

14. A ball is thrown horizontally off a cliff at the same time that an identical ball is dropped off a cliff. How long after the dropped ball hits the ground will the thrown ball hit?

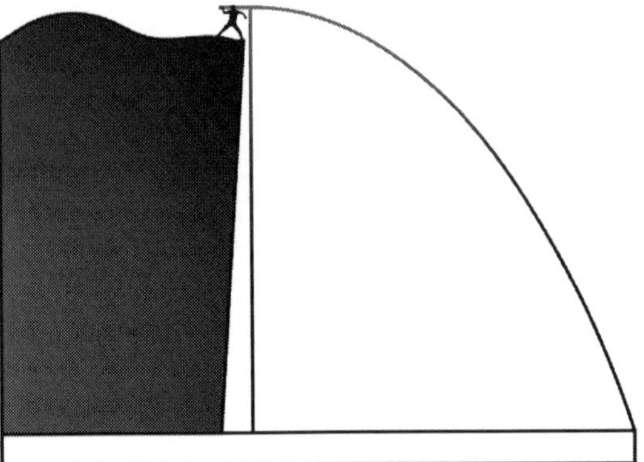

a. approximately 1 second after
b. approximately 2 seconds after
c. they will hit at the same time

15. The cam rotates at 5 rpm. How many times will the follower (needle) move up and down in a minute?

a. 20
b. 72
c. 140

16. Which of the following are not ways to increase the torque applied to a wrench?

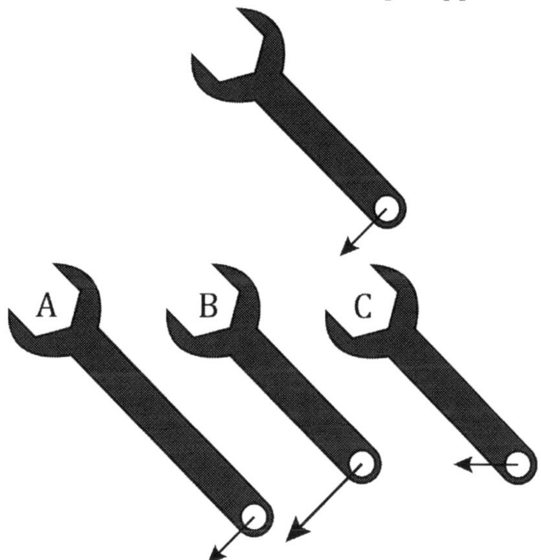

a. increase the length from the center to the applied force
b. increase the force
c. angle the force toward the center

17. A ball is pushed down into a vertical spring. The ball is released and flies upward. Which best describes the states of energy the ball underwent?

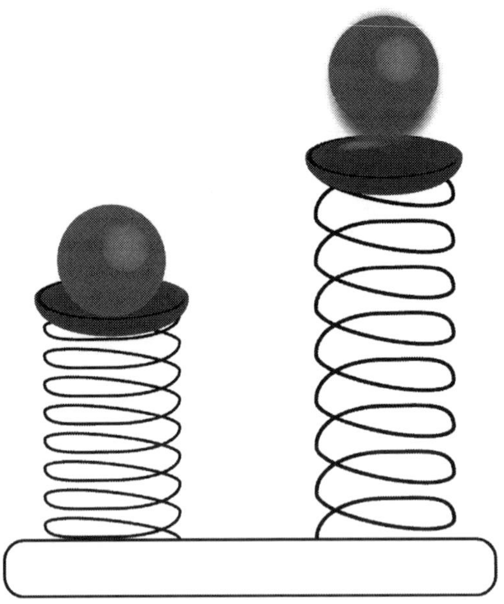

a. convective energy to potential energy
b. potential energy to kinetic energy
c. kinetic energy to potential energy

18. A vacuum tank is held by weights at a depth of 50 feet underwater. If the tank is raised to a depth of 25 feet, will the pressure on the walls of the tank increase, decrease, or stay the same?

a. increase
b. decrease
c. stay the same

19. Adding salt to water raises its density. Will salt water have a lower, higher, or the same specific gravity than 1?

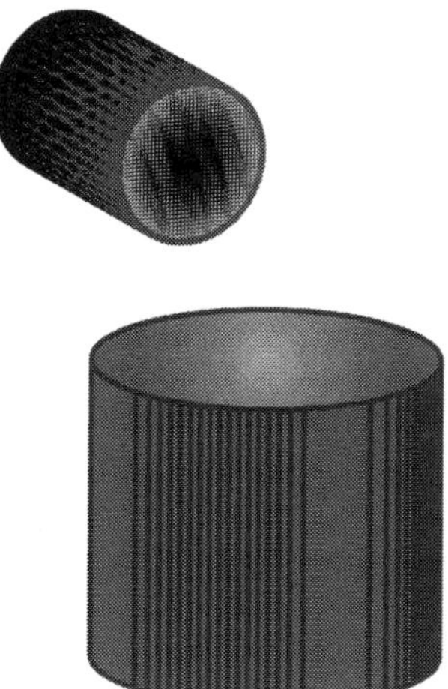

a. lower
b. higher
c. the same

20. Which of the following is an example of convective heat transfer?

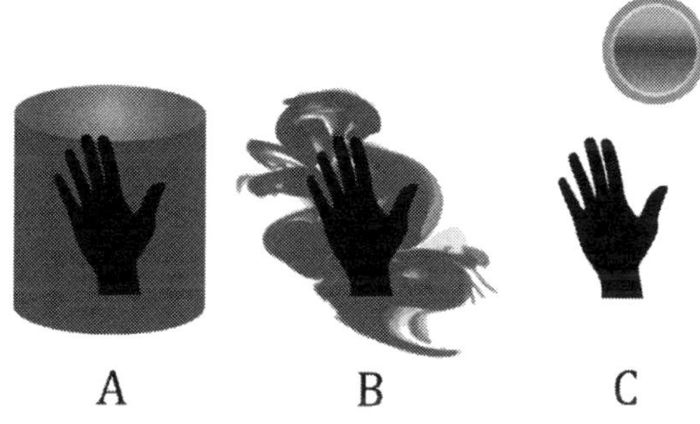

a. a man burns his hand on a hot pot
b. a man burns his hand in steam
c. a man gets a sun burn

21. Which of the following is the electrical component which holds a voltage across a gap between two conductive materials?

a. resistor
b. inductor
c. capacitor

22. Which of these wrenches is likely to provide the greatest torque with a set force?

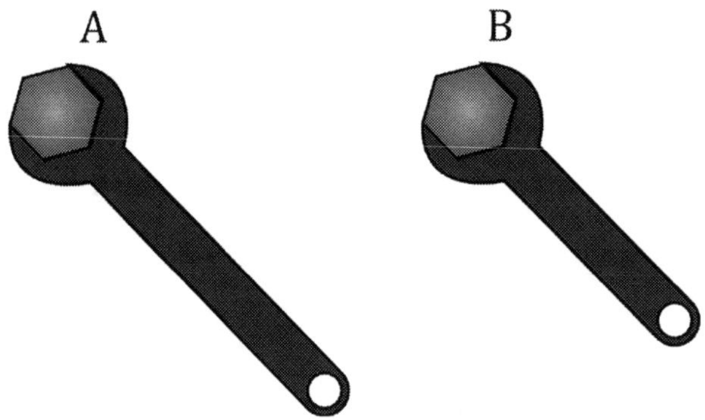

a. wrench A
b. wrench B
c. both wrenches will provide the same torque

23. Which of the following is true of this circuit?

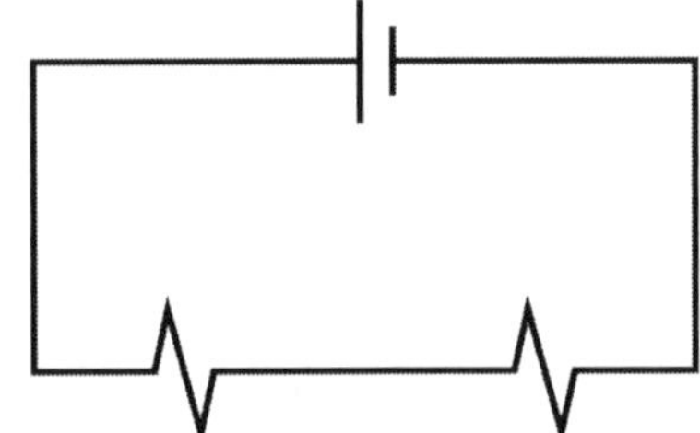

a. the voltage is the same everywhere
b. the current is the same everywhere
c. there is no current

24. Which device does not measure current in an electrical system?

a. ammeter
b. multimeter
c. voltmeter

25. A ball is thrown straight into the air with an initial kinetic energy of 100 ft-lb. What is the potential energy of the ball at half of the height of the flight path?

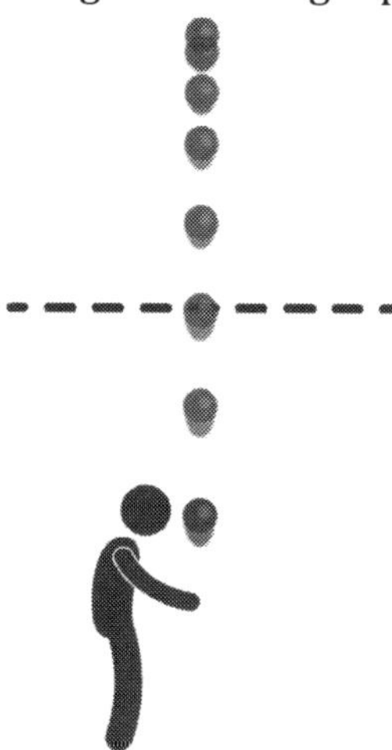

a. 33 ft-lb
b. 50 ft-lb
c. 66 ft-lb

26. An increase in mechanical advantage with a set motion for the load and a set applied force necessitates an increase in ______ the applied force?

a. the distance traveled by
b. the angle of action of
c. the potential energy behind

27. A windlass drum has two sections with different circumferences. When winding the drum, one side of the rope winds around the large section and the other unwinds from the small section. If the large section of the drum has a circumference of 3.5 ft and the other section has a circumference of 1 ft, how far will the weight lift with two full turns of the drum?

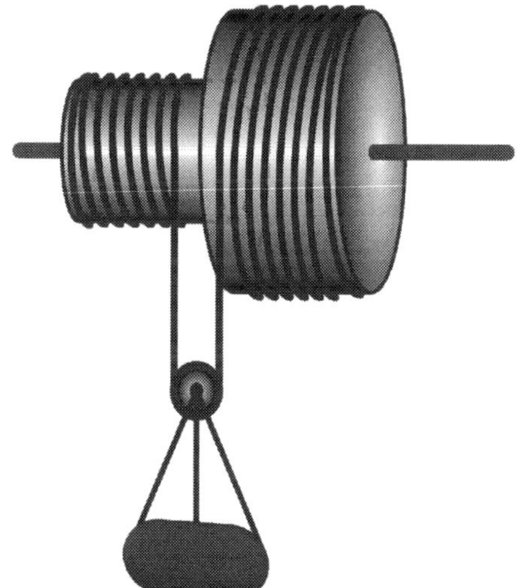

a. 2.5 feet
b. 9 feet
c. 4.5 feet

28. Which type of situation will lead to condensation on the outside of pipes?

a. hot liquid in the pipe and cold air outside the pipe
b. cold liquid in the pipe and colder air outside the pipe
c. cold liquid in the pipe and hot air outside the pipe

29. Which color will absorb the most radiation?

a. black
b. green
c. dark yellow

30. Two gears (30 and 18 teeth) mesh. If the smaller gear rotates 3 times, how many times will the larger gear rotate?

a. 1.6 times
b. 1.8 times
c. 3 times

Answer Key and Explanations

Simple Drawings Test

Question	Answer	Question	Answer	Question	Answer	Question	Answer
1	C	26	C	51	B	76	B
2	B	27	A	52	D	77	E
3	E	28	E	53	E	78	C
4	A	29	C	54	C	79	B
5	B	30	D	55	B	80	A
6	A	31	D	56	A	81	B
7	D	32	A	57	A	82	D
8	C	33	C	58	C	83	E
9	B	34	A	59	D	84	A
10	A	35	E	60	B	85	C
11	D	36	B	61	A	86	D
12	C	37	B	62	D	87	E
13	B	38	D	63	B	88	C
14	D	39	C	64	C	89	D
15	A	40	D	65	E	90	B
16	E	41	A	66	A	91	C
17	C	42	B	67	D	92	A
18	B	43	E	68	C	93	B
19	E	44	B	69	A	94	B
20	B	45	B	70	A	95	E
21	A	46	B	71	B	96	C
22	D	47	E	72	C	97	B
23	C	48	E	73	B	98	E
24	D	49	C	74	A	99	B
25	B	50	A	75	A	100	C

Hidden Figures Test

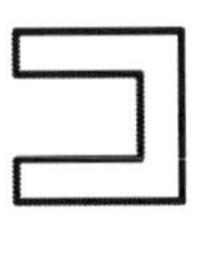
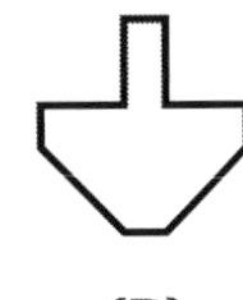

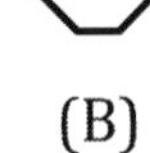

(A) (B) (C) (D) (E)

1. (B)

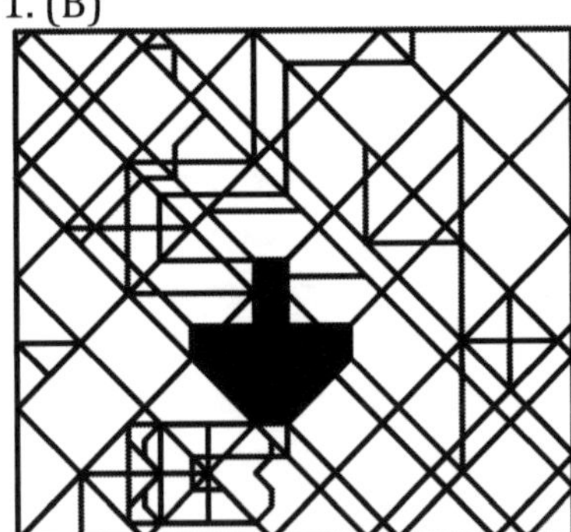

4. (C)

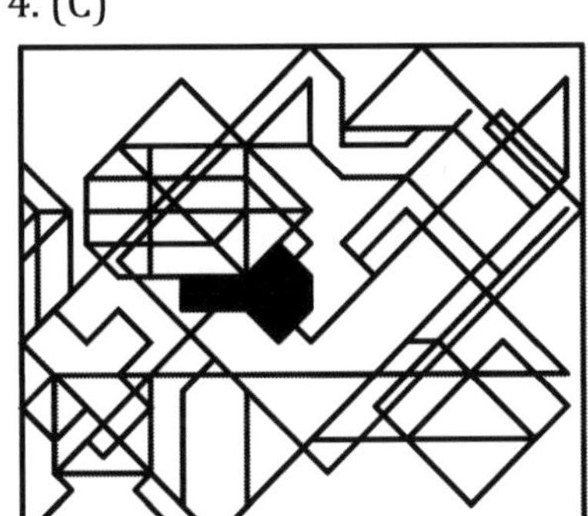

2. (D)

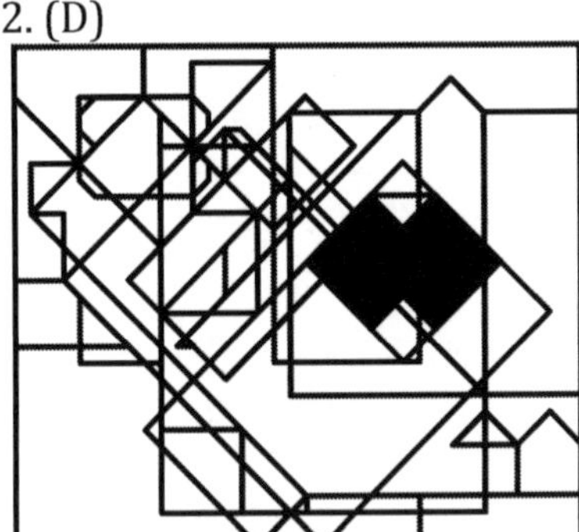

5. (A)

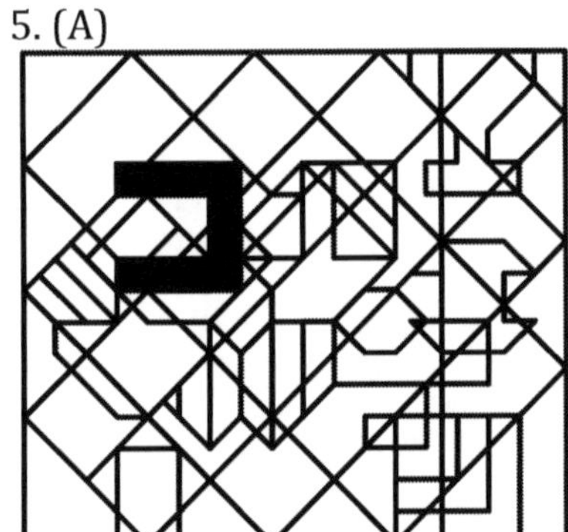

3. (E)

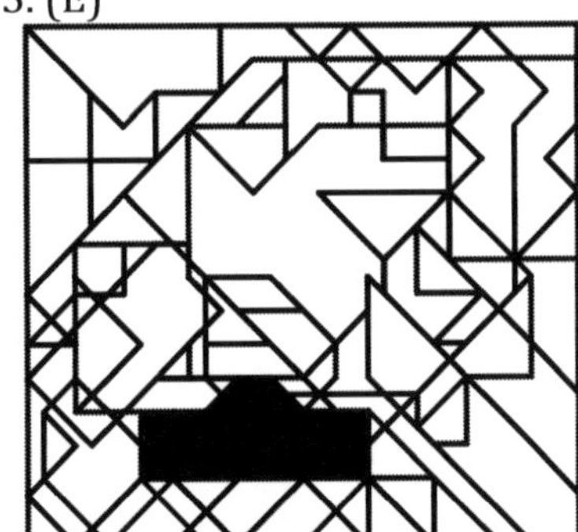

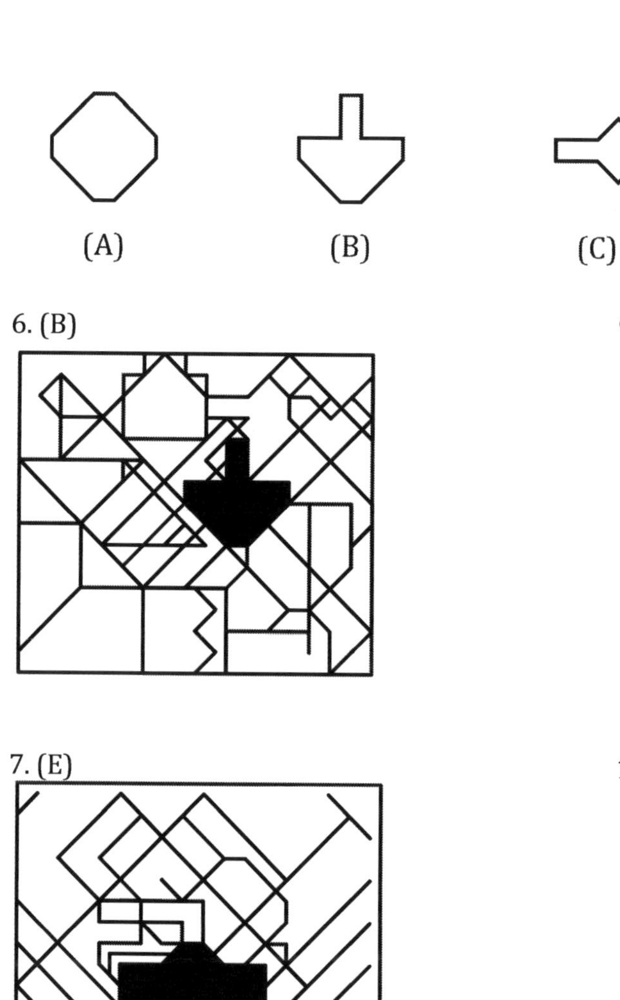

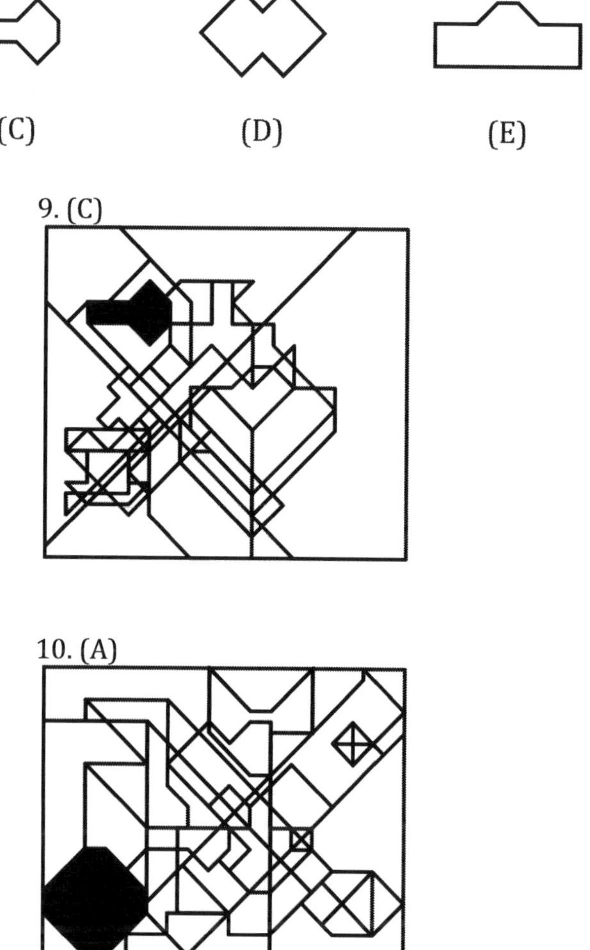

(A) (B) (C) (D) (E)

6. (B)

9. (C)

7. (E)

10. (A)

8. (D)

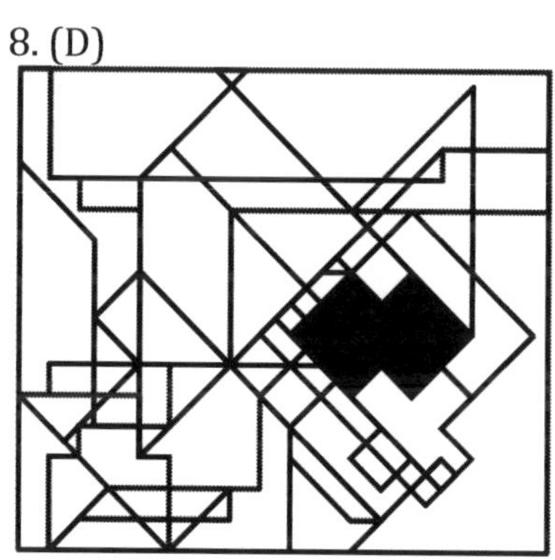

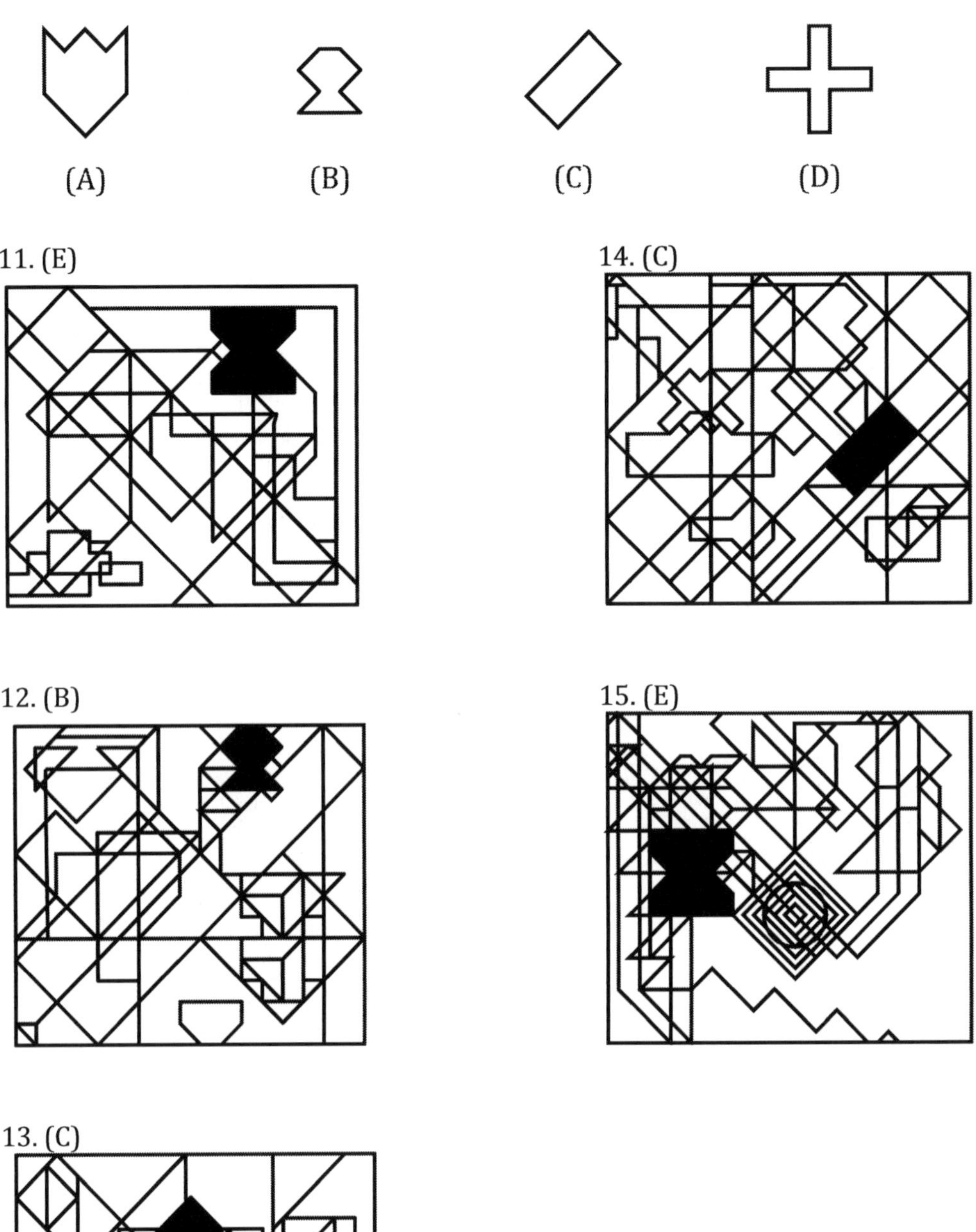
(A)
(B)
(C)
(D)
(E)
11. (E)
14. (C)
12. (B)
15. (E)
13. (C)

(A)

(B)

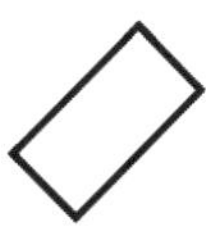

(C)

(D)

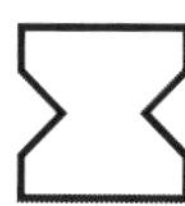

(E)

16. (A)

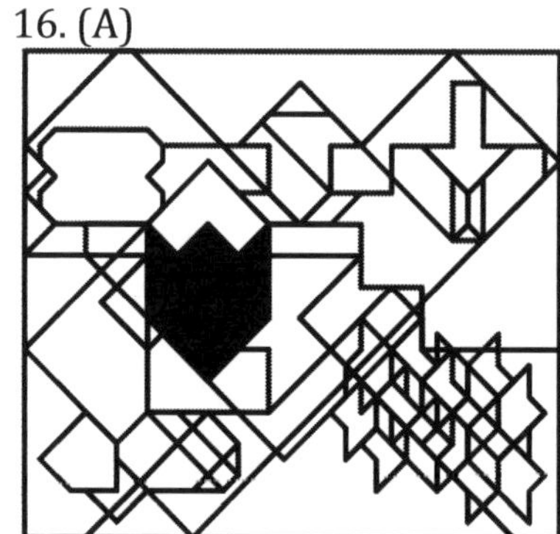

19. (B)

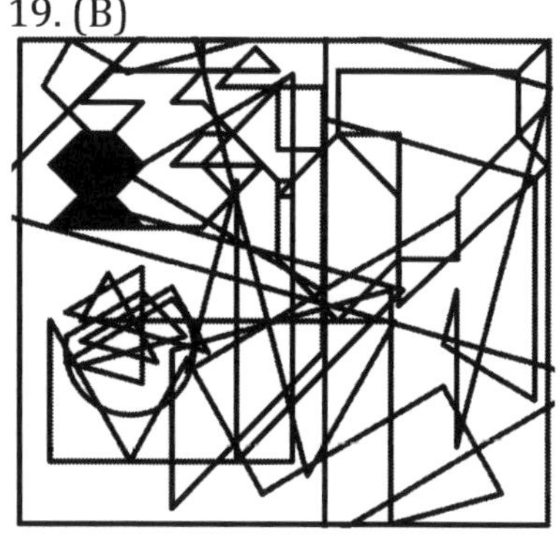

17. (D)

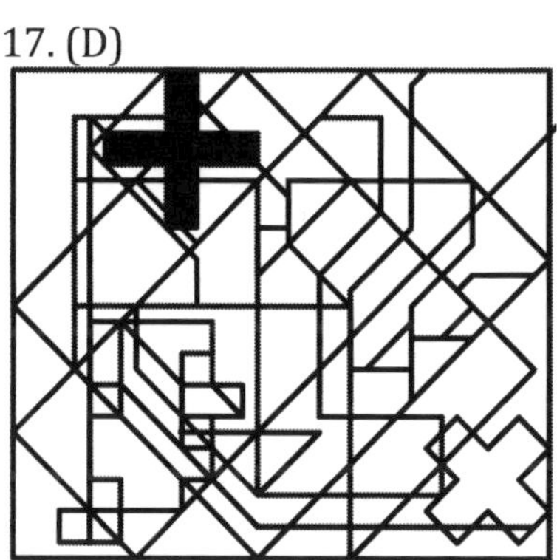

20. (C)

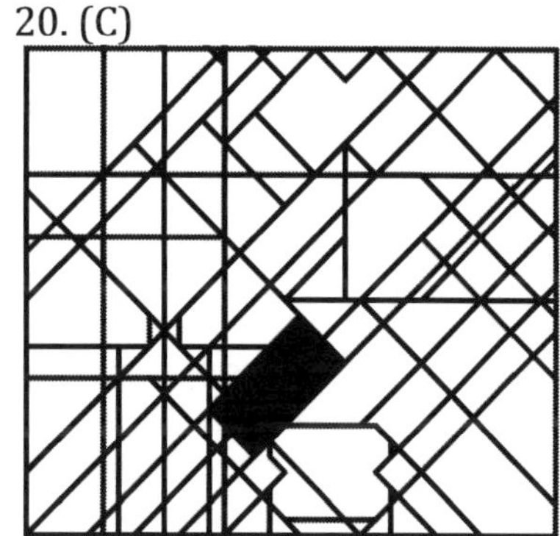

18. (A)

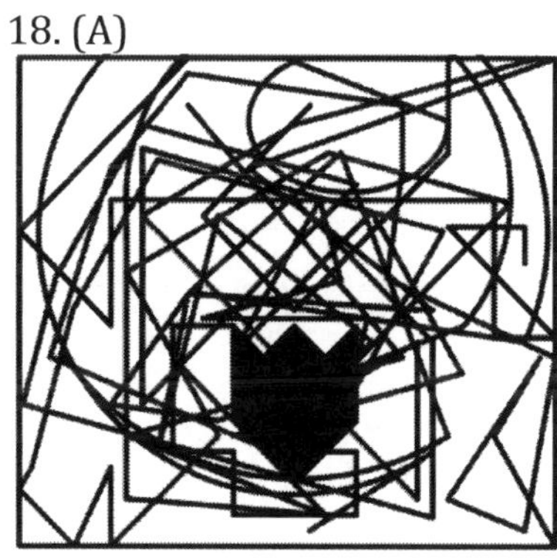

(A)

(B)

(C)

(D)

(E)

21. (E)

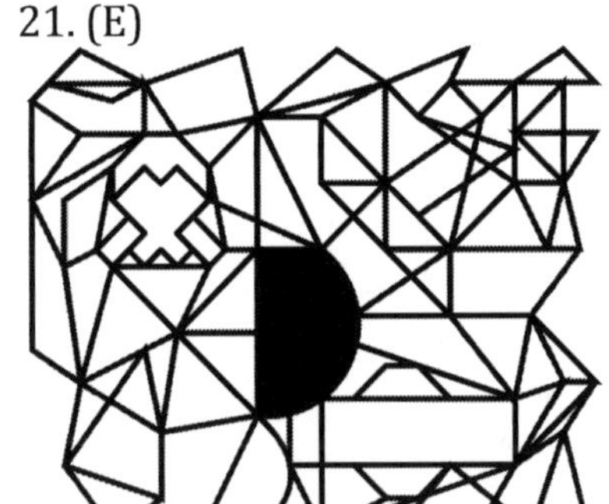
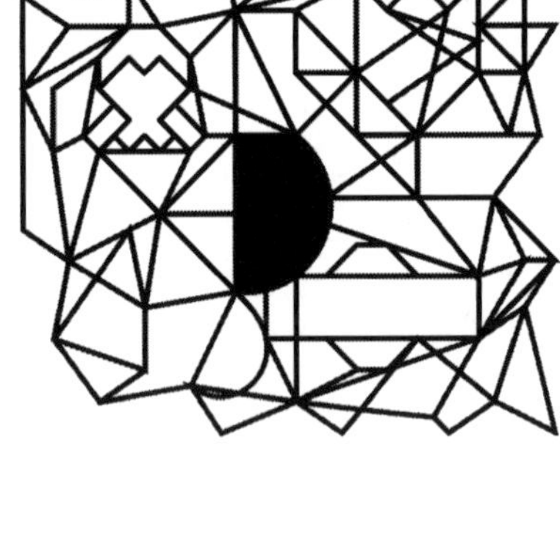

22. (A)

23. (D)

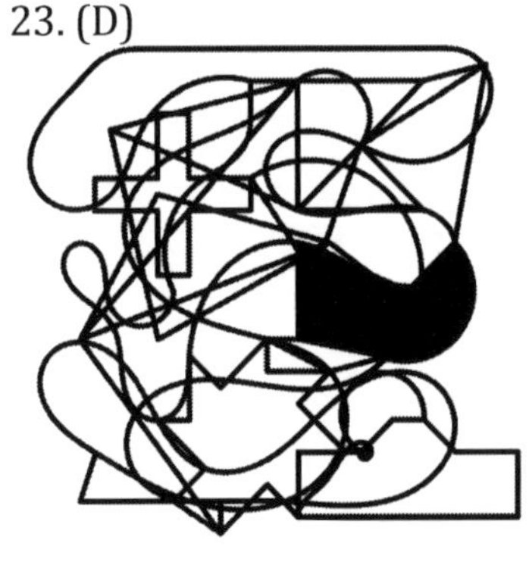

24. (B)

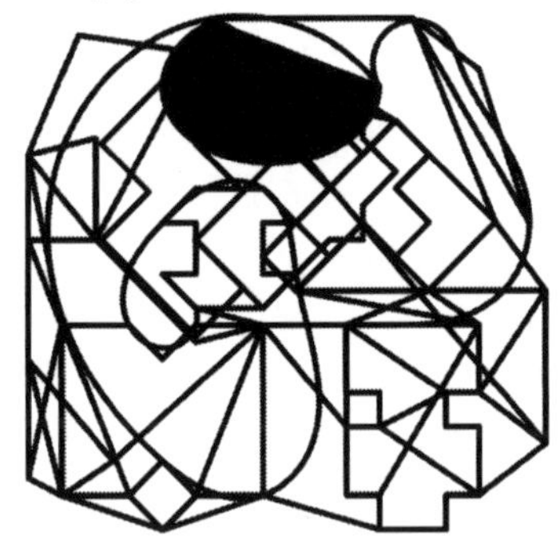

25. (C)

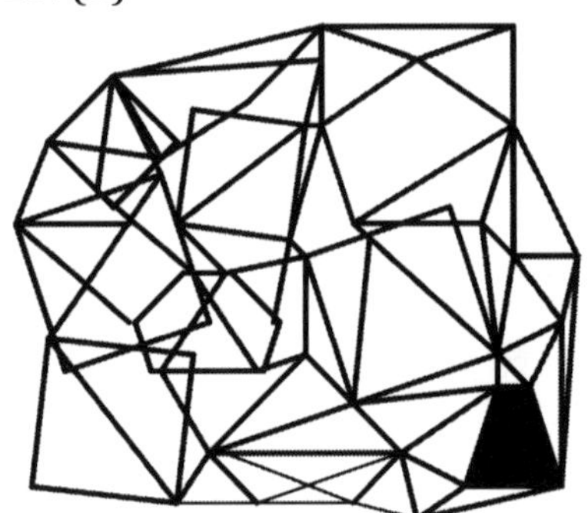

(A)

(B)

(C)

(D)

(E)

26. (A)

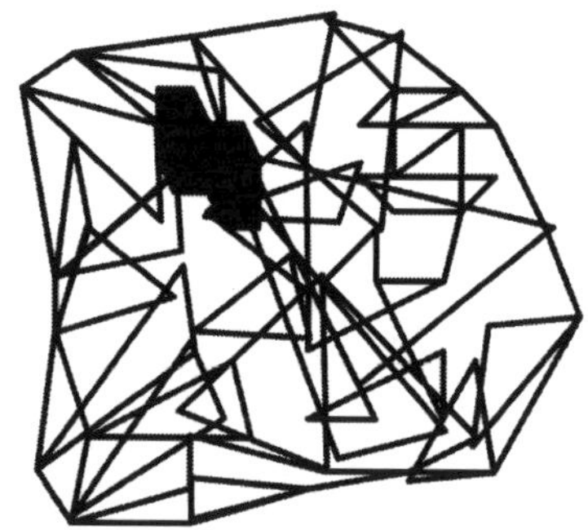

29. (B)

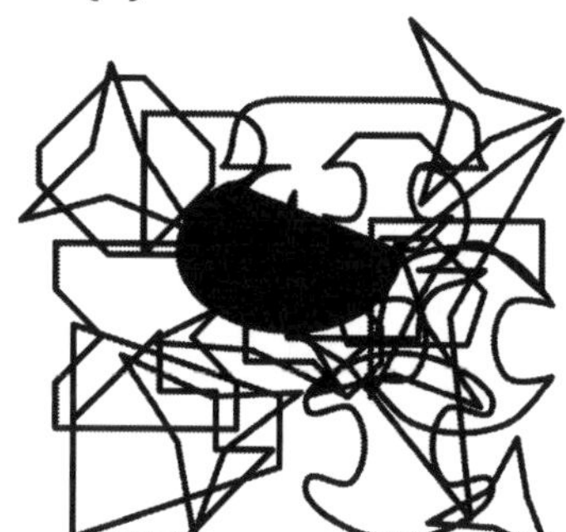

27. (E)

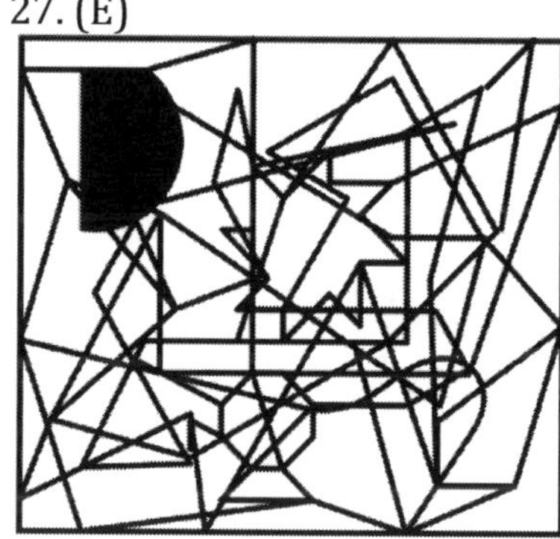

30. (C)

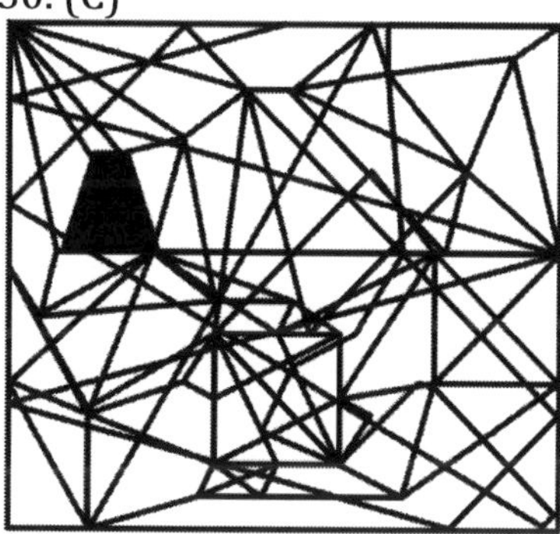

28. (D)

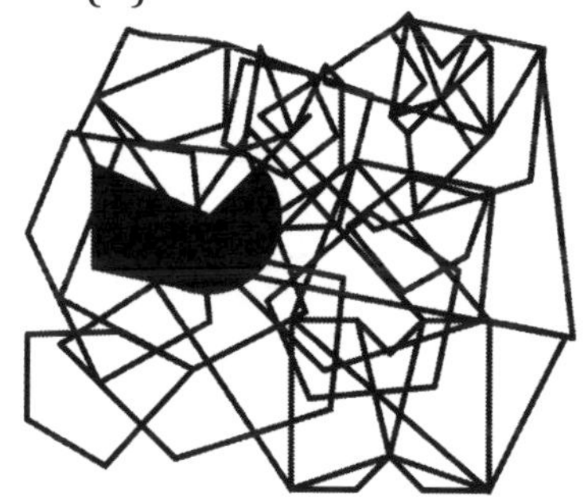

(A)

(B)

(C)

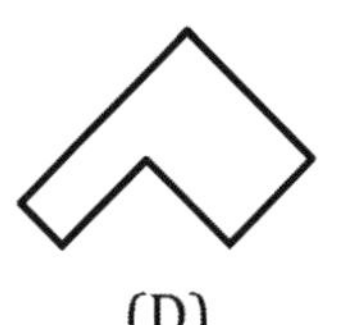
(D)

(E)

31. (A)

34. (B)

32. (D)

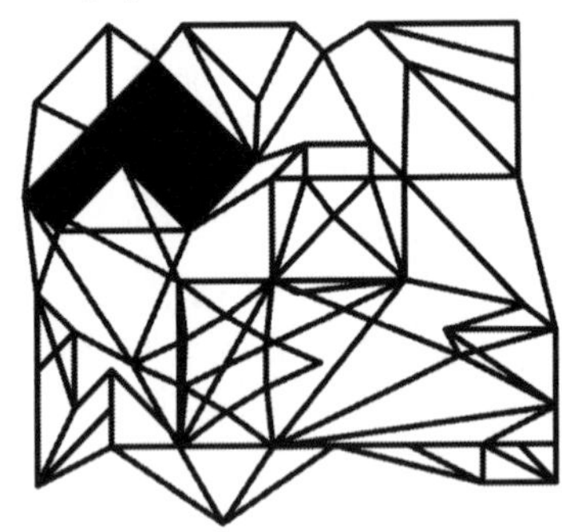

35. (D)

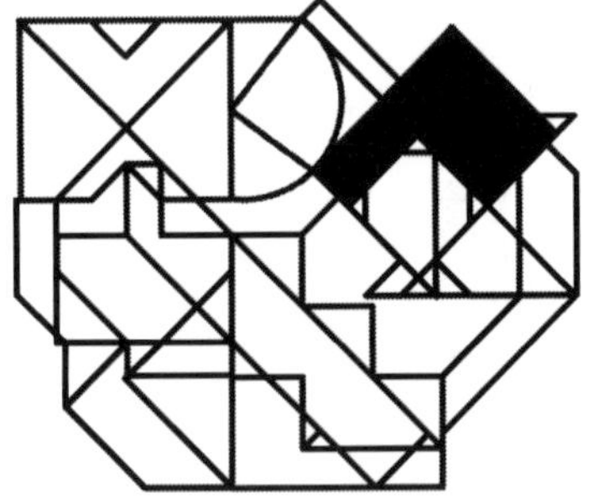

33. (C)

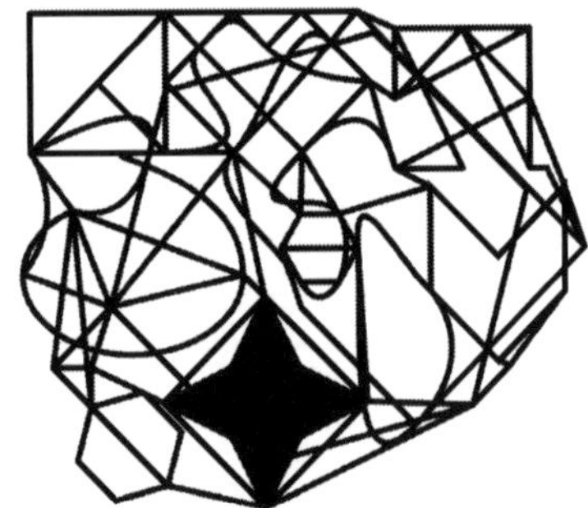

(A)

(B)

(C)

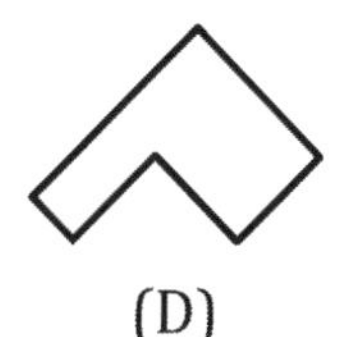
(D)

(E)

36. (C)

37. (A)

38. (E)

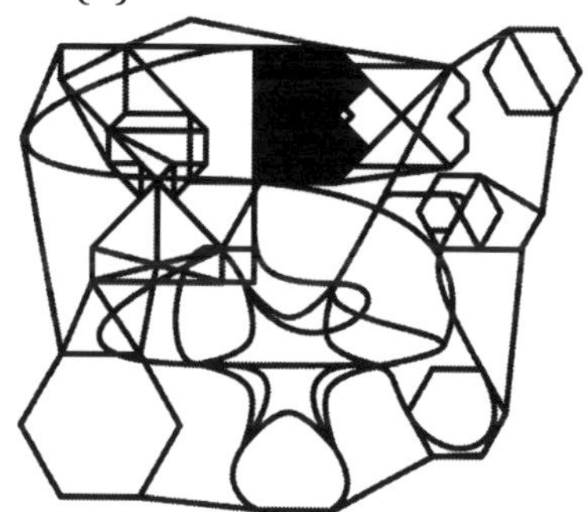

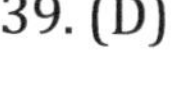
39. (D)

40. (A)

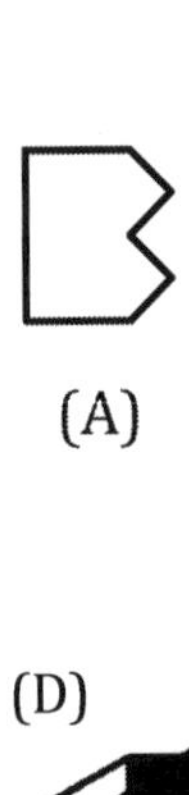
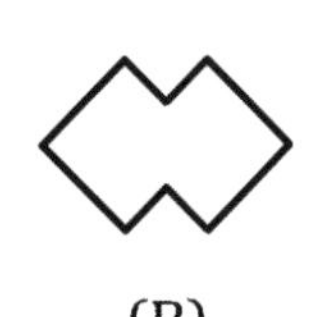

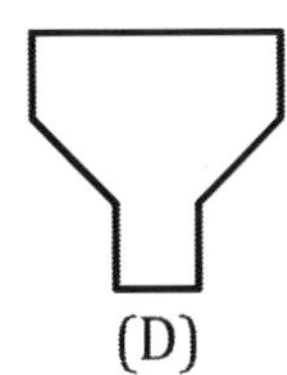

(A) (B) (C) (D) (E)

41. (D)

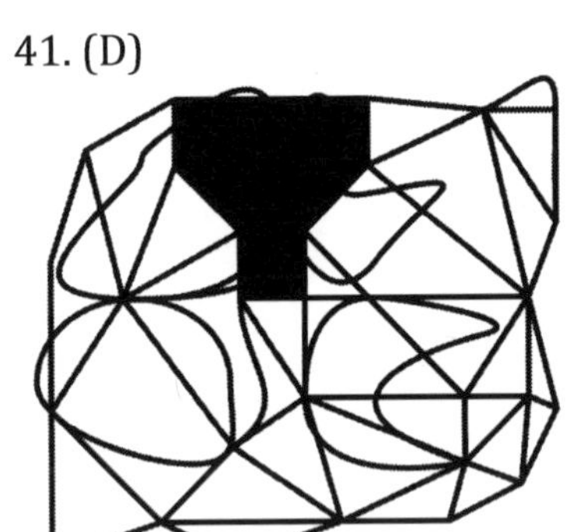

42. (A)

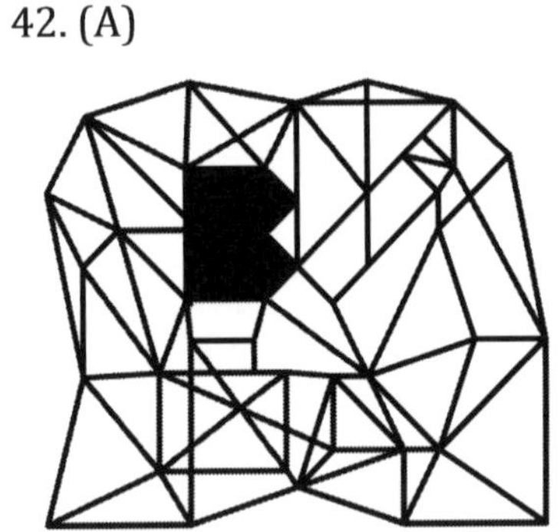

43. (B)

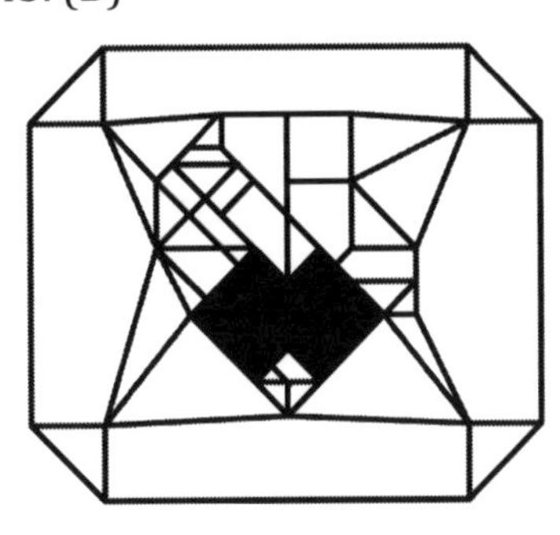

44. (A)

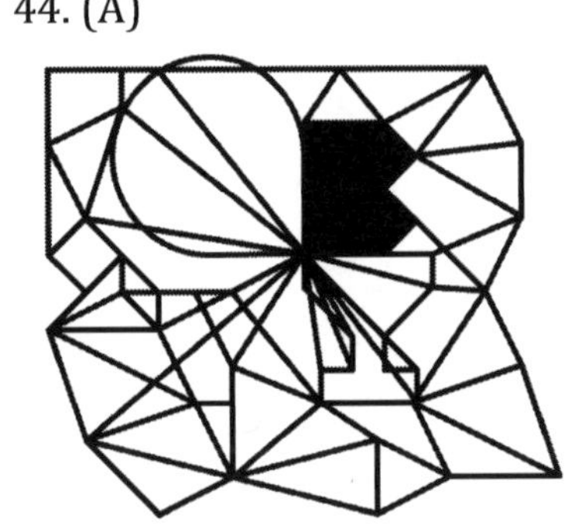

45. (E)

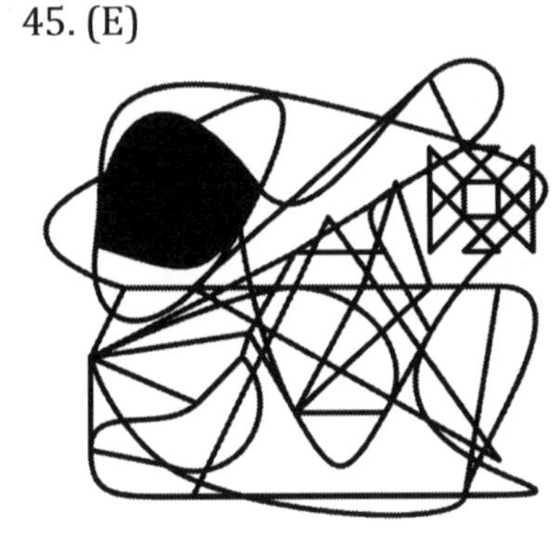

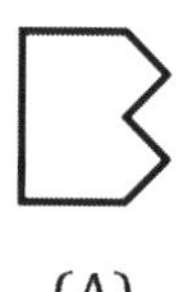
(A)

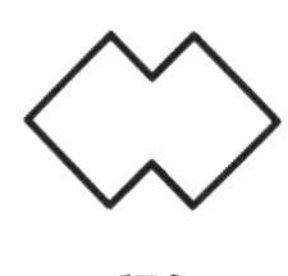
(B)

(C)

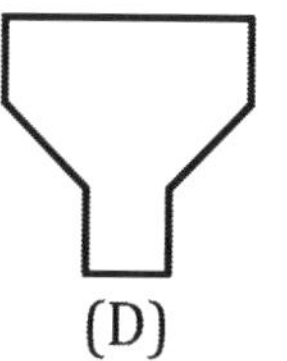
(D)

(E)

46. (C)

47. (B)

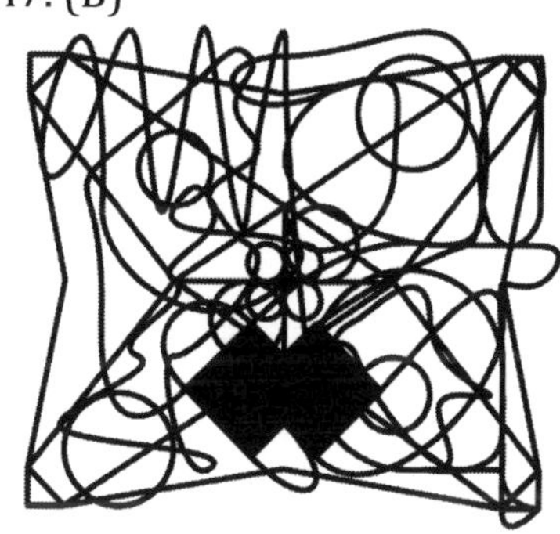

48. (A)

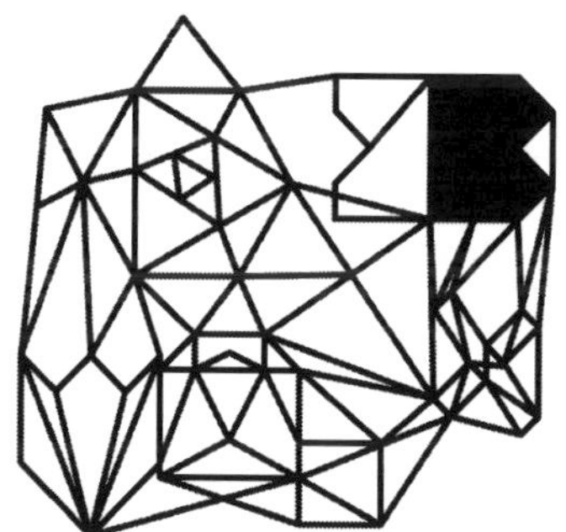

49. (D)

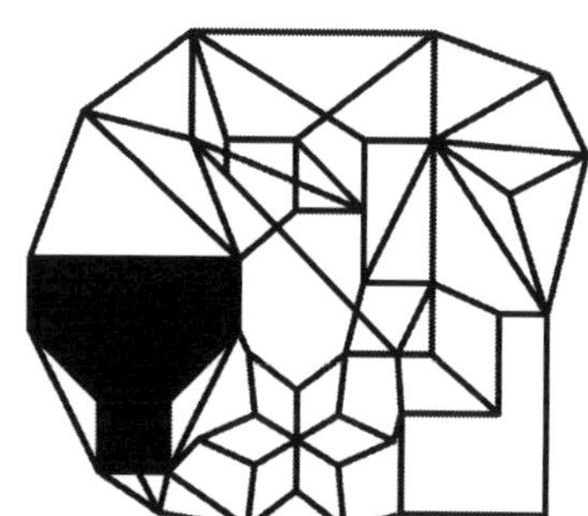

50. (C)

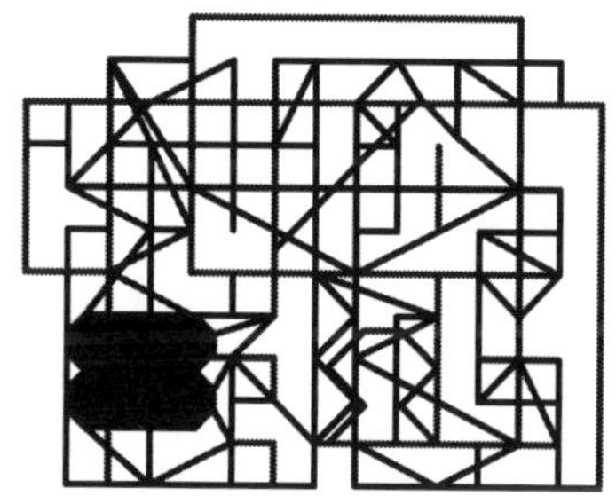

Army Aviation Information Test

1. E: Parasite. The force that resists the movement of a helicopter through the air and is produced when lift is developed is called drag. Drag must be overcome by the engine to turn the rotor. Drag always acts parallel to the relative wind. Total drag is composed of three types of drag: profile, induced, and parasite.

2. A: Governors are common on all turbine helicopters (as it is a function of the fuel control system of the turbine engine), and used on some piston powered helicopters.

3. E: The horizontal reference datum is an imaginary vertical plane or point, arbitrarily fixed somewhere along the longitudinal axis of the helicopter, from which all horizontal distances are measured for weight and balance purposes. There is no fixed rule for its location. It is established by the helicopter manufacturer.

4. B: The cyclic position relative to the horizon determines the helicopter's travel and attitude.

5. D: 45 knots. Training maneuvers for rapid deceleration should always be done into the wind. After leveling off at an altitude between 25 and 40 feet, depending upon the manufacturer's recommendations, accelerate to the desired entry speed, which is approximately 45 knots for most training helicopters.

6. B: The Bell TH-67 has been the Army's primary training helicopter since 1993.

7. D: Translational thrust occurs when the tail rotor becomes more aerodynamically efficient during the transition from hover to forward flight. As the tail rotor works in progressively less turbulent air, this improved efficiency produces more antitorque thrust, causing the nose of the aircraft to yaw left (with a main rotor turning counterclockwise) and forces the pilot to apply right pedal (decreasing the AOA in the tail rotor blades) in response.

8. C: The solidity ratio is the ratio of the total rotor blade area, which is the combined area of all the main rotor blades, to the total rotor disk area. This ratio provides a means to measure the potential for a rotor system to provide thrust and lift.

9. B: Torque pedals. There are three major controls in a helicopter that the pilot must use during flight. They are the collective pitch control, the cyclic pitch control, and the antitorque pedals or tail rotor control. In addition to these major controls, the pilot must also use the throttle control, which is usually mounted directly to the collective pitch control in order to fly the helicopter.

10. C: Each gallon of reciprocating engine oil weighs 7.5 pounds.

11. D: 100. In steep turns, the nose drops. In most cases, energy (airspeed) must be traded to maintain altitude as the required excess engine power may not be available (to maintain airspeed in a 2G/60° turn, rotor thrust/engine power must increase by 100 percent).

12. D: 300 and 500. It is important to strike a balance between a reconnaissance conducted too high and one too low. It should not be flown so low that a pilot must divide attention between studying the area and avoiding obstructions to flight. A high reconnaissance should be flown at an altitude of 300 to 500 feet above the surface.

13. C: The CH-47 Chinook came to prominence in the Vietnam War and is still in current use.

14. C: Cyclic feathering changes angle of incidence differentially around the rotor system. Cyclic feathering creates a differential lift in the rotor system by changing the AOA differentially across the rotor system. Aviators use cyclic feathering to control attitude of the rotor system.

15. C: Bernoulli's principle describes the relationship between internal fluid pressure and fluid velocity. It is a statement of the law of conservation of energy and helps explain why an airfoil develops an aerodynamic force.

16. D: 100% of maximum. Normal helicopter landings usually require high power settings, with terminations to a hover requiring the highest power setting.

17. C: Should be about the pace of a brisk walk. During an approach to a pinnacle or ridgeline, groundspeed is more difficult to judge because visual references are farther away than during approaches over trees or flat terrain. Pilots must continually perceive the apparent rate of closure by observing the apparent change in size of the landing zone features. Avoid the appearance of an increasing rate of closure to the landing site. The apparent rate of closure should be that of a brisk walk.

18. C: The OH-58A Kiowa has an empty weight of 1,583 pounds.

19. B: Translating tendency. During hovering flight, a single main rotor helicopter tends to move in the direction of tail rotor thrust. This lateral (or sideward) movement is called translating tendency.

20. D: Cyclic pitch. An increase in pitch angle increases angle of attack; a decrease in pitch angle decreases angle of attack.

21. B: Effective weight. When a helicopter is maneuvering, centrifugal force adds extra weight to the fuselage. This extra weight, when added to the weight of the helicopter, crew, passengers, and cargo, becomes the effective weight of the helicopter, or load factor.

22. E: None - the first four answers are all true in most helicopters.

23. A: Parallel to the ridgeline and into the wind. If there is a need to climb to a pinnacle or ridgeline, it should be done on the upwind side, when practicable, to take advantage of any updrafts. The approach flightpath should be parallel to the ridgeline and into the wind as much as possible.

24. E: The UH-72 Lakota is the US Army's primary light utility helicopter.

25. A: The Coriolis Effect is also referred to as the law of conservation of angular momentum. It states that the value of angular momentum of a rotating body does not change unless an external force is applied. In other words, a rotating body continues to rotate with the same rotational velocity until some external force is applied to change the speed of rotation.

26. A: The collective pitch control (or simply "collective" or "thrust lever") is located on the left side of the pilot's seat and is operated with the left hand.

27. D: Hovering in a strong headwind. A forward CG is easily recognized when coming to a hover following a vertical takeoff, but not as obvious when hovering into a strong wind, since less rearward cyclic displacement is required than when hovering with no wind.

28. C: Increase the collective. To enter a climb in a helicopter while maintaining airspeed, the first actions are increasing the collective and throttle, and adjusting the pedals as necessary to maintain a centered ball in the slip/skid indicator.

29. D: 13 and 15. An approach angle of approximately 13° to 15° is considered a steep approach.

30. D: The AH-64 Apache features four hardpoints mounted on stub-wing pylons, and usually carries a combination of AGM-114 Hellfire missiles and Hydra 70 rocket pods.

31. A: Factors that can make it unsafe to take off operating at maximum gross weight include high altitude, high temperature, and high humidity conditions, which result in a high-density altitude.

32. B: In a standard airplane traffic pattern, the second of the five legs is known as the crosswind leg.

33. B: 5. The slope must be shallow enough to hold the helicopter against it with the cyclic during the entire landing. A slope of 5° is considered maximum for normal operation of most helicopters. Pilots should always consult the RFM or POH for the specific limitations of the helicopter being flown.

34. C: The CH-47 Chinook has a maximum speed of 170 knots.

35. C: 16 and 24. While transitioning to forward flight at about 16 to 24 knots, the helicopter goes through effective translational lift (ETL).

36. C: The antitorque pedals control in which direction the nose of the helicopter is pointing.

37. D: Each gallon of JP-4 jet fuel weighs 6.5 pounds.

38. C: 25. A hover taxi is used when operating below 25 feet above ground level (AGL).

39. B: 100. The helicopter should be kept in trim just prior to loss of effective translational lift (approximately 25 knots). Below 100' AGL, the antitorque pedals should be adjusted to align the helicopter with the intended touchdown point.

40. A: The primary use of OH-58 Kiowa helicopters is armed reconnaissance in support of ground troops.

Spatial Apperception Test

Problem	Answer	Description
1	B	out to sea, diving, and banking right
2	D	coastline right, diving, and wings level
3	E	coastline right, level flight, and banking left
4	B	coastline right, diving, and banking right
5	E	coastline left, climbing, and wings level
6	D	out to sea, level flight, and banking left
7	A	out to sea, diving, and banking left
8	A	out to sea, climbing, and wings level
9	B	coastline left, diving, and banking right
10	B	coastline left, level flight, and banking right
11	B	coastline right, climbing, and wings level
12	D	out to sea, climbing, and banking left
13	C	coastline left, diving, and banking left
14	B	coastline left, climbing, and banking right
15	D	out to sea, climbing, and banking right
16	C	coastline right, level flight, and banking right
17	C	coastline right, level flight, and wings level
18	B	coastline left, level flight, and banking left
19	C	coastline left, level flight, and wings level
20	D	coastline left, climbing, and banking left
21	D	coastline left, diving, and wings level
22	C	coastline right, climbing, and banking right
23	A	out to sea, level flight, and wings level
24	D	out to sea, diving, and wings level
25	B	out to sea, level flight, and banking right

Reading Comprehension Test

1. C: Taking the entire passage as a whole, it shows that the development of turbine engine powered helicopters is the factor that was most responsible for a huge increase in the number of helicopters in use.

2. D: Twin tilt rotors are not mentioned in the passage, while all the other answer choices are.

3. A: The passages states: "The variation from absolutely level depends on the particular helicopter and the horizontal stabilizer function."

4. C: This statement is the only one backed up by the contents of the passage.

5. D: Fools rush in where angels fear to tread expresses the idea that people who are new or inexperienced at something will often take dangerous chances that wiser or more experienced people would steer clear of, which most closely matches the author's theme that unbridled curiosity in a pilot can lead to disaster. He is not saying curiosity is bad in and of itself; only that it needs to have limits. That's why Curiosity killed the cat is incorrect.

6. C: Environment. While the pilot has less control over external pressures than over himself/herself and the aircraft, a pilot still has some control over these pressures. A pilot can refuse to yield to pressure to take risky chances in order to meet a schedule or accomplish a mission. However, when it comes to weather and other environmental factors, the pilot has no control whatsoever, and must deal with them as they are.

7. A: The passage is a broad overview of single-pilot resource management (SRM).

8. E: Improving a pilot's knowledge and skills is an effective way to promoting safe operation is a good summary of the message the author is trying to get across.

9. D: The Minimum Equipment List (MEL) is the correct answer, based on this part of the passage: The FAA considers an approved MEL to be a supplemental type certificate (STC) issued to an aircraft by serial number and registration number. It therefore becomes the authority to operate that aircraft in a condition other than originally type certificated.

10. E: The briefing covers the information in the first four answer choices, but does not instruct passengers on where to collect items stowed for the flight.

11. C: The main reason pilots should avoid leaving the cockpit with the engines running and rotors going during turnarounds is that it's unsafe.

12. B: The author's main point in this passage is that pilots can best prepare for emergencies by planning ahead – taking the time to master the helicopter and its systems, and anticipating emergencies and how to respond to them before they happen.

13. C: The passage states that high frequency vibrations can cause numbness in the pilot's leg.

14. B: According to the passage, the amount the collective can be lowered depends on altitude.

15. A: While many factors go into an exact technical definition of attitude, the relation of the helicopter to the horizon is a good thumbnail description.

16. E: While some of the errors listed are more common during attitude instrument flying, that doesn't imply that the less common ones are any less dangerous. Any of the mistakes listed can be extremely dangerous, and can lead to an accident.

17. D: From the passage: The semirigid rotor is also capable of feathering, which means that the pitch angle of the blade changes.

18. C: The author says that rigid rotor systems offer the best properties of semirigid and fully articulated systems, and are easier to design, too.

19. D: The passage states that information on how to deal with non-emergency malfunctions are usually found in RFMs for larger helicopters, which implies that this information doesn't appear in most RFMs.

20. A: This passage is mainly about how to create a takeoff plan in an unfamiliar location.

Math Skills Test

1. A: First, subtract 4 from both sides to isolate x:

$$16x + 4 - 4 = 100 - 4$$
$$16x = 96$$

Then, divide both sides by 16 to solve for x:

$$16x/16 = 96/16$$
$$x = 6$$

2. A: Use the FOIL method (first, outside, inside, and last) to get rid of the brackets:

$10x^2 + 20x - 100x - 200$

Then, combine like terms to simplify the expression:

$10x^2 - 80x - 200$

3. A: Complementary angles are two angles that equal 90° when added together.

4. D: To simplify this expression, the law of exponents that states that $(x^m)^n = x^{m*n}$ must be observed:

$2^3x^{4*3} + 2\ (y^{5*5})$

$8x^{12} + 2y^{25}$

5. A: The sum of the measures of the three angles of any triangle is 180. The equation of the angles of this triangle can be written as $2x + 6x + 10x = 180$, or $18x = 180$. Therefore, $x = 10$. Therefore, the measure of the smallest angle is 20.

6. B: The formula for the area of a circle is $\pi\ r^2$. The diameter of a circle is equal to twice its radius. Therefore, to find the radius of this circle, it is necessary to divide the diameter by 2: 12 / 2 = 6cm

Then, use the formula to find the area of the circle: $\pi\ 6^2$

$\pi *36 = 113cm^2$

7. D: The general equation to find the area of a quadrilateral is length * width.

Since the length and width of a square are equal, we can calculate the area of the square described in the question:

$A = l * w$

$A = 15cm * 15cm$

$A = 225cm^2$

8. C: To find the volume of a rectangular solid, the formula is length * width * height.

Therefore, this solid's volume = 12cm * 3cm * 9cm = $324cm^3$

9. C: First, add $4x^2$ to both sides to isolate x:

$$2x^2 + 4x^2 = -4x^2 + 4x^2 + 216$$
$$6x^2 = 216$$

Then, divide both sides by 6:

$$6x^2/6 = 216/6$$
$$x^2 = 36$$

Finally, take the square root of both sides to solve for x:

$$\sqrt{x^2} = \sqrt{36}$$
$$x = 6$$

10. B: The general equation to find the area of a quadrilateral is length * width.

Since the length and width of a square are equal, we can calculate the area of the square described in the question. We can divide the perimeter by 4 since all sides are equal length. Once we know each side is 6 m we can multiply 6*6 to get an area of 36 m^2.

11. B: The formula for the area of a rectangle is length * width. Using the measurements given in the question, the area of the rectangle can be calculated:

A = length * width

A = 5cm * 7cm

A = $35cm^2$

12. B: On a six-sided die, the probability of throwing any number is 1 in 6. The probability of throwing a 3 or a 4 is double that, or 2 in 6. This can be simplified by dividing both 2 and 6 by 2.

Therefore, the probability of throwing either a 3 or 4 is 1 in 3.

13. C: First, add the 24 and the 6:

$-2y \geq 30$

Then, divide both sides by -2 to solve for y:

$-2y/-2 \geq 30/-2$

$y \geq -15$

Finally, when both sides are divided by a negative number, the direction of the sign must be reversed:

$y \leq -15$

14. A: First, bring the 5x to the left side of the equation to make it easier to solve:

$$2x - 5x = -30$$
$$-3x = -30$$

Then, divide both sides by -3 to solve for x:

$$-3x/-3 = -30/-3$$
$$x = 10$$

15. C: The solution of $f(x) = g(x)$ can be determined by setting the two functions equal to one another. Thus, the following may be written $3x + 6 = 2x - 8$. Solving for x gives $x = -14$.

16. A: The area of a square is equal to the square of the length of one side. If the area is 64 in^2, the side length must therefore be $\sqrt{64in^2} = 8$ in. The circle is inscribed in the square, so the side length of the square is the same as the circle's diameter. If the circle's diameter is 8 in, then the circle's radius must be half of that, or 4 in. The area of a circle is equal to $A = \pi r^2 = \pi(4\text{ in})^2 = 16\pi\text{ in}^2$.

17. A: First, bring the -3x to the left side of the equation and the 23 to the right side of the equation to make it easier to solve:

4x + 3x > -6 – 23

7x > -29

Then, divide both side by 7 to solve for x:

7x/7> -29/7

x > -4.14

18. D: First, bring all of the terms containing x to the left side of the equation to make it easier to solve: 2x + 5x – 3x – x = 30

$$7x - 4x = 30$$
$$3x = 30$$

Then, divide both sides by 3 to solve for x:

$$3x/3 = 30/3$$
$$x = 10$$

19. B: First, substitute the given values for x and y into the expression:

$3(4)^2$ 10 + 10/2 – 6(4)

Then, calculate the value of the expression:

According to the order of operations, any multiplying and dividing must be done first:

3*16*10 + 5 – 24

480 + 5 – 24

Then, any addition or subtraction should be completed:

485 – 24

461

20. B: The average is the total amount spent divided by the number of students. The first three students spend an average of \$10, so the total amount they spend is $3 \times \$10 = \$30$. The other six students spend an average of \$4, so the total amount they spend is $6 \times \$4 = \$24$. The total amount spent by all nine students is $\$30 + \$24 = \$54$, and the average amount they spend is $\$54 \div 9 = \$6$.

21. C: First, substitute the given value of w (7) into the expression each time it appears.

$8*7^2 - 12(7) + (4*7 - 5) + 6$

According to the order of operations, any calculations inside of the brackets must be done first:

$8*7^2 - 12(7) + (23) + 6$

Finally, calculate the value of the expression:

$8*49 - 84 + 23 + 6$

$392 - 84 + 23 + 6$

337

22. C: First, subtract 7 from both sides to isolate x:

$$x/3 + 7 - 7 = 35 - 7$$
$$x/3 = 28$$

Then, multiply both sides by three to solve for x:

$$x/3 * 3 = 28 * 3$$
$$x = 84$$

23. B: First, bring all terms to the left side of the equation to make it easier to solve:

$2x^2 - 7x - x^2 + 12 = 0$

Combine like terms:

$x^2 - 7x + 12 = 0$

Then, factor the equation:

$(x - 4)(x - 3) = 0$

Finally, solve for x in both instances:

$x - 4 = 0$

$x = 4$

$x - 3 = 0$

$x = 3$

$x = 3, 4$

24. A: Another way of expressing the fact that x is 25% of 250 is:

x = (0.25)250

Then, it is simply a matter of multiplying out the right side of the equation to calculate the value of x: x = 62.5

25. B: The volume of a cube is calculated by cubing the length, width, or height of the cube (the value for all three of these is the same.

Therefore, the volume of a cube equals = length^3

In this case 8cm^3= x * x * x, where x can represent the length of the cube.

To find the length, we must figure out which number cubed equals 8.

The answer is 2cm: 2cm * 2cm * 2cm = 8cm^3

26. B: One way to compare fractions is to convert them to equivalent fractions which have common denominators. In this case the lowest common denominator of the three fractions is $7 \times 12 = 84$. Converting each of the fractions to this denominator, $\frac{1}{3} = \frac{1 \times 28}{3 \times 28} = \frac{28}{84}$, $\frac{2}{7} = \frac{2 \times 12}{7 \times 12} = \frac{24}{84}$, and $\frac{5}{12} = \frac{5 \times 7}{12 \times 7} = \frac{35}{84}$. Since $24 < 28 < 35$, it must be the case that $\frac{2}{7} < \frac{1}{3} < \frac{5}{12}$.

27. A: Use the FOIL (first, outside, inside, last) to expand the expression:

$4x^3 - 2x^2 + 6x - 3$

There are no like terms, so the expression cannot be simplified any further.

28. D: To simplify this expression, the law of exponents that states that $x^m * x^n = x^{m+n}$ must be observed.

$10x^{4+2}y^{7+3}m^{2+8}z$

Therefore, $10x^6y^{10}m^{10}z$ is the simplified expression.

29. C: First, find the total number of students in the classroom: 13 + 18 = 31

There is an 18 in 31 chance that a name chosen randomly will be a girl's name.

To express this as a percentage, divide 18 by 31, then multiply that number by 100:

18/31 * 100% = 58%

30. A: *x* percent is the same thing as $\frac{x}{100}$, and finding *x* percent of a number is the same as multiplying that number by *x* percent. This is true even when the number is itself a percent. So, 10% of 40% is $40\% \times 10\% = 40\% \times \frac{10}{100} = 40\% \times \frac{1}{10} = 4\%$.

Mechanical Comprehension Test

1. A: The velocity is made up of two components, the x and y components. The x component is not changing during flight, but the weight of the projectile decreases the positive y component of the velocity. Thus, the total velocity will be greatest before the y component has decreased.

2. A: Because the linear speed of two connected pulleys is the same, the pulley with the smaller radius spins faster. The largest pulley will spin slower than the middle pulley. The smallest pulley will spin faster than the middle pulley, making it the fastest pulley.

3. C: Gear A and gear C have the same number of teeth. Thus, gears A and C will have the same speed. Since gear C is rotating at 10 rpm, the total number of rotations is calculated by multiplying the rpm by the number of minutes.

4. A: Because the large mass will produce a greater torque at the same distance from the fulcrum as the small mass, the distance from the large mass to the fulcrum should be shortened. Then, the torque produced by the large mass will decrease and the torque produced by the small mass will increase.

5. A: When the rope is not parallel to the intended path of motion, the force is divided into useful force (x direction) and not useful force (y direction). If only some of the force is useful, then the man will need to apply more force to achieve the same pulling force as if the rope were parallel to the table.

6. B: Because the volume of the liquid doesn't change, when the small piston is compressed, the volume decrease in one piston is the volume increase in the other piston. As the volume is the area times the height, the height of the larger piston only needs to raise one fourth the height that the small piston moved.

7. A: The downward force decreases part of the y component of the top force, but does not affect the x component of the force. Thus, the resultant force is up and to the right.

8. B: because the same volume of water has to flow through all parts of the river, the water will slow down to fill the wide section.

9. C: The negative side of magnet 2 will be attracted to the positive side of magnet 1. The positive side of magnet 2 will be attracted to the negative side of magnet 3 with the same force. Because the magnitudes of the forces are equal and the directions are opposite, the sum of the forces will be zero.

10. C: The first phase change is from solid to liquid at -21°C. The next phase change is from liquid to gas at 81°C. 90°C is only slightly higher than 81°C, making it safe to say that the substance is still a gas.

11. A: Substitute token values for the resistors to solve. Using 1 Ω resistors, the resistance of circuit A, having resistors in series, is the simple sum of the two resistors: 2 Ω. Because the resistors in circuit B are in parallel, the resistance of circuit B is the reciprocal of the sum of the reciprocals of the resistances, or $\frac{1}{\frac{1}{1}+\frac{1}{1}}$. the result is 1/2 Ω.

12. A: To find the number of swings in a time period from the frequency, multiply the frequency times the time period, after converting the time period into seconds to match the frequency. The final calculation is $\frac{1.4\ swings}{second} * 1\ minute * \frac{60\ seconds}{1\ minute} = 84\ swings$

13. B: The mechanical advantage is calculated by the output force divided by the input force. Because both pistons are the same size, the output force will equal the input force, resulting in a mechanical advantage of one.

14. C: Because the horizontal component of the thrown ball's velocity will not affect the vertical component, the vertical component of the thrown ball's velocity will be identical to the dropped ball's velocity. The balls will hit at the same time.

15. A: The cam has four bumps on it. The needle will move up and down for each bump. The cam will rotate five times in the time period of one minute. The total times the needle will move up and down will be five times four.

16. C: Torque is the product of a force perpendicular to the arm and the length of the arm. Options A and B each increase one part of the torque calculation. However, angling the force towards the center would decrease the part of the force that is acting perpendicular to the arm, as some of the force will be acting inward.

17. B: When the ball is compressed into the spring, the ball has potential stored in the spring. When the ball is flying upwards, the ball has kinetic energy associated with the motion.

18. B: Pressure increases with depth in water. When the tank was lower it experienced more pressure. Thus, when the tank is higher it experiences less pressure.

19. B: Specific gravity can be calculated as the ratio of the density of the liquid in question to the density of water. Because salt water has a higher density than water, the ratio will be greater than one.

20. B: Convective heat transfer deals with the transfer of heat by fluids (including gas). Steam is a fluid which transfers heat to objects, like a hand, with lower temperatures than it.

21. C: A capacitor stores voltage across a gap between two conductive materials.

22. A: Torque is the product of a force perpendicular to the arm and the length of the arm. Wrench A, with the longer arm, will be able to achieve greater amounts of torque with a set force.

23. B: Because the circuit only has one path and the two resistors are in series, the current is the same everywhere in the circuit. The voltage will drop over both resistors. Also, because the circuit is complete, there is current in the circuit.

24. C: Ammeters measure current (think amps). Multimeters measure current and voltage. Voltmeters only measure voltage.

25. B: When the ball is flying upwards, the kinetic energy is being converted into potential energy. Potential energy increases linearly with height, meaning that an object at 2 feet over the ground has twice the potential energy of the object at 1 foot over the ground. Thus, if all of the energy of the ball will be converted from kinetic energy, and half of the energy will be converted at half the height, the potential energy of the ball will be 50 ft-lb.

26. A: Because mechanical advantage is the ratio of output force to input force, an increase in mechanical advantage means, in this case, that the output force will be increasing. However, energy in simple machines is conserved. This means that the work, or force times distance, done to the input will need to increase, while keeping the force the same. Increasing the distance of the applied force will increase the work, allowing for an increased force for the output.

27. A: As the drum spins one full turn, the hanging rope increases length by 1 foot and decreases length by 3.5 feet. Thus, every spin decreases the rope length by 2.5 feet. In two turns, the rope will decrease length by 5 feet. The pulley makes the weight lift half the distance that the rope decreased. Thus, the weight raises 2.5 feet.

28. C: Condensation from the air occurs when the water vapor in the air cools down enough to change phase from vapor to liquid water. If a pipe is cold and the air is warm, the water vapor will condense on the pipe.

29. A: The color, black, will absorb the most heat from radiation.

30. B: The gear ratio between the small and large gears is 18/30 or 3/5. Multiply the number of rotations of the small gear times the gear ratio to get (3 rotations)*(3/5) = 1.8 rotations.

How to Overcome Test Anxiety

Just the thought of taking a test is enough to make most people a little nervous. A test is an important event that can have a long-term impact on your future, so it's important to take it seriously and it's natural to feel anxious about performing well. But just because anxiety is normal, that doesn't mean that it's helpful in test taking, or that you should simply accept it as part of your life. Anxiety can have a variety of effects. These effects can be mild, like making you feel slightly nervous, or severe, like blocking your ability to focus or remember even a simple detail.

If you experience test anxiety—whether severe or mild—it's important to know how to beat it. To discover this, first you need to understand what causes test anxiety.

Causes of Test Anxiety

While we often think of anxiety as an uncontrollable emotional state, it can actually be caused by simple, practical things. One of the most common causes of test anxiety is that a person does not feel adequately prepared for their test. This feeling can be the result of many different issues such as poor study habits or lack of organization, but the most common culprit is time management. Starting to study too late, failing to organize your study time to cover all of the material, or being distracted while you study will mean that you're not well prepared for the test. This may lead to cramming the night before, which will cause you to be physically and mentally exhausted for the test. Poor time management also contributes to feelings of stress, fear, and hopelessness as you realize you are not well prepared but don't know what to do about it.

Other times, test anxiety is not related to your preparation for the test but comes from unresolved fear. This may be a past failure on a test, or poor performance on tests in general. It may come from comparing yourself to others who seem to be performing better or from the stress of living up to expectations. Anxiety may be driven by fears of the future—how failure on this test would affect your educational and career goals. These fears are often completely irrational, but they can still negatively impact your test performance.

Review Video: 3 Reasons You Have Test Anxiety
Visit mometrix.com/academy and enter code: 428468

Elements of Test Anxiety

As mentioned earlier, test anxiety is considered to be an emotional state, but it has physical and mental components as well. Sometimes you may not even realize that you are suffering from test anxiety until you notice the physical symptoms. These can include trembling hands, rapid heartbeat, sweating, nausea, and tense muscles. Extreme anxiety may lead to fainting or vomiting. Obviously, any of these symptoms can have a negative impact on testing. It is important to recognize them as soon as they begin to occur so that you can address the problem before it damages your performance.

Review Video: 3 Ways to Tell You Have Test Anxiety
Visit mometrix.com/academy and enter code: 927847

The mental components of test anxiety include trouble focusing and inability to remember learned information. During a test, your mind is on high alert, which can help you recall information and stay focused for an extended period of time. However, anxiety interferes with your mind's natural processes, causing you to blank out, even on the questions you know well. The strain of testing during anxiety makes it difficult to stay focused, especially on a test that may take several hours. Extreme anxiety can take a huge mental toll, making it difficult not only to recall test information but even to understand the test questions or pull your thoughts together.

Review Video: How Test Anxiety Affects Memory
Visit mometrix.com/academy and enter code: 609003

Effects of Test Anxiety

Test anxiety is like a disease—if left untreated, it will get progressively worse. Anxiety leads to poor performance, and this reinforces the feelings of fear and failure, which in turn lead to poor performances on subsequent tests. It can grow from a mild nervousness to a crippling condition. If allowed to progress, test anxiety can have a big impact on your schooling, and consequently on your future.

Test anxiety can spread to other parts of your life. Anxiety on tests can become anxiety in any stressful situation, and blanking on a test can turn into panicking in a job situation. But fortunately, you don't have to let anxiety rule your testing and determine your grades. There are a number of relatively simple steps you can take to move past anxiety and function normally on a test and in the rest of life.

Review Video: How Test Anxiety Impacts Your Grades
Visit mometrix.com/academy and enter code: 939819

Physical Steps for Beating Test Anxiety

While test anxiety is a serious problem, the good news is that it can be overcome. It doesn't have to control your ability to think and remember information. While it may take time, you can begin taking steps today to beat anxiety.

Just as your first hint that you may be struggling with anxiety comes from the physical symptoms, the first step to treating it is also physical. Rest is crucial for having a clear, strong mind. If you are tired, it is much easier to give in to anxiety. But if you establish good sleep habits, your body and mind will be ready to perform optimally, without the strain of exhaustion. Additionally, sleeping well helps you to retain information better, so you're more likely to recall the answers when you see the test questions.

Getting good sleep means more than going to bed on time. It's important to allow your brain time to relax. Take study breaks from time to time so it doesn't get overworked, and don't study right before bed. Take time to rest your mind before trying to rest your body, or you may find it difficult to fall asleep.

Review Video: The Importance of Sleep for Your Brain
Visit mometrix.com/academy and enter code: 319338

Along with sleep, other aspects of physical health are important in preparing for a test. Good nutrition is vital for good brain function. Sugary foods and drinks may give a burst of energy but this burst is followed by a crash, both physically and emotionally. Instead, fuel your body with protein and vitamin-rich foods.

Also, drink plenty of water. Dehydration can lead to headaches and exhaustion, especially if your brain is already under stress from the rigors of the test. Particularly if your test is a long one, drink water during the breaks. And if possible, take an energy-boosting snack to eat between sections.

Review Video: How Diet Can Affect your Mood
Visit mometrix.com/academy and enter code: 624317

Along with sleep and diet, a third important part of physical health is exercise. Maintaining a steady workout schedule is helpful, but even taking 5-minute study breaks to walk can help get your blood pumping faster and clear your head. Exercise also releases endorphins, which contribute to a positive feeling and can help combat test anxiety.

When you nurture your physical health, you are also contributing to your mental health. If your body is healthy, your mind is much more likely to be healthy as well. So take time to rest, nourish your body with healthy food and water, and get moving as much as possible. Taking these physical steps will make you stronger and more able to take the mental steps necessary to overcome test anxiety.

Review Video: How to Stay Healthy and Prevent Test Anxiety
Visit mometrix.com/academy and enter code: 877894

Mental Steps for Beating Test Anxiety

Working on the mental side of test anxiety can be more challenging, but as with the physical side, there are clear steps you can take to overcome it. As mentioned earlier, test anxiety often stems from lack of preparation, so the obvious solution is to prepare for the test. Effective studying may be the most important weapon you have for beating test anxiety, but you can and should employ several other mental tools to combat fear.

First, boost your confidence by reminding yourself of past success—tests or projects that you aced. If you're putting as much effort into preparing for this test as you did for those, there's no reason you should expect to fail here. Work hard to prepare; then trust your preparation.

Second, surround yourself with encouraging people. It can be helpful to find a study group, but be sure that the people you're around will encourage a positive attitude. If you spend time with others who are anxious or cynical, this will only contribute to your own anxiety. Look for others who are motivated to study hard from a desire to succeed, not from a fear of failure.

Third, reward yourself. A test is physically and mentally tiring, even without anxiety, and it can be helpful to have something to look forward to. Plan an activity following the test, regardless of the outcome, such as going to a movie or getting ice cream.

When you are taking the test, if you find yourself beginning to feel anxious, remind yourself that you know the material. Visualize successfully completing the test. Then take a few deep, relaxing breaths and return to it. Work through the questions carefully but with confidence, knowing that you are capable of succeeding.

Developing a healthy mental approach to test taking will also aid in other areas of life. Test anxiety affects more than just the actual test—it can be damaging to your mental health and even contribute to depression. It's important to beat test anxiety before it becomes a problem for more than testing.

Review Video: Test Anxiety and Depression
Visit mometrix.com/academy and enter code: 904704

Study Strategy

Being prepared for the test is necessary to combat anxiety, but what does being prepared look like? You may study for hours on end and still not feel prepared. What you need is a strategy for test prep. The next few pages outline our recommended steps to help you plan out and conquer the challenge of preparation.

Step 1: Scope Out the Test

Learn everything you can about the format (multiple choice, essay, etc.) and what will be on the test. Gather any study materials, course outlines, or sample exams that may be available. Not only will this help you to prepare, but knowing what to expect can help to alleviate test anxiety.

Step 2: Map Out the Material

Look through the textbook or study guide and make note of how many chapters or sections it has. Then divide these over the time you have. For example, if a book has 15 chapters and you have five days to study, you need to cover three chapters each day. Even better, if you have the time, leave an extra day at the end for overall review after you have gone through the material in depth.

If time is limited, you may need to prioritize the material. Look through it and make note of which sections you think you already have a good grasp on, and which need review. While you are studying, skim quickly through the familiar sections and take more time on the challenging parts. Write out your plan so you don't get lost as you go. Having a written plan also helps you feel more in control of the study, so anxiety is less likely to arise from feeling overwhelmed at the amount to cover. A sample plan may look like this:

- Day 1: Skim chapters 1–4, study chapter 5 (especially pages 31–33)
- Day 2: Study chapters 6–7, skim chapters 8–9
- Day 3: Skim chapter 10, study chapters 11–12 (especially pages 87–90)
- Day 4: Study chapters 13–15
- Day 5: Overall review (focus most on chapters 5, 6, and 12), take practice test

Step 3: Gather Your Tools

Decide what study method works best for you. Do you prefer to highlight in the book as you study and then go back over the highlighted portions? Or do you type out notes of the important information? Or is it helpful to make flashcards that you can carry with you? Assemble the pens, index cards, highlighters, post-it notes, and any other materials you may need so you won't be distracted by getting up to find things while you study.

If you're having a hard time retaining the information or organizing your notes, experiment with different methods. For example, try color-coding by subject with colored pens, highlighters, or post-it notes. If you learn better by hearing, try recording yourself reading your notes so you can listen while in the car, working out, or simply sitting at your desk. Ask a friend to quiz you from your flashcards, or try teaching someone the material to solidify it in your mind.

Step 4: Create Your Environment

It's important to avoid distractions while you study. This includes both the obvious distractions like visitors and the subtle distractions like an uncomfortable chair (or a too-comfortable couch that makes you want to fall asleep). Set up the best study environment possible: good lighting and a comfortable work area. If background music helps you focus, you may want to turn it on, but otherwise keep the room quiet. If you are using a computer to take notes, be sure you don't have any other windows open, especially applications like social media, games, or anything else that could distract you. Silence your phone and turn off notifications. Be sure to keep water close by so you stay hydrated while you study (but avoid unhealthy drinks and snacks).

Also, take into account the best time of day to study. Are you freshest first thing in the morning? Try to set aside some time then to work through the material. Is your mind clearer in the afternoon or evening? Schedule your study session then. Another method is to study at the same time of day that you will take the test, so that your brain gets used to working on the material at that time and will be ready to focus at test time.

Step 5: Study!

Once you have done all the study preparation, it's time to settle into the actual studying. Sit down, take a few moments to settle your mind so you can focus, and begin to follow your study plan. Don't give in to distractions or let yourself procrastinate. This is your time to prepare so you'll be ready to fearlessly approach the test. Make the most of the time and stay focused.

Of course, you don't want to burn out. If you study too long you may find that you're not retaining the information very well. Take regular study breaks. For example, taking five minutes out of every hour to walk briskly, breathing deeply and swinging your arms, can help your mind stay fresh.

As you get to the end of each chapter or section, it's a good idea to do a quick review. Remind yourself of what you learned and work on any difficult parts. When you feel that you've mastered the material, move on to the next part. At the end of your study session, briefly skim through your notes again.

But while review is helpful, cramming last minute is NOT. If at all possible, work ahead so that you won't need to fit all your study into the last day. Cramming overloads your brain with more information than it can process and retain, and your tired mind may struggle to recall even previously learned information when it is overwhelmed with last-minute study. Also, the urgent nature of cramming and the stress placed on your brain contribute to anxiety. You'll be more likely to go to the test feeling unprepared and having trouble thinking clearly.

So don't cram, and don't stay up late before the test, even just to review your notes at a leisurely pace. Your brain needs rest more than it needs to go over the information again. In fact, plan to finish your studies by noon or early afternoon the day before the test. Give your brain the rest of the day to relax or focus on other things, and get a good night's sleep. Then you will be fresh for the test and better able to recall what you've studied.

Step 6: Take a practice test

Many courses offer sample tests, either online or in the study materials. This is an excellent resource to check whether you have mastered the material, as well as to prepare for the test format and environment.

Check the test format ahead of time: the number of questions, the type (multiple choice, free response, etc.), and the time limit. Then create a plan for working through them. For example, if you have 30 minutes to take a 60-question test, your limit is 30 seconds per question. Spend less time on the questions you know well so that you can take more time on the difficult ones.

If you have time to take several practice tests, take the first one open book, with no time limit. Work through the questions at your own pace and make sure you fully understand them. Gradually work up to taking a test under test conditions: sit at a desk with all study materials put away and set a timer. Pace yourself to make sure you finish the test with time to spare and go back to check your answers if you have time.

After each test, check your answers. On the questions you missed, be sure you understand why you missed them. Did you misread the question (tests can use tricky wording)? Did you forget the information? Or was it something you hadn't learned? Go back and study any shaky areas that the practice tests reveal.

Taking these tests not only helps with your grade, but also aids in combating test anxiety. If you're already used to the test conditions, you're less likely to worry about it, and working through tests until you're scoring well gives you a confidence boost. Go through the practice tests until you feel comfortable, and then you can go into the test knowing that you're ready for it.

Test Tips

On test day, you should be confident, knowing that you've prepared well and are ready to answer the questions. But aside from preparation, there are several test day strategies you can employ to maximize your performance.

First, as stated before, get a good night's sleep the night before the test (and for several nights before that, if possible). Go into the test with a fresh, alert mind rather than staying up late to study.

Try not to change too much about your normal routine on the day of the test. It's important to eat a nutritious breakfast, but if you normally don't eat breakfast at all, consider eating just a protein bar. If you're a coffee drinker, go ahead and have your normal coffee. Just make sure you time it so that the caffeine doesn't wear off right in the middle of your test. Avoid sugary beverages, and drink enough water to stay hydrated but not so much that you need a restroom break 10 minutes into the test. If your test isn't first thing in the morning, consider going for a walk or doing a light workout before the test to get your blood flowing.

Allow yourself enough time to get ready, and leave for the test with plenty of time to spare so you won't have the anxiety of scrambling to arrive in time. Another reason to be early is to select a good seat. It's helpful to sit away from doors and windows, which can be distracting. Find a good seat, get out your supplies, and settle your mind before the test begins.

When the test begins, start by going over the instructions carefully, even if you already know what to expect. Make sure you avoid any careless mistakes by following the directions.

Then begin working through the questions, pacing yourself as you've practiced. If you're not sure on an answer, don't spend too much time on it, and don't let it shake your confidence. Either skip it and come back later, or eliminate as many wrong answers as possible and guess among the remaining ones. Don't dwell on these questions as you continue—put them out of your mind and focus on what lies ahead.

Be sure to read all of the answer choices, even if you're sure the first one is the right answer. Sometimes you'll find a better one if you keep reading. But don't second-guess yourself if you do immediately know the answer. Your gut instinct is usually right. Don't let test anxiety rob you of the information you know.

If you have time at the end of the test (and if the test format allows), go back and review your answers. Be cautious about changing any, since your first instinct tends to be correct, but make sure you didn't misread any of the questions or accidentally mark the wrong answer choice. Look over any you skipped and make an educated guess.

At the end, leave the test feeling confident. You've done your best, so don't waste time worrying about your performance or wishing you could change anything. Instead, celebrate the successful completion of this test. And finally, use this test to learn how to deal with anxiety even better next time.

Review Video: 5 Tips to Beat Test Anxiety
Visit mometrix.com/academy and enter code: 570656

Important Qualification

Not all anxiety is created equal. If your test anxiety is causing major issues in your life beyond the classroom or testing center, or if you are experiencing troubling physical symptoms related to your anxiety, it may be a sign of a serious physiological or psychological condition. If this sounds like your situation, we strongly encourage you to seek professional help.

How to Overcome Your Fear of Math

The word *math* is enough to strike fear into most hearts. How many of us have memories of sitting through confusing lectures, wrestling over mind-numbing homework, or taking tests that still seem incomprehensible even after hours of study? Years after graduation, many still shudder at these memories.

The fact is, math is not just a classroom subject. It has real-world implications that you face every day, whether you realize it or not. This may be balancing your monthly budget, deciding how many supplies to buy for a project, or simply splitting a meal check with friends. The idea of daily confrontations with math can be so paralyzing that some develop a condition known as *math anxiety*.

But you do NOT need to be paralyzed by this anxiety! In fact, while you may have thought all your life that you're not good at math, or that your brain isn't wired to understand it, the truth is that you may have been conditioned to think this way. From your earliest school days, the way you were taught affected the way you viewed different subjects. And the way math has been taught has changed.

Several decades ago, there was a shift in American math classrooms. The focus changed from traditional problem-solving to a conceptual view of topics, de-emphasizing the importance of learning the basics and building on them. The solid foundation necessary for math progression and confidence was undermined. Math became more of a vague concept than a concrete idea. Today, it is common to think of math, not as a straightforward system, but as a mysterious, complicated method that can't be fully understood unless you're a genius.

This is why you may still have nightmares about being called on to answer a difficult problem in front of the class. Math anxiety is a very real, though unnecessary, fear.

Math anxiety may begin with a single class period. Let's say you missed a day in 6th grade math and never quite understood the concept that was taught while you were gone. Since math is cumulative, with each new concept building on past ones, this could very well affect the rest of your math career. Without that one day's knowledge, it will be difficult to understand any other concepts that link to it. Rather than realizing that you're just missing one key piece, you may begin to believe that you're simply not capable of understanding math.

This belief can change the way you approach other classes, career options, and everyday life experiences, if you become anxious at the thought that math might be required. A student who loves science may choose a different path of study upon realizing that multiple math classes will be required for a degree. An aspiring medical student may hesitate at the thought of going through the necessary math classes. For some this anxiety escalates into a more extreme state known as *math phobia*.

Math anxiety is challenging to address because it is rooted deeply and may come from a variety of causes: an embarrassing moment in class, a teacher who did not explain concepts well and contributed to a shaky foundation, or a failed test that contributed to the belief of math failure.

These causes add up over time, encouraged by society's popular view that math is hard and unpleasant. Eventually a person comes to firmly believe that he or she is simply bad at math. This belief makes it difficult to grasp new concepts or even remember old ones. Homework and test grades begin to slip, which only confirms the belief. The poor performance is not due to lack of ability but is caused by math anxiety.

Math anxiety is an emotional issue, not a lack of intelligence. But when it becomes deeply rooted, it can become more than just an emotional problem. Physical symptoms appear. Blood pressure may rise and heartbeat may quicken at the sight of a math problem – or even the thought of math! This fear leads to a mental block. When someone with math anxiety is asked to perform a calculation, even a basic problem can seem overwhelming and impossible. The emotional and physical response to the thought of math prevents the brain from working through it logically.

The more this happens, the more a person's confidence drops, and the more math anxiety is generated. This vicious cycle must be broken!

The first step in breaking the cycle is to go back to very beginning and make sure you really understand the basics of how math works and why it works. It is not enough to memorize rules for multiplication and division. If you don't know WHY these rules work, your foundation will be shaky and you will be at risk of developing a phobia. Understanding mathematical concepts not only promotes confidence and security, but allows you to build on this understanding for new concepts. Additionally, you can solve unfamiliar problems using familiar concepts and processes.

Why is it that students in other countries regularly outperform American students in math? The answer likely boils down to a couple of things: the foundation of mathematical conceptual understanding and societal perception. While students in the US are not expected to *like* or *get* math, in many other nations, students are expected not only to understand math but also to excel at it.

Changing the American view of math that leads to math anxiety is a monumental task. It requires changing the training of teachers nationwide, from kindergarten through high school, so that they learn to teach the *why* behind math and to combat the wrong math views that students may develop. It also involves changing the stigma associated with math, so that it is no longer viewed as unpleasant and incomprehensible. While these are necessary changes, they are challenging and will take time. But in the meantime, math anxiety is not irreversible—it can be faced and defeated, one person at a time.

False Beliefs

One reason math anxiety has taken such hold is that several false beliefs have been created and shared until they became widely accepted. Some of these unhelpful beliefs include the following:

There is only one way to solve a math problem. In the same way that you can choose from different driving routes and still arrive at the same house, you can solve a math problem using different methods and still find the correct answer. A person who understands the reasoning behind math calculations may be able to look at an unfamiliar concept and find the right answer, just by applying logic to the knowledge they already have. This approach may be different than what is taught in the classroom, but it is still valid. Unfortunately, even many teachers view math as a subject where the best course of action is to memorize the rule or process for each problem rather than as a place for students to exercise logic and creativity in finding a solution.

Many people don't have a mind for math. A person who has struggled due to poor teaching or math anxiety may falsely believe that he or she doesn't have the mental capacity to grasp mathematical concepts. Most of the time, this is false. Many people find that when they are relieved of their math anxiety, they have more than enough brainpower to understand math.

Men are naturally better at math than women. Even though research has shown this to be false, many young women still avoid math careers and classes because of their belief that their math abilities are inferior. Many girls have come to believe that math is a male skill and have given up trying to understand or enjoy it.

Counting aids are bad. Something like counting on your fingers or drawing out a problem to visualize it may be frowned on as childish or a crutch, but these devices can help you get a tangible understanding of a problem or a concept.

Sadly, many students buy into these ideologies at an early age. A young girl who enjoys math class may be conditioned to think that she doesn't actually have the brain for it because math is for boys, and may turn her energies to other pursuits, permanently closing the door on a wide range of opportunities. A child who finds the right answer but doesn't follow the teacher's method may believe that he is doing it wrong and isn't good at math. A student who never had a problem with math before may have a poor teacher and become confused, yet believe that the problem is because she doesn't have a mathematical mind.

Students who have bought into these erroneous beliefs quickly begin to add their own anxieties, adapting them to their own personal situations:

I'll never use this in real life. A huge number of people wrongly believe that math is irrelevant outside the classroom. By adopting this mindset, they are handicapping themselves for a life in a mathematical world, as well as limiting their career choices. When they are inevitably faced with real-world math, they are conditioning themselves to respond with anxiety.

I'm not quick enough. While timed tests and quizzes, or even simply comparing yourself with other students in the class, can lead to this belief, speed is not an indicator of skill level. A person can work very slowly yet understand at a deep level.

If I can understand it, it's too easy. People with a low view of their own abilities tend to think that if they are able to grasp a concept, it must be simple. They cannot accept the idea that they are capable of understanding math. This belief will make it harder to learn, no matter how intelligent they are.

I just can't learn this. An overwhelming number of people think this, from young children to adults, and much of the time it is simply not true. But this mindset can turn into a self-fulfilling prophecy that keeps you from exercising and growing your math ability.

The good news is, each of these myths can be debunked. For most people, they are based on emotion and psychology, NOT on actual ability! It will take time, effort, and the desire to change, but change is possible. Even if you have spent years thinking that you don't have the capability to understand math, it is not too late to uncover your true ability and find relief from the anxiety that surrounds math.

Math Strategies

It is important to have a plan of attack to combat math anxiety. There are many useful strategies for pinpointing the fears or myths and eradicating them:

Go back to the basics. For most people, math anxiety stems from a poor foundation. You may think that you have a complete understanding of addition and subtraction, or even decimals and percentages, but make absolutely sure. Learning math is different from learning other subjects. For example, when you learn history, you study various time periods and places and events. It may be important to memorize dates or find out about the lives of famous people. When you move from US history to world history, there will be some overlap, but a large amount of the information will be new. Mathematical concepts, on the other hand, are very closely linked and highly dependent on each other. It's like climbing a ladder – if a rung is missing from your understanding, it may be difficult or impossible for you to climb any higher, no matter how hard you try. So go back and make sure your math foundation is strong. This may mean taking a remedial math course, going to a tutor to work through the shaky concepts, or just going through your old homework to make sure you really understand it.

Speak the language. Math has a large vocabulary of terms and phrases unique to working problems. Sometimes these are completely new terms, and sometimes they are common words, but are used differently in a math setting. If you can't speak the language, it will be very difficult to get a thorough understanding of the concepts. It's common for students to think that they don't understand math when they simply don't understand the vocabulary. The good news is that this is fairly easy to fix. Brushing up on any terms you aren't quite sure of can help bring the rest of the concepts into focus.

Check your anxiety level. When you think about math, do you feel nervous or uncomfortable? Do you struggle with feelings of inadequacy, even on concepts that you know you've already learned? It's important to understand your specific math anxieties, and what triggers them. When you catch yourself falling back on a false belief, mentally replace it with the truth. Don't let yourself believe that you can't learn, or that struggling with a concept means you'll never understand it. Instead, remind yourself of how much you've already learned and dwell on that past success. Visualize grasping the new concept, linking it to your old knowledge, and moving on to the next challenge. Also, learn how to manage anxiety when it arises. There are many techniques for coping with the irrational fears that rise to the surface when you enter the math classroom. This may include controlled breathing, replacing negative thoughts with positive ones, or visualizing success. Anxiety interferes with your ability to concentrate and absorb information, which in turn contributes to greater anxiety. If you can learn how to regain control of your thinking, you will be better able to pay attention, make progress, and succeed!

Don't go it alone. Like any deeply ingrained belief, math anxiety is not easy to eradicate. And there is no need for you to wrestle through it on your own. It will take time, and many people find that speaking with a counselor or psychiatrist helps. They can help you develop strategies for responding to anxiety and overcoming old ideas. Additionally, it can be very helpful to take a short course or seek out a math tutor to help you find and fix the missing rungs on your ladder and make sure that you're ready to progress to the next level. You can also find a number of math aids online: courses that will teach you mental devices for figuring out problems, how to get the most out of your math classes, etc.

Check your math attitude. No matter how much you want to learn and overcome your anxiety, you'll have trouble if you still have a negative attitude toward math. If you think it's too hard, or just have general feelings of dread about math, it will be hard to learn and to break through the anxiety. Work on cultivating a positive math attitude. Remind yourself that math is not just a hurdle to be cleared, but a valuable asset. When you view math with a positive attitude, you'll be much more likely to understand and even enjoy it. This is something you must do for yourself. You may find it helpful to visit with a counselor. Your tutor, friends, and family may cheer you on in your endeavors. But your greatest asset is yourself. You are inside your own mind – tell yourself what you need to hear. Relive past victories. Remind yourself that you are capable of understanding math. Root out any false beliefs that linger and replace them with positive truths. Even if it doesn't feel true at first, it will begin to affect your thinking and pave the way for a positive, anxiety-free mindset.

Aside from these general strategies, there are a number of specific practical things you can do to begin your journey toward overcoming math anxiety. Something as simple as learning a new note-taking strategy can change the way you approach math and give you more confidence and understanding. New study techniques can also make a huge difference.

Math anxiety leads to bad habits. If it causes you to be afraid of answering a question in class, you may gravitate toward the back row. You may be embarrassed to ask for help. And you may procrastinate on assignments, which leads to rushing through them at the last moment when it's too late to get a better understanding. It's important to identify your negative behaviors and replace them with positive ones:

Prepare ahead of time. Read the lesson before you go to class. Being exposed to the topics that will be covered in class ahead of time, even if you don't understand them perfectly, is extremely helpful in increasing what you retain from the lecture. Do your homework and, if you're still shaky, go over some extra problems. The key to a solid understanding of math is practice.

Sit front and center. When you can easily see and hear, you'll understand more, and you'll avoid the distractions of other students if no one is in front of you. Plus, you're more likely to be sitting with students who are positive and engaged, rather than others with math anxiety. Let their positive math attitude rub off on you.

Ask questions in class and out. If you don't understand something, just ask. If you need a more in-depth explanation, the teacher may need to work with you outside of class, but often it's a simple concept you don't quite understand, and a single question may clear it up. If you wait, you may not be able to follow the rest of the day's lesson. For extra help, most professors have office hours outside of class when you can go over concepts one-on-one to clear up any uncertainties. Additionally, there may be a *math lab* or study session you can attend for homework help. Take advantage of this.

Review. Even if you feel that you've fully mastered a concept, review it periodically to reinforce it. Going over an old lesson has several benefits: solidifying your understanding, giving you a confidence boost, and even giving some new insights into material that you're currently learning! Don't let yourself get rusty. That can lead to problems with learning later concepts.

Teaching Tips

While the math student's mindset is the most crucial to overcoming math anxiety, it is also important for others to adjust their math attitudes. Teachers and parents have an enormous influence on how students relate to math. They can either contribute to math confidence or math anxiety.

As a parent or teacher, it is very important to convey a positive math attitude. Retelling horror stories of your own bad experience with math will contribute to a new generation of math anxiety. Even if you don't share your experiences, others will be able to sense your fears and may begin to believe them.

Even a careless comment can have a big impact, so watch for phrases like *He's not good at math* or *I never liked math*. You are a crucial role model, and your children or students will unconsciously adopt your mindset. Give them a positive example to follow. Rather than teaching them to fear the math world before they even know it, teach them about all its potential and excitement.

Work to present math as an integral, beautiful, and understandable part of life. Encourage creativity in solving problems. Watch for false beliefs and dispel them. Cross the lines between subjects: integrate history, English, and music with math. Show students how math is used every day, and how the entire world is based on mathematical principles, from the pull of gravity to the shape of seashells. Instead of letting students see math as a necessary evil, direct them to view it as an imaginative, beautiful art form – an art form that they are capable of mastering and using.

Don't give too narrow a view of math. It is more than just numbers. Yes, working problems and learning formulas is a large part of classroom math. But don't let the teaching stop there. Teach students about the everyday implications of math. Show them how nature works according to the laws of mathematics, and take them outside to make discoveries of their own. Expose them to math-related careers by inviting visiting speakers, asking students to do research and presentations, and learning students' interests and aptitudes on a personal level.

Demonstrate the importance of math. Many people see math as nothing more than a required stepping stone to their degree, a nuisance with no real usefulness. Teach students that algebra is used every day in managing their bank accounts, in following recipes, and in scheduling the day's events. Show them how learning to do geometric proofs helps them to develop logical thinking, an invaluable life skill. Let them see that math surrounds them and is integrally linked to their daily lives: that weather predictions are based on math, that math was used to design cars and other machines, etc. Most of all, give them the tools to use math to enrich their lives.

Make math as tangible as possible. Use visual aids and objects that can be touched. It is much easier to grasp a concept when you can hold it in your hands and manipulate it, rather than just listening to the lecture. Encourage math outside of the classroom. The real world is full of measuring, counting, and calculating, so let students participate in this. Keep your eyes open for numbers and patterns to discuss. Talk about how scores are calculated in sports games and how far apart plants are placed in a garden row for maximum growth. Build the mindset that math is a normal and interesting part of daily life.

Finally, find math resources that help to build a positive math attitude. There are a number of books that show math as fascinating and exciting while teaching important concepts, for example: *The Math Curse; A Wrinkle in Time; The Phantom Tollbooth;* and *Fractals, Googols and Other Mathematical Tales*. You can also find a number of online resources: math puzzles and games, videos that show math in nature, and communities of math enthusiasts. On a local level, students can compete in a variety of math competitions with other schools or join a math club.

The student who experiences math as exciting and interesting is unlikely to suffer from math anxiety. Going through life without this handicap is an immense advantage and opens many doors that others have closed through their fear.

Self-Check

Whether you suffer from math anxiety or not, chances are that you have been exposed to some of the false beliefs mentioned above. Now is the time to check yourself for any errors you may have accepted. Do you think you're not wired for math? Or that you don't need to understand it since you're not planning on a math career? Do you think math is just too difficult for the average person?

Find the errors you've taken to heart and replace them with positive thinking. Are you capable of learning math? Yes! Can you control your anxiety? Yes! These errors will resurface from time to time, so be watchful. Don't let others with math anxiety influence you or sway your confidence. If you're having trouble with a concept, find help. Don't let it discourage you!

Create a plan of attack for defeating math anxiety and sharpening your skills. Do some research and decide if it would help you to take a class, get a tutor, or find some online resources to fine-tune your knowledge. Make the effort to get good nutrition, hydration, and sleep so that you are operating at full capacity. Remind yourself daily that you are skilled and that anxiety does not control you. Your mind is capable of so much more than you know. Give it the tools it needs to grow and thrive.

Thank You

We at Mometrix would like to extend our heartfelt thanks to you, our friend and patron, for allowing us to play a part in your journey. It is a privilege to serve people from all walks of life who are unified in their commitment to building the best future they can for themselves.

The preparation you devote to these important testing milestones may be the most valuable educational opportunity you have for making a real difference in your life. We encourage you to put your heart into it—that feeling of succeeding, overcoming, and yes, conquering will be well worth the hours you've invested.

We want to hear your story, your struggles and your successes, and if you see any opportunities for us to improve our materials so we can help others even more effectively in the future, please share that with us as well. **The team at Mometrix would be absolutely thrilled to hear from you!** So please, send us an email (support@mometrix.com) and let's stay in touch.

Additional Bonus Material

Due to our efforts to try to keep this book to a manageable length, we've created a link that will give you access to all of your additional bonus material.

Please visit https://www.mometrix.com/bonus948/sift to access the information.

Made in the USA
Middletown, DE
18 August 2019